The Christmas Almanack

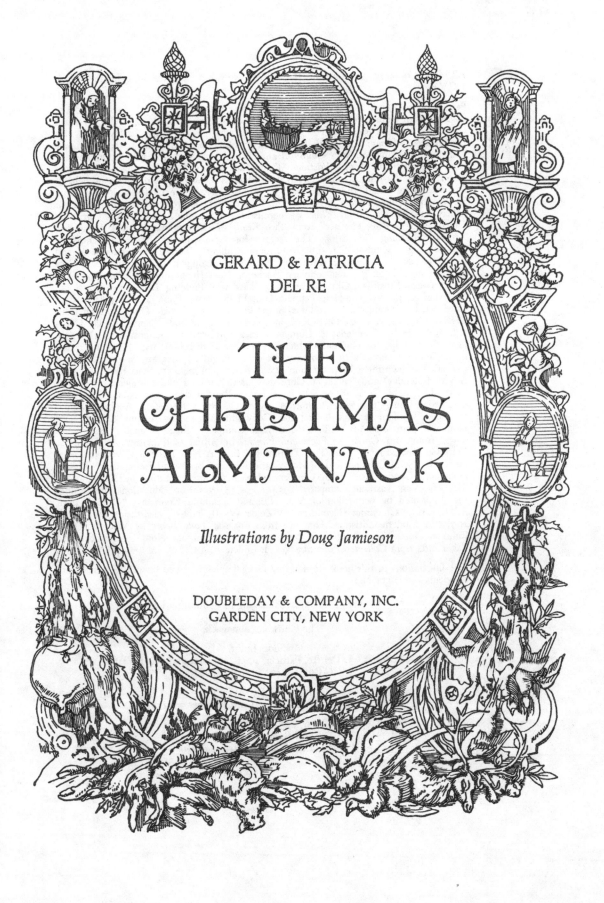

GERARD & PATRICIA
DEL RE

THE CHRISTMAS ALMANACK

Illustrations by Doug Jamieson

DOUBLEDAY & COMPANY, INC.
GARDEN CITY, NEW YORK

All biblical quotations throughout this volume are taken from the King James Version (KJV).

Permission to quote material from the following sources is gratefully acknowledged: "1521" taken from *The Gentleman of Renaissance France* by H. L. Wiley, Harvard University Press, 1954; "A Too White Christmas" by William Lashly from *Old Christmases*, William Strode, ed., Sampson Low Marston & Co., Ltd., 1947; "A Strange Christmas Eve" by Winston Churchill and "Toothpick Stars and Edible Ornaments" from *The LIFE Book of Christmas*, Time, Inc., 1963; "The Aftermath—December Twenty-sixth" by Julia Boynton Green from *Days We Celebrate*, Robert Haven Schauffler, ed., Dodd, Mead, 1940; "To Jesus on His Birthday" from *Collected Poems*, Edna St. Vincent Millay, Harper & Row, 1928. Copyright 1928, 1955 by Edna St. Vincent Millay and Norma Millay Ellis. By permission of Norma Millay Ellis; "Christmas Greetings from Ring Lardner" from *Two Kinds of Christmases*, H. Jack Lang, ed., World Publishing Co., 1965; The recipes for Goose (except stuffing), Pheasant, Suckling Pig (including Chestnut Mushroom Stuffing), Turkey (including Sage and Onion Dressing), Panettone (including Basic Sweet Dough), Stollen (including Easy White Icing), Eggnog (nonalcoholic), Bûche de Noël (including Mocha or Chocolate Butter Cream Frosting), Gingerbread Boys, Baked Rice Pudding, Lebkuchen, Marzipan, Moravian Christmas Cookies, Pepparkakor, Pfeffernüsse, Plum Pudding (including Hard Sauce), Springerle, Sugarplums, Sugar Pretzels, and Cookie Ornaments all from THE DOUBLEDAY COOKBOOK by Jean Anderson and Elaine Hanna. Copyright © 1975 by Doubleday & Company, Inc. Reprinted by permission of the publisher; The recipe for Glorious Golden Fruitcake and directions for "Natural Decorations" from *Christmas with a Country Flavor*, copyright © 1973, 1974, 1975 by Farm Journal, Inc. Reprinted by permission of the Farm Journal; Directions for "Christmas Advent Calendar" and "Medieval Christmas Castle" from *Holiday Magic* by Margaret Perry. Copyright © 1978 by Margaret Perry. Reprinted by permission of Nelson Doubleday, Inc.; "Pomanders" from *A Merry Christmas Herbal* by Adelma Grenier Simmons, William Morrow & Co., Inc. Copyright © 1968 by Adelma Grenier Simmons. By permission of William Morrow & Company, Inc.; "Stained 'Glass' Windows" from 1001 *Christmas Facts and Fancies* by Alfred Carl Hottes, A. T. de La Mare Co., Inc., 1937; "Some Tree Trimmings" from *A New Look at Christmas Decorations* by N. Hildebrand and Sr. M. Gratia Listaite, Bruce Publishing Co.; "Kissing Hoop and Goody Tree" from *Christmas Lighting and Decorating* by Theodore A. Saros, D. Van Nostrand Company, 1954. © 1954 by Litton Educational Publishing, Inc. Reprinted by permission of Van Nostrand Reinhold Company; "Ceppo" from *A Treasury of Christmas Decorations* by Zelda Wyatt Schulke, Hearthside Press, Inc., 1957; "A Modern Christmas Lament" from *For the Time Being* by W. H. Auden, Random House, 1945. Reprinted by permission of Random House and Faber and Faber Ltd., from *Collected Poems* by W. H. Auden.

The illustrations in this book are done by Doug Jamieson, based on nineteenth-century woodcuts and engravings.

Library of Congress Cataloging in Publication Data
Del Re, Gerard, 1944–
The Christmas almanack.

Includes index.
1. Christmas.   I. Del Re, Patricia, 1944–   joint author.   II. Title.
GT4985.D47   394.2′68282

ISBN: 0-385-13353-7
Library of Congress Catalog Card Number 77-12842

With love to Richard S. Lane
and Barbara Zena Wallace

Our sincere gratitude goes to William J. Brooke
for all his help in compiling this book.

"I will honor Christmas in my heart
and try to keep it all the year."

—Ebeneezer Scrooge
A Christmas Carol
1843

Contents

CHRISTMAS IN THE GOSPELS

CHRISTMAS ON THE CALENDAR

IT HAPPENED ON CHRISTMAS

CHRISTMAS AROUND THE WORLD
IN CUSTOM AND TRADITION

CHRISTMAS MUSIC

CHRISTMAS ON THE PAGE

CHRISTMAS ON FILM

CHRISTMAS ON THE SMALL SCREEN

CHRISTMAS ON THE TABLE

CHRISTMAS AROUND THE HOUSE

CHRISTMAS ON MY MIND

The Christmas Almanack

CHRISTMAS
in the
GOSPELS

Luke 2:1–20

[1] And it came to pass in those days, that there went out a decree from Caesar Augustus, that all the world should be taxed. [2] (*And* this taxing was first made when Cyrenius was governor of Syria.) [3] And all went to be taxed, every one into his own city. [4] And Joseph also went up from Galilee, out of the city of Nazareth, into Judaea, unto the city of David, which is called Bethlehem; (because he was of the house and lineage of David:) [5] To be taxed with Mary his espoused wife, being great with child. [6] And so it was, that, while they were there, the days were accomplished that she should be delivered. [7] And she brought forth her firstborn son, and wrapped him in swaddling clothes, and laid him in a manger; because there was no room for them in the inn. [8] And there were in the same country shepherds abiding in the field, keeping watch over their flock by night. [9] And, lo, the angel of the Lord came upon them, and the glory of the Lord shone round about them: and they were sore afraid. [10] And the angel said unto them, Fear not: for, behold, I bring you good tidings of great joy, which shall be to all people. [11] For unto you is born this day in the city of David a Saviour, which is Christ the Lord. [12] And this *shall be* a sign unto you; Ye shall find the babe wrapped in swaddling clothes, lying in a manger. [13] And suddenly there was with the angel a multitude of the heavenly host praising God, and saying, [14] Glory to God in the highest, and on earth peace, good will toward men. [15] And it came to pass, as the angels were gone away from them into heaven, the shepherds said one to another, Let us now go even unto Bethlehem, and see this thing which is come to pass, which the Lord hath made known unto us. [16] And they came with haste, and found Mary, and Joseph, and the babe lying in a manger. [17] And when they had seen *it*, they made known abroad the saying which was told them

concerning this child. [18] And all they that heard *it* wondered at those things which were told them by the shepherds. [19] But Mary kept all these things, and pondered *them* in her heart. [20] And the shepherds returned, glorifying and praising God for all the things that they had heard and seen, as it was told unto them. (KJV)

Matthew 2:1–23

[1] Now when Jesus was born in Bethlehem of Judaea in the days of Herod the king, behold, there came wise men from the east to Jerusalem, [2] Saying, Where is he that is born King of the Jews? for we have seen his star in the east, and are come to worship him. [3] When Herod the king had heard *these things*, he was troubled, and all Jerusalem with him. [4] And when he had gathered all the chief priests and scribes of the people together, he demanded of them where Christ should be born. [5] And they said unto him, In Bethlehem of Judaea: for thus it is written by the prophet, [6] And thou Bethlehem, *in* the land of Juda, art not the least among the princes of Juda: for out of thee shall come a Governor, that shall rule my people Israel. [7] Then Herod, when he had privily called the wise men, inquired of them diligently what time the star appeared. [8] And he sent them to Bethlehem, and said, Go and search diligently for the young child; and when ye have found *him*, bring me word again, that I may come and worship him also. [9] When they had heard the king, they departed; and, lo, the star, which they saw in the east, went before them, till it came and stood over where the young child was. [10] When they saw the star, they rejoiced with exceeding great joy. [11] And when

they were come into the house, they saw the young child with Mary his mother, and fell down, and worshipped him: and when they had opened their treasures, they presented unto him gifts; gold, and frankincense, and myrrh. [12] And being warned of God in a dream that they should not return to Herod, they departed into their own country another way. [13] And when they were departed, behold, the angel of the Lord appeareth to Joseph in a dream, saying, Arise, and take the young child and his mother, and flee into Egypt, and be thou there until I bring thee word: for Herod will seek the young child to destroy him. [14] When he arose, he took the young child and his mother by night, and departed into Egypt: [15] And was there until the death of Herod: that it might be fulfilled which was spoken of the Lord by the prophet, saying, Out of Egypt have I called my son. [16] Then Herod, when he saw that he was mocked of the wise men, was exceeding wroth, and sent forth, and slew all the children that were in Bethlehem, and in all the coasts thereof, from two years old and under, according to the time which he had diligently inquired of the wise men. [17] Then was fulfilled that which was spoken by Jeremy the prophet, saying, [18] In Rama was there a voice heard, lamentation, and weeping, and great mourning, Rachel weeping *for* her children, and would not be comforted, because they are not. [19] But when Herod was dead, behold, an angel of the Lord appeareth in a dream to Joseph in Egypt, [20] Saying, Arise, and take the young child and his mother, and go into the land of Israel: for they are dead which sought the young child's life. [21] And he arose, and took the young child and his mother, and came into the land of Israel. [22] But when he heard that Archelaus did reign in Judaea in the room of his father Herod, he was afraid to go thither: notwithstanding, being warned of God in a dream, he turned aside into the parts of Galilee: [23] And he came and dwelt in a city called Nazareth: that it might be fulfilled which was spoken by the prophets, He shall be called a Nazarene. (KJV)

The Old Familiar Story

We are all familiar with the biblical Christmas story, or at least with the two verses we had to memorize as our part of the Sunday School Christmas Pageant. Most of us would say we know the story backwards and forwards. Yet most of us know it better backwards in that our real understanding of the first Christmas has come from the paintings, music, stories, Christmas cards, commercials, and movies that have appeared in the last two thousand years. Hollywood has probably affected our idea of Christmas more than the Bible ever has.

To prove the point, herewith:

A POP QUIZ

Go back to the first page and read the Gospel story again if you feel you need to cram, but then do not cheat while the test is in progress. Remember, we just want to know what the Gospel writers had to say about each question. Ready?

1. What did Mary ride on the road to Bethlehem?
2. How soon after they reached Bethlehem was Jesus born?
3. What sort of building was Jesus born in?
4. What animals were gathered about the manger?
5. How many Wise Men were there?
6. How did the star compare in brightness with other stars?
7. Who else besides the Wise Men saw the star?
8. Did Joseph meet the Wise Men?

On the next page are the answers as given in Matthew and Luke.

5

1. *They don't say.*
2. *They don't say.*
3. *They don't say.*
4. *They don't say.*
5. *They don't say.*
6. *They don't say.*
7. *They don't say.*
8. *They don't say.*

If you don't believe these answers, go back and read the Gospel story again. Then read on to see what the Bible *does* say and where we picked up some of our ideas.

The Journey to Bethlehem

In popular myth, the journey from Nazareth to Bethlehem has Mary seated on a donkey and is one of great tribulation, which would never have been undertaken but for the census. In fact, no donkey is mentioned although it may possibly have existed. As to the hardship of the journey, undoubtedly all travel in that time was difficult, but this trip was not to be unique for Joseph and Mary. Bethlehem is just five miles from Jerusalem and, according to Luke 2:41, Jesus' "parents went to Jerusalem every year at the feast of the passover." Thus the trip was to be an annual pilgrimage for them.

The phrase "great with child" conjures up in the modern mind an image of Mary being near the time of delivery. In fact, this King James translation is just a seventeenth-century euphemism for "pregnant," with no indication of how far along that pregnancy might be. There is no hint as to how long Mary and Joseph were at Bethlehem before the birth took place. People assume it was within the first night or two because there was no room at the inn, but such a crowded situation might have arisen at any time, and the Bible does not give an answer.

The Stable

No stable is mentioned in the texts of Matthew and Luke. The word translated as "manger" may mean either that or "stall." A stall could be either in a stable or outdoors. Moreover, an inn of the time does not fit our modern conception with individual rooms and a stable out back. An inn could often be a large, one-roomed structure where the travelers slept elevated on cots or platforms and the animals were in the same room on the floor. Thus a manger might be indoors, on a different level from the sleeping facilities but in the same room. We really can't say where Christ was born.

Popular tradition made the stable a cave. Thus, when Constantine became Christian and sought the birthplace of Jesus, he decided on a series of caves near Bethlehem. In keeping the general trend of adapting the pagan to the Christian, he tore down a temple to Adonis and erected the Church of the Nativity on the same spot, over the cave where he believed Jesus was born.

The Animals

There is no mention of the friendly animals that popular art and fiction have clustered around the manger, giving warmth and adoration. However, since a manger was for the feeding of such animals, it is probably safe to assume that animals were around somewhere. The image of the King of Heaven humbling Himself to be surrounded by the beasts of the field has proved to be enduring as well as inspiring. Countless legends tell how all animals kneel in adoration on Christmas Eve at midnight, just as their ancestors did in the original stable, and how the animals can also speak at that time.

Several medieval carols and pageants presented the charming story of the animals seeking to worship the newborn king with their own voices. Each response is cleverly suited to the "language" of each animal. The rooster crows out, "Christus natus est," Latin for "Christ is born." "Ubi?" "Where?" muses the taciturn ox. The excitable sheep bleat out, "Bethlehem!" "Hihamus" or "eamus," brays the donkey, "let's go." And a young calf replies, "Volo!" "I'm going!"

The Shepherds and the Angels' Song

The shepherds of the time were not regarded as they are now. We see shepherds as they were pictured in the Arcadian myths and pastorals of a much later time, as men who lolled in the fields playing on pipes and passing the days in rustic meditation. Such a description applies better to the sheep than to the shepherds. At the time of Jesus' birth, shepherds were rough men considered to be outside the law. Coming upon them at night, alone, would probably terrify anyone.

The song of the angels is a blessing to biblical scholars since its exact translation has given them gainful employment for centuries and shows no sign of letting up. "And on earth peace, good will toward men" is what we all learned, but "peace toward men of good will" is just as correct a translation of the ambiguous Greek that Luke uses at this point. The examination of fine details of grammar, usage, and prosody and textual comparisons have not produced a definitive answer on who should expect God's peace and good will, all men or only those who have tried to deserve them. It is probably safest to try to be in the second category, just in case.

The Wise Men

Matthew does not tell us how many Wise Men there were, nor who they were and where they came from. Tradition finally settled on three since three gifts are mentioned, but as late as the third century there were paintings of four Wise Men and earlier there had been as many as a dozen.

The word that Matthew uses for the Wise Men is *magoi*. This word was applied to a multitude of practitioners of the occult arts. Fortunetellers, astronomers, augurers, and general magicians were all referred to as magi. One widely held theory is that the Magi of the Bible were priests of Zoroaster from Persia. Their functions in this religion would have included the interpretation of signs and astrology. Babylonia and Arabia are also very possible sources for the magicians we call Wise Men.

The idea of the Wise Men as kings (as in "We Three Kings of Orient Are") does not appear in the Gospels but was added in popular tradition later. This idea probably arose from application of Psalm 72:10–11: "The kings of Sheba and Seba shall offer gifts. Yea, all kings shall fall down before him."

Whatever their origin and status, the Magi caught the popular imagination with their exotic and mysterious story. The early Church paid far more attention to them than to the prosaic shepherds. In the Roman catacombs, the Magi appear in paintings at least two centuries earlier than the shepherds, and far more prominently. It would not be until the Protestants arose to decry the adoration of relics and the elaborate symbolism accorded the Magi that the simple shepherds who did not bear such a "taint" would be elevated to the major position in nativity scenes that they now occupy.

With the intense interest that the early Church had in them, it is natural that the Magi should begin to acquire names and homes and even physical manifestations. Numerous traditions arose with such tongue-twisting names as Yazdegerd, Hormizdah, and Perozadh, Kings of Persia, Saba, Sheba, or, less specifically, "the East." The sixth century marks the first appearance in a Greek manuscript, which is known only from a later Latin translation, of the names Balthasar, Melchior, and Gaspar or Caspar. Each was a king and each was assigned a kingdom and a particular royal gift. Balthasar, a black King of Ethiopia and forty years old, brought myrrh in a gold-mounted horn. Melchior, also forty or sometimes older, King of Arabia, brought a casket of gold in the form of a shrine. Gaspar was King of Tarsus and a beardless youth of twenty when he brought frankincense in a jar or censer. Thus the Magi represented people of all races and all ages kneeling in adoration.

The gifts of the Wise Men have been taken symbolically to mean many different things, but the general symbolic value of each is clear. Gold was the purest material and therefore worthy of a king. Incense is used in the worship of a god, carrying prayers upward with its sweet scent. Myrrh was a balm for physical suffering. Thus, it has been suggested, Jesus was being worshiped as king, god, and great physician, or sacrifice. The gifts may also suggest what each Christian must offer up to God: virtue, prayer, and suffering.

The time allowed for the Wise Men's journey is not specified in the Gospels. As nothing says whether the star arose at Jesus' birth or before it, there is really no way of telling when they set out. Popular tradition varies from twelve days to two years and puts their arrival on January 6, Epiphany, although no one thinks twice of Christmas manger scenes that show them arriving a few minutes after the shepherds, who came from just down the road.

However long that first trip to Bethlehem, the Wise Men's journeys were far from ended. The cathedral at Cologne, Germany, contains a shrine that is said to hold the still-uncorrupt remains of the Three Kings. These bodies were taken to Constantinople either by Empress Helena, mother of Constantine, in the third century or by Emperor Zeno in the fifth century. After the First Crusade, they turned up in Milan and then were moved to Cologne by the emperor Frederick Barbarossa. In 1903 the cardinal of Cologne returned some of the relics to the cardinal of Milan. Let us hope that the Magi have finally reached journey's end and rest.

The Star

The Star of Bethlehem appears in pictures as a great shining light that would have created astonishment in anyone seeing it. But Matthew does not indicate that anyone besides the Magi paid it any notice. Herod asks them the time when they first saw it as though it had not been seen or particularly noticed in Jerusalem. Yet it must have been something that would have special meaning to trained observers of the skies such as the Wise Men. Three major theories have been put forward as natural explanations of the star:

1. A nova is a star that explodes, becoming suddenly very bright where it may have been dim before, and remaining highly visible, sometimes even during the day, for weeks at a time. Astronomers in many parts of the world, however, had been keeping records since long before this time, and none indicated a nova occurring in the last few years B.C. or the first few years A.D.

2. A comet is a celestial body that appears as a bright head trailing a luminous tail of gases and particles. A comet has the advantage over a star as candidate for Star of Bethlehem in that it moves and could conceivably seem to lead the Wise Men. By stretching our dates somewhat, it is possible to put Halley's comet, which returns about every seventy-seven years, into approximately the right place. It would have appeared in 12 B.C. in the constellation Leo, which might be interpreted symbolically as the Lion of Judah. But comets were known to the people of the time as comets, not as stars, and they were more often thought to presage catastrophes than joyous occasions.

3. The most popular theory is that of a planetary conjunction. An ordinary conjunction occurs whenever two planets are passing each other at their closest point as viewed from the earth. This happens as often as every twenty years or so, depending upon the specific planets.

11

Much rarer is a conjunction of three planets. The great astronomer Kepler saw such a conjunction of Mars, Jupiter, and Saturn in October 1604. His calculations showed that there is such a conjuction every 805 years. This would mean that one occurred in the year 7–6 B.C., appearing most brightly in the months of May–June, September–October, and December of 7 B.C. This would result in a particularly bright star or pattern of stars that might be noticed by anyone but would have special significance for an astrologer.

These are the scientific explanations put forward to account for the star. Most Christians are satisfied with the simple words of Matthew: "When they had heard the king, they departed; and, lo, the star, which they saw in the east, went before them, till it came and stood over where the young child was. When they saw the star, they rejoiced with exceeding great joy. And when they were come into the house, they saw the young child with Mary his mother, and fell down, and worshipped him: and when they had opened their treasures, they presented unto him gifts; gold, and frankincense, and myrrh." (KJV)

CHRISTMAS
on the
CALENDAR

Jesus' Birthday

We celebrate Christmas as the birthday of Jesus Christ, and we shall continue to do so even though scholars tell us there is no hard evidence that would let us know on what date Jesus was born. In fact, there is no certainty even about the year.

Luke does give certain clues to the year. The appearance of the angel to Elisabeth happened "in the days of Herod," and we know that Herod, the king of Judaea, died in March or April of 4 B.C.

Luke also tells us that shortly before Jesus' birth "there went out a decree from Caesar Augustus, that all the world should be taxed," and that this happened "when Cyrenius was governor of Syria." Records show that the only census taking place during the governorship of Quirinius (the accepted modern spelling of "Cyrenius") took place in 7–6 B.C. Generally, modern scholarship places the birth of Christ in approximately 6 B.C. This would be two years before the death of Herod. Since Matthew says Herod ordered the massacre of all male children under two years of age in Bethlehem in an attempt to kill the Messiah, it would appear that Jesus was probably approaching two years of age before Herod died, meaning that Jesus was born in 6 B.C.

The year 6 B.C. would also accord roughly with Luke's statement that Jesus was about thirty years of age in "the fifteenth year of the reign of Tiberius Caesar" (Luke 3:1, 23), which would have been A.D. 27–28.

The earliest reference to Christmas being celebrated on December 25 appeared in Antioch in the middle of the second century. As the Christian Church was still a persecuted minority, no official determination was made until the fourth century, when the Roman emperor Constantine embraced Christianity, thereby ensuring its legality and eventual domination of Western culture. According to the Philocalian Calendar, a Roman almanac of the year 336, December 25 was the date for the Nativity Feast, indicating the popular acceptance given that date. In 350, December 25 was finally declared officially to be Christmas by Pope Julius I.

By the fifth century, Christmas had become so important in the Church calendar that it was considered to be the beginning of the ecclesiastical year. The start of the Church calendar was later moved back to include Advent, the season of preparation for the coming of Christ. In 529 the Emperor Justinian made December 25 a civic holiday, thereby prohibiting any work on that day. The Council of Tours in 567 established the period of Advent as a time of fasting before Christmas and proclaimed the twelve days from Christmas to Epiphany a sacred, festive season.

Other Winter Solstice Celebrations

There are indications, though no hard evidence, that as Christians went on from year to year and century to century developing the rites of Christmas, they borrowed, adopted, or simply carried over elements of other midwinter celebrations. The time of the winter solstice has always been an important season in the mythology of all peoples. The sun, the giver of life, is at its lowest ebb. It is shortest daylight of the year; the promise of spring is buried in cold and snow. It is the time when the forces of chaos that stand against the return of light and life must once again be defeated by the gods. At the low point of the solstice, the people must help the gods through imitative magic and religious ceremonies. The sun begins to return in triumph. The days lengthen and, though winter remains, spring is once again conceivable. For all people, it is a time of great festivity.

In Mesopotamia, there was a year's-end celebration called Zagmuk. A criminal was set up as a mock king and eventually executed as a scapegoat for the people's sins of the previous year. In the Mesopotamian creation myth, the great god Marduk had subdued the monsters of chaos before the world began, but their restraint was loosened with the dying of the sun and they had to be conquered again at the end of each year. To help, a wooden image was made of his opponents by the Mesopotamians and was burned in a great bonfire. It may well be this wooden image which traveled a circuitous route over the course of hundreds of years to become the Yule log of northern celebrations.

Persia and Babylonia also had solstice festivals, called Sacaea. Slaves and masters exchanged places. Two criminals were chosen: one was set free; one was treated as a king and then executed.

In Greek mythology, Zeus overthrew Kronos and the Titans at this time of year to establish his own reign. In Rome, Zeus became identified with Jupiter and Kronos with Saturn. When he escaped from the defeat by Jupiter, Saturn established his realm in Italy. It was a time of great peace and prosperity known ever afterward as the Golden Age. Goodness and plenty were available for all (though only men existed at the time—women would come with the plagues of later times). All men were equal. But the Golden Age did not last. Saturn was forced out again by Jupiter. In his temple at Rome, the feet of Saturn were bound in chains all the year as a symbol of his defeat except for one brief period. This was the Saturnalia, the celebration of the return of the Golden Age.

The Saturnalia ran from December 17 to 24 and was followed shortly by the kalends (first day of the month) of January, which was also a great celebration. All businesses were closed except those that provided food or revelry. Slaves were made equal to masters or even set over them. Gambling, drinking, and feasting were encouraged. People exchanged gifts, called *strenae*, from the vegetation goddess Strenia, whom it was important to honor at midwinter. Originally these gifts were merely twigs from her sacred grove, but they later became fruits or cakes and finally small figures and more elaborate gifts. Men dressed as women or in the hides of animals and caroused in the streets. Candles and lamps were used to frighten the spirits of darkness, which were powerful at this time of year. At its most decadent and barbaric, Saturnalia may have been the excuse among Roman soldiers in the East for the human sacrifice of the king of the revels. This, however, was the extreme. Generally, Saturnalia was a boisterous, noisy revel celebrating the Golden Age and helping to overcome the forces that threaten the earth at the sun's ebb.

Why December 25?

Saturnalia and the kalends were the celebrations most familiar to early Christians, December 17–24 and January 1–3, but the tradition of celebrating December 25 as Christ's birthday came to the Romans from Persia. Mithra, the Persian god of light and sacred contracts, was born out of a rock on December 25. Rome was famous for its flirtations with strange gods and cults, and in the third century the emperor Aurelian established the festival of Dies Invicti Solis, the Day of the Invincible Sun, on December 25. Mithra was an embodiment of the sun, so this period of its rebirth was a major day in Mithraism, which had become Rome's latest official religion with the patronage of Aurelian. It is believed that the emperor Constantine adhered to Mithraism up to the time of his conversion to Christianity. He was probably instrumental in seeing that the major feast of his old religion was carried over to his new faith.

Early Christians were familiar with the symbolic identification of Christ with the Sun, as in Malachi 4:2: "But unto you that fear my name shall the Sun of righteousness arise with healing in his wings." It was easy to replace the Invincible Sun symbolically with the new Sun of Righteousness, and most of the festivities were carried over whole into the new religion.

Yule

Finally, as the Christian faith was carried into the dark nights of northern Europe, two important festivals celebrated by the Germanic and Celtic peoples of these lands found their way into the celebration of Christmas. The first was generally in mid-November when the first snows covered the fields and made it difficult for herds to forage. Faced with the impossible task of finding food for all the herd throughout the winter, the barbarian Teutons and Celts made a delight of necessity with a great slaughter and feasting.

In December, ten to twelve days were set aside for celebrating the *Julmond*. The origins of the word *Jul*, which became our familiar "Yule," remain shrouded in mystery. It may relate to the Germanic word *Iul* or *Giul*, which means "a turning wheel." This would relate to the turning of the seasons or the rising of the wheel of the sun. More probably it derives from the word *Geola*, which means "a feast" and was sometimes used to mean the whole month of December.

In the celebration of Jul, wheat was worshiped and its products, bread and liquor distilled from the grains of the field, were exchanged as gifts and heavily indulged in. In midwinter, the idea of rebirth and fertility was tremendously important. In the snows of winter, the evergreen was a symbol of the life that would return in the spring, so evergreens were used for decoration. The boar, which was the symbol of Frey, a god of regeneration, was killed and eaten. Light was important in dispelling the growing darkness of the solstice, so a Yule log was lighted with the remains of the previous year's log.

This was the background that the Christian missionaries found as they moved north, starting in the fifth century. It was very much like Rome with its Saturnalia before the acceptance of Christianity, and, as before, the local customs were swallowed up into the practice of the new faith. The various saints' days festivities throughout November and December took on the aspects of the harvest feasts, and Christmas absorbed the characteristics of Jul. By the end of the ninth century, Christmas was observed throughout Europe with feasting and celebration, the giving of presents, decorating with evergreens, light, and noise. As many customs lost their religious reasons for being, they passed into the realm of superstition, becoming good luck traditions and eventually merely enjoyable customs without rationale. Thus the mistletoe was no longer worshiped but became eventually an excuse for rather nonreligious activities.

Christmas Festivities at Their Peak

The celebration of Christmas as feast reached its height in medieval England. The twelve days of Christmas were a time to call the court together and indulge in unequaled revelry. Kings and bishops vied to outdo each other in the splendor of their retinue's apparel, the elaborateness of their entertainments, the pageantry of their tournaments, and the groaning bounty of their banquet tables. One course of such a banquet, a Christmas pie, was described as being 9 feet in diameter, weighing 165 pounds, and containing 2 bushels of flour, 20 pounds of butter, 4 geese, 2 rabbits, 4 wild ducks, 2 woodcocks, 6 snipes, 4 partridges, 2 neats' tongues, 2 curlews, 6 pigeons, and 7 blackbirds. At one Christmas Henry III had 600 oxen slaughtered, not to mention the game and fish or the veritable oceans of wine needed to ease the passage of such a herd down the throats of king and court.

Christmas also became the time for all good nobles and merchants to show their fealty to their king by making him splendid gifts. There was an understanding as to how much each should give, and cash was considered an appropriate present. In the mid-thirteenth century, when the merchant class was backward about doing its share, Henry III closed the shops for two weeks until the merchants agreed to come up with the stipulated two thousand pounds.

Gambling was very popular at Christmas. It was considered a quiet sport and therefore more suitable in fashionable circles than some of the rowdier entertainments that were popular among the common people. Edward IV actually passed an act restricting card play to the twelve days of Christmas. It is said that Queen Elizabeth I's indulgent nobles gave her loaded dice to play with so that she would always win.

By the sixteenth century, the celebration of Christmas had become

19

a boisterous affair. Bands of mummers, dressed like beasts and women as in the days of Saturnalia, begged money and caroused, even invading churches to disrupt services with their merriment.

"No Christmas!"

Inevitably, there were reactions against what Christmas had become. Since the earliest days of the Church, the religious had inveighed against the way Christ's birthday was celebrated. There was even great controversy over whether His birthday should be celebrated at all. As early as A.D. 245, the Church father Origen was proclaiming it heathenish to celebrate Christ's birthday as if He were merely a temporal ruler when His spiritual nature should be the main concern. This view was echoed throughout the centuries, but found strong, widespread advocacy only with the rise of Protestantism. To these serious-minded, sober clerics, the celebration of Christmas flew in the face of all they believed. Drunken revelry on Christmas! The day was not even known to be Christ's birthday. It was merely an excuse to continue the customs of pagan Saturnalia. The Protestants found their own quieter ways of celebrating, in calm and meditation. The strict Puritans refused to celebrate at all, saying that no celebration should be more important than the Sabbath. The Pilgrims in Massachusetts made a point of working on Christmas as on any other day.

This made little difference to the world at large until the Puritans came to power in England, beheading King Charles I and establishing Oliver Cromwell as Lord Protector of the country.

On June 3, 1647, Parliament established punishments for observing Christmas and certain other holidays. This policy was reaffirmed in 1652 with these words:

Resolved by the Parliament
That no Observation shall be had of the Five and twentieth day of *December* commonly called *Christmas-Day*; nor any Solemnity used or exercised in Churches upon the Day in respect thereof.

The town criers passed through the streets ringing their bells and shouting, "No Christmas! No Christmas!" For those who celebrated Christmas quietly in their churches, this caused a good deal of soul-searching and some martyrlike acts of courage. For the common people, however, it provided a new form of Christmas entertainment: the riot.

Christmas Under the Puritans

from a contemporary account

Upon Wednesday, Decem. 22, the Cryer of Canterbury by the appointment of Master Major [Mayor] openly proclaimed that Christmas day, and all other Superstitious Festivals should be put downe, and that a Market should be kept upon Christmas day. Which not being observed (but very ill taken by the Country) the towne was thereby unserved with provision, and trading very much hindered; which occasioned great discontent among the people, causing them to rise in a Rebellious way.

The Major being slighted, and his Commands observed only of a few who opened their Shops, to the number of 12 at the most: They were commanded by the multitude to shut up again, but refusing to obey, their ware was thrown up and down, and they, at last forced to shut in.

The Major and his assistants used their best endeavours to qualifie this tumult, but the fire being once kindled, was not easily quenched. The Sheriffe laying hold of a fellow, was stoutly resisted; which the Major perceiving, took a Cudgell and strook the man; who, being no puny, pulled up his courage, and knockt down the Major, whereby his Cloak was much torne and durty, beside the hurt he received. The Major thereupon made strict Proclamation for keeping the Peace and that every man depart to his own house. The multitude hollowing thereat, in disorderly manner; the Aldermen and Constables caught two or three of the rout, and sent them to Jayle, but they soon broke loose, and jeered Master Alderman.

Soon after, issued forth the Commanders of the Rabble, with an addition of Souldiers, into the high street, and brought with them two

Foot-balls, whereby their company increased. Which the Major and Aldermen perceiving, took what prisoners they had got, and would have carried them to the Jayle. But the multitude following after to the King's Bench, were opposed by Captain Bridg, who was straight knoct down, and had his head broke in two places, not being able to withstand the multitude, who, getting betwixt him and the Jayle, rescued their fellowes, and beat the Major and Aldermen into their houses, and then cried Conquest.

Christmas Restored

In 1647, ten thousand men from Canterbury and the surrounding area gathered and passed their own resolution that "if they could not have their Christmas day, they would have the King back on his throne again." Eventually the monarchy was restored in 1660. Christmas regained its official acceptance. As the court had less and less real power and as the middle class rose, Christmas became more a celebration of the people and less an excuse for royal display. The middle class had its own versions of the Christmas feast, and the popular dramatic forms, the pantomime and the St. George play, replaced the royal masque as the primary form of Christmas entertainment.

America was later in recovering from the Puritan influence than England. Christmas was outlawed in New England until the middle of the nineteenth century. In 1856 Christmas Day was still an ordinary workday in Boston and failure to report to a job was grounds for dismissal. Classes were held in Boston public schools as late as 1870. It was probably the influence of immigrants from Germany and Ireland that finally convinced the Yankees that Christmas could be a harmless, pleasant, and even religious festivity. The first state to declare Christmas a legal holiday was Alabama in 1836. The last was Oklahoma in 1890.

Today (Almost) Everyone Celebrates
on December 25

A curious quirk of history resulted in some Englishmen being the last holdouts in the struggle to establish December 25 as Christmas. Tradition held that Joseph of Arimathea, who provided the tomb for Jesus, had later wandered as far as England, bringing with him the Holy Grail. When he landed at Glastonbury, he planted his thorn staff, which took root and grew. Moreover, it and its alleged offspring magically blossomed every Christmas Eve.

In 1752 Britain adopted the Gregorian calendar, which had already been accepted throughout Europe. This calendar had been created to correct the mistakes in the Julian calendar, which had misjudged the length of the year very slightly. Over the centuries, the mistake had built up to a total of eleven days. Thus Christmas under the new calendar was still December 25, but it fell eleven days earlier that year. At Quainton in Buckinghamshire, two thousand people gathered on December 24 to watch a thorn tree that was said to be descended from Joseph's staff. It had not blossomed by midnight, and they refused to celebrate Christmas. They came back on January 5, which would have been Christmas under the old calendar. The thorn tree had blossomed, and the people celebrated on the assumption that the tree knew best.

The Gregorian calendar was gradually accepted, although there were still a few die-hard tree-watchers as late as 1950. But it can now be said that Christmas is celebrated by everyone on December 25 except for the Armenians. (See *Armenia* in the section "Christmas Around the World in Custom and Tradition.")

IT HAPPENED ON CHRISTMAS

A.D. 496

The first important step toward the unification of the French nation came on Christmas Day 496. Clovis I was the king of the Franks, one of the tribes that inhabited Gaul (as France was then called). In order to gain the support of the bishops and the backing of the Church, Clovis and three thousand of his followers converted to Christianity and were baptized on Christmas Day. The combined power of Church and state was then great enough to begin forging a nation out of the scattered and disorganized tribes.

King Arthur

According to Sir Thomas Malory's *Morte d'Arthur*, the fifteenth-century romance of the semimythical British king, Merlin the magician called the nobles together on Christmas Day for a sign as to who was their rightful king. There was a sword embedded in an anvil or stone. Whoever could draw it out would be king. All tried and failed. It was young Arthur, who knew nothing of the sword's significance, who finally succeeded. He was just trying to find a sword for his brother who had left his own behind, and the sword in the stone seemed the handiest source.

A.D. 800

In return for defending the Pope, Charlemagne was crowned Emperor of the Romans, beginning one of the most brilliant periods of the Middle Ages. Pope Leo III himself crowned the Emperor on Christmas Day 800.

1066

The year 1066 is well known as the one when William the Conqueror led his Norman French army against the Saxon inhabitants of England in the Battle of Hastings. It was on Christmas Day that William assumed the English throne with the Pope's blessing.

1214

On Christmas Day 1214 the English barons presented King John with a list of demands. The king ignored them. Eventually, hostilities broke out and after the confrontation at Runnymede the following June, the king was finally forced to sign the Magna Carta, the "Great Charter," which was the first guarantee of a subject's rights against the king and the foundation of all later English constitutional law.

1492

On Christmas Eve 1492 the *Santa María* ran aground on the island of Hispaniola. Columbus left a group of men to form a colony and sailed for Spain in the *Niña*. He thought he had discovered a new, short route to Japan.

Christmas Masquing

In this year, 1512, the King [Henry VIII] kept his Christmas at Greenwich where was such abundance of viands served to all comers of any honest behaviour as hath been few times seen. And against New Year's night was made in the hall a castle, gates, towers and dungeon, garnished with artillery and weapons after the most warlike fashion: and on the front of the castle was written *Le Fortresse dangereux*, and within the castle were six ladies clothed in russet satin, laid all over with leaves of gold, and every one knit with laces of blue silk and gold. On their heads, coifs and caps all of gold. After this castle had been carried about the hall, and the Queen had beheld it, in came the King with five others apparelled in coats, the one half of russet satin, the other half of rich cloth of gold; on their heads caps of russet satin embroidered with works of fine gold bullion.

These six assaulted the castle. The ladies seeing them so lusty and courageous, were content to solace with them, and upon further communication to yield the castle, and so they came down and danced a long space. And after the ladies led the knights into the castle, and then the castle suddenly vanished out of their sights.

On the day of the Epiphany at night, the King, with eleven others, were disguised after the manner of Italy, called a masque, a thing not seen before in England: they were apparelled in garments long and broad, wrought all with gold, with visors and caps of gold. And after the banquet done these masquers came in with six gentlemen disguised in silk, bearing staff torches, and desired the ladies to dance: some were content, and some refused. And after they had danced: and communed together, as the fashion of the masque is, they took their leave and departed, and so did the Queen and all the ladies.

from Edward Hall's *The Union
of the Noble and Illustre Families
of Lancaster and York,* 1542

1521

The King [Francis I of France] and his retinue, after having made a little sojourn at Amboise around Christmas, went on north a few miles to spend the *fête des Rois* (or Twelfth Night) of 1521 at Romorantin. It all started when the news came to Francis that the Comte de Saint-Pol in his house nearby had just chosen a king for the festival: some courtier had already by chance found in the Twelfth Night cake the large bean that made him king for the day, a gay ceremony that is still done in France on the sixth of January. The King, in high good spirits, decided "with the young gentlemen of his court" to challenge the authority of this king that had got his crown so easily. Saint-Pol and a group in his domain accepted the challenge, and laid in a supply of ammunition to defend the temporarily royal castle against the besiegers. The defense material consisted of a "prodigious quantity of snowballs, eggs, and apples," which turned out not to be enough to repel the assault, for the attackers were soon pushing in the doors and the ammunition was all gone. In the excitement, someone snatched a burning chunk of wood from a fireplace upstairs and threw it out a window. It struck the King on the side of the head, wounding him quite seriously. Nevertheless, he would permit no investigations to be made as to who had thrown the almost deadly missile, saying that if he indulged in such tomfoolery, he would have to take his chances on any accident. . . . It seems likely that the episode caused the King to have a permanent scar . . . which he covered with a beard—and thus popularized beards at Court.

from *The Gentleman of Renaissance France* by H. L. Wiley

A Sixteenth-century English Christmas

Before the coming of Cromwell and the Commonwealth with its prohibition on the celebration of Christmas, the common people's festivities had become more than slightly boisterous. Philip Stubbs described it thus in the sixteenth century:

Thus things sette in order, they have their hobbie-horses, dragons, and other antiques, together with their baudie pipers, and thunderyng drommers, to strike up the Deville's daunce withall: then marche these heathen companie towards the church and churchyarde, their pipers pipyng, drommers thonderyng, their stumppes dauncyng, their bells jynglyng, their hande-kercheefes swyngyng about their heades like madmen, their hobbie horses, and other monsters skyrmishyng amongest the throng: and in this sort they goe to the churche (though the minister bee at praier or preachyng) dauncyng and swingyng their handkercheefs over their heades in the churche, like devilles incarnate, with suche a confused noise, that no man can hear his owne voice.

Then the foolishe people, they looke, they stare, they laugh, they fleere, and mount upon formes and pewes, to see these goodly pageauntes solemnized in this sort. Then after this, about the churche they goe againe and againe, and so forthe into the churcheyarde, where they have commonly their sommer haules, their bowers, arbours, and banquettyng houses set up, wherein they feaste, banquet, and daunce all that daie, and (peradventure) all that night too. And thus these terrestrial furies spend their Sabbaoth daie.

Christmas in America, 1621

The Puritans who settled New England refused to celebrate Christmas on the grounds that no day was more important than the Sabbath and, besides, Christ's birthday was not actually known. Sometimes new settlers had to be forced to work on Christmas Day. From the journal of Governor Bradford of Plymouth Colony, December 25, 1621:

On ye day called Christmas day, ye Govr. caled them out to worke (as he was used), but the most of this new company excused themselves and said it went against their consciences to worke on ye day. So the Govr. tould them that if they made it a mater of conscience, he would spare them till they were better informed. So he led away ye rest, and left them; but when they came home at noone from their worke, he found them in ye streete at play, openly: some pitching ye barr, and some at stoole-ball and such like sports. So he went to them and took away their implements and tould them that it was against his conscience that they should play and others worke. If they made the keeping of it a matter of devotion, let them kepe their houses, but ther should be no gameing or revelling in ye streete. Since which time nothing hath been attempted that way, at least openly.

1776

The American colonials did not celebrate Christmas at this time because of the continuing Puritan influence. The Hessians, who were German mercenaries hired by the British, did celebrate. On Christmas night 1776 Washington crossed the Delaware and caught the

Hessians by surprise, as they were still involved in their celebrations. Their camp probably contained the first Christmas tree seen in America. This initial decisive action led to later victory at the Battle of Trenton, America's first major victory in the Revolutionary War.

Yellow Fever

Christmas Day 1900 provided an odd reason for rejoicing: in American Army barracks in Cuba, a young soldier named Moran contracted yellow fever. That may seem a strange reason for happiness, but the sickness occurred as the result of a carefully controlled experiment by Walter Reed. The soldier's sickness proved conclusively that yellow fever could be transmitted only by the *Stegomyia* mosquito. This opened the way to developing the treatment for this dread disease and helped save countless lives.

A Too White Christmas

In 1911 the great English explorer Robert Scott set out overland across Antarctica to reach the South Pole. The expedition was to be a tragic one, as he and a four-man team would reach the Pole one month after the Norwegian explorer Amundsen, and none of them would survive the homeward journey. There was no sense of foreboding or hardship in this diary entry by one of the survivors of the expedition, William Lashly, only hope, courage, and good humor:

> Christmas Day and a good one. We have done fifteen miles over a very changing surface. First of all it was very much crevassed and pretty rotten; we were often in difficulties as to which way we should tackle it. I had the misfortune to drop clean through, but was stopped with a jerk

when at the end of my harness. It was not of course a very nice sensation, especially on Christmas Day, and being my birthday as well. While spinning round in space like I was it took me a few seconds to gather together my thoughts and see what kind of a place I was in. It certainly was not a fairy's palace. When I had collected myself I heard someone calling from above, "Are you all right, Lashly?" I was all right it is true, but I did not care to be dangling in the air on a piece of rope, especially when I looked round and saw what kind of a place it was. It seemed about fifty feet deep and eight feet wide, and 120 feet long. This information I had ample time to gain while dangling there. I could measure the width with my ski sticks, as I had them on my wrists. It seemed a long time before I saw the rope come down alongside me with a bowline in it for me to put my foot in and get dragged out. It was not a job I should care to have to go through often, as by being in the crevasse I had got cold and a bit frost-bitten on the hands and face, which made it more difficult for me to help myself. Anyhow Evans, Bowers and Crean hauled me out and Crean wished me many happy returns of the day, and of course I thanked him politely and the others laughed. . . .

1915

During World War I the Western Front gave the world the term "war of attrition," endless bloody fighting that neither gained nor lost anything except lives. On Christmas afternoon 1915 the Germans from Saxony laid down their rifles and crawled out of the muddy trenches into the no man's land between the lines. They carried food. They began to sing. The disbelieving British heard the sound of carols they knew in their own language. They joined in, English words and German words blending in songs that knew nothing of national boundaries. They ate and sang together in the slush and the snow until their officers came and broke it up. The officers couldn't allow fraternizing with the enemy. "Fraternize" is from the Latin word that means "brother." Even in the midst of mud and blood and horror, Christmas can make brothers of men.

"A Strange Christmas Eve"

It was not long after Pearl Harbor when Winston Churchill visited the newly-at-war America and made this Christmas speech in 1941:

> I spend this anniversary and festival far from my country, far from my family, and yet I cannot truthfully say that I feel far from home. Whether it be the ties of blood on my mother's side, or the friendships I have developed here over many years of active life, or the commanding sentiment of comradeship in the common cause of great peoples who speak the same language, who kneel at the same altars and, to a very large extent, pursue the same ideals; I cannot feel myself a stranger here in the centre and at the summit of the United States. I feel a sense of unity and fraternal association which, added to the kindliness of your welcome, convinces me that I have a right to sit at your fireside and share your Christmas joys.
>
> Fellow workers, fellow soldiers in the cause, this is a strange Christmas Eve. Almost the whole world is locked in deadly struggle. Armed with the most terrible weapons which science can devise, the nations advance upon each other. Ill would it be for us this Christmastide if we were not sure that no greed for the lands or wealth of any other people, no vulgar ambitions, no morbid lust for material gain at the expense of others, had led us to the field. Ill would it be for us if that were so. Here, in the midst of war, raging and roaring over all the lands and seas, sweeping nearer to our hearths and homes; here, amid all these tumults, we have tonight the peace of the spirit in each cottage home and in every generous heart. Therefore we may cast aside, for this night at least, the cares and dangers which beset us and make for the children an evening of happiness in a world of storm. Here then, for one night only, each home throughout the English-speaking world should be a brightly-lighted island of happiness and peace.
>
> Let the children have their night of fun and laughter, let the gifts of Father Christmas delight their play. Let us grown-ups share to the full in their unstinted pleasures before we turn again to the stern tasks and the formidable years that lie before us, resolved that by our sacrifice and

daring these same children shall not be robbed of their inheritance or denied their right to live in a free and decent world.

And so, in God's mercy, a happy Christmas to you all.

from *The LIFE Book of Christmas*, 1963

1941

Within weeks of their sneak attack on Pearl Harbor, the Japanese were sweeping across the Pacific. On Christmas Day, Hong Kong fell to them. It would not return to British control until 1945.

1944

For the American force at Bastogne during World War II, Christmas was not a joyful affair. It was the Battle of the Bulge and they were surrounded and outnumbered. Three days before Christmas, the German commander sent his ultimatum, demanding unconditional surrender with annihilation as the only alternative. The American commander returned the immortal Christmas message "Nuts."

CHRISTMAS AROUND the WORLD in CUSTOM and TRADITION

The joys of Christmas burst forth in celebrations as varied and colorful as the people who celebrate. A hundred languages sing the happiness of Christ's coming around the ceppo, the crèche, the bonfire, or the Christmas tree. In a thousand different ways, the peoples of the earth join their hearts in the great communion of humankind that only this season can bring. There are traditions as old as Bethlehem to remind us of all that has gone before; there are constantly newborn customs as fresh and spontaneous as the wonder of a child's first Christmas. Let us look at some of the celebrations from around the world so that we can learn new forms of joy.

Abbot of Unreason

In the Middle Ages the Abbot of Unreason performed the same functions as the Lord of Misrule except that he was dressed in clerical robes. He was particularly popular in Scotland. He would supervise the mumming and merrymaking in courts and in large households. As with most of the medieval Christmas festivities, he tended to get out of hand and turn into a rather sacrilegious character. For that reason he was banned in England by Act of Parliament in 1555. However, it was not until the time of the Commonwealth and the ban on all Christmas festivities in both England and Scotland that he really disappeared, and as the Scottish never fully resumed their Christmas celebrations, he never returned.

Advent Calendar

The Advent calendar originated in Germany and Scandinavia, but it has now become very popular in America as well. Sometimes the Advent calendar is the picture of a house with windows that can be opened to reveal the tiny pictures behind them. Other times it is a picture of a typical Christmas scene or snowscape with perforated areas that can be removed or opened, again to reveal the pictures behind. There is one window or flap for each day of Advent, the season before Christmas, or, sometimes, one for each day of December leading up to Christmas. Each day, the children are allowed to reveal one picture. If there are several children in the family, the privilege rotates from one to another, usually with much confusion, since everyone wants it to be his or her day each time. The pictures thus revealed are of toys or Christmas scenes or anything else appropriate to the season. The last and largest picture is revealed on December 25. It is the nativity scene, which gives meaning to all the joy and fun that the other pictures represent.

Advent Wreath

The Advent wreath is of Lutheran origin, but its sense of joyous anticipation has made it popular with many other religious groups in England and America. It is an evergreen wreath with four candles set in holders attached to it. Beginning four Sundays before Christmas, on the first Sunday of Advent, one candle is lighted each week as a symbol of the light that will come into the world with the birth of Jesus. On the last Sunday before Christmas, all four are lighted to give a radiance to the church altar or the dining room table, wherever one wishes to set up the wreath. In some countries, Advent candles are similarly burned each week, but without being set in a wreath.

Ale Posset

A traditional hot drink of Yorkshire, England, ale posset consists of milk curdled with ale, beer, and wine, and very often spiced. It was the final beverage taken by families of old Yorkshire on Christmas Eve. As part of the annual ritual, each family member at this time would take a sip or "sup" for good luck.

Armenia

Christmas is celebrated in Armenia on January 19. This is caused by two factors. First, the early Armenian Church rejected the idea of December 25 as Christmas and clung to the earlier notion that Christ's birthday should be celebrated on the same day as his baptism, January 6. Second, when Pope Gregory XIII created his calendar to correct the mistakes in the earlier Julian calendar, the Armenian Church rejected it for religious purposes. Therefore, the thirteen days' difference between Gregorian and Julian in this century makes their January 6 the same day as our January 19. Clear?

The Armenians prepare for Christmas with a fast. They eat no animal food for a week and no food at all on the last day before Christmas. The fast is broken only after the Christmas Eve service, when they return home to a dinner of rice pilaf. The children then go onto the roofs with handkerchiefs and sing carols. Adults fill up the handkerchiefs with presents of raisins or fried wheat or sometimes money. There are also morning services on Christmas Day.

Asalto

Traditional Christmas fun in Puerto Rico begins on Christmas Night, when one's lawn is invaded by merrymakers, very often in the middle of the night when all sane people are asleep. This *asalto*, or invasion, begins with much shouting and laughing and leads to the singing of the traditional light, joyous carols known as *aguinaldos*. These songs appeal to the host's sense of generosity and the appeal is seldom in vain. The host climbs out of bed and acknowledges his cheerful guests, often as many as thirty people, by opening his home to them. Singing and feasting take place, and in an hour or so the happy host joins his guests as they hurry off to invade someone else's peace and quiet.

Australia

As Australia was settled by the British, Australian Christmas customs are the descendants of the traditional British Christmas. But as the climate is the reverse of that of the mother country, there are no sleigh rides, or Yule logs, or any of the other snug comforts against the cold. The main articles of decoration are the Christmas bell and the Christmas bush, and after the hearty afternoon feast, supper may be a picnic in the countryside or at the beach. Swimsuits are perfectly ordinary attire for the Christmas weather.

One tradition that is purely Australian began in 1937. On Christmas Eve, radio announcer Norman Banks saw a lonely old woman listening to Christmas carols on the radio while a lone candle burned forlornly in her window. Thinking about how to make the world brighter for such people at that time of year made the words "Carols by Candlelight" spring into his head, along with an idea. The next Christmas Eve he broadcast a great carol sing by all who wanted to join in, from the Alexandra Gardens along the banks of Melbourne's main river. "Carols by Candlelight" became a joyous annual tradition and was eventually broadcast in many other countries around the world. Each year, more than a quarter of a million people gather to sing carols and join hands at midnight for "Auld Lang Syne." It is a great showing of community and Christmas spirit that is almost unequaled anywhere else in the world.

Austria

Christmas in Austria is a very musical time. Many of the world's greatest carols, including "Silent Night," have come to us from Austria, and they can be heard everywhere throughout the country as Christmas approaches.

December 6 is the day when St. Nicholas and his grotesque assistant, Krampus, may pay a visit, just as the Wise Men are often on hand for January 6. But the gifts are brought on Christmas Eve by the Christkind. Sometimes the Christkind will even help to decorate the Christmas tree before the big Christmas Eve supper, which will probably feature carp as a main course. Dinner on Christmas Day will be roast goose with all the trimmings.

A curious figure still lurks in Austrian Christmas season tradition, most especially on New Year's Eve. He is old and bearded and ugly, and he hides in the shadows wearing a wreath of mistletoe. If a young beauty is unfortunate enough to linger too long beneath the magic pine bough, Sylvester is liable to leap out and kiss her vigorously. His rights are severely limited, however, as he is banished with the arrival of the New Year; and, besides, if one knows who it is lurking behind the false whiskers, it is not necessarily an unpleasant experience at all.

Babouschka

Babouschka was the gift-giver in Russia when Christmas was an acceptable festivity, and probably continues in a quiet way under the Communist regime. She was something between a witch and an old woman, her name meaning simply "grandmother." Legend says she refused shelter to Mary and Joseph and misdirected the Wise Men on their way to Bethlehem. As atonement for these sins, she must wander the earth on Epiphany Eve, looking for the Christ Child but never finding him, and dropping off presents for good little boys and girls on her way.

Bambino

Bambino is the Italian word for "baby," but at Christmastime it is used specifically to refer to the representations of the baby Jesus that are placed in the countless manger scenes in homes and churches all over Italy. The most famous Bambino is one dating from medieval times in the Church of Santa Maria in Aracoeli in Rome. It is brought to the crib every year at Christmas with elaborate ceremonies, and children preach sermons before it. Offerings are sent to the church from all over the world for candles to be placed at the manger in which it lies. It is credited with a number of miracles.

One famous story concerns a woman who feigned sickness in order to be left alone with the miraculous image. She replaced it with a false image and stole the real one. None of the priests knew of the exchange, but that night there was a great ringing of bells and hammering at the main door of the church. When the priests hurried to open it, they found no one there except the image of the Christ Child, which had come home of its own accord.

Befana

Befana is a female Santa Claus to Italian children and is very active at Christmastime in that country, particularly on January 6, the Feast of the Epiphany. In fact, her name is probably just a popular corruption of the word "Epiphany." The legend has it that Befana, a very old and decrepit woman, refused to interrupt her household duties and avail herself of an invitation extended to her by the Magi to accompany them on their journey to Bethlehem to find the Christ Child. She was too busy sweeping the floor! The Magi, according to some legends, needed a guide in their search and asked Befana to help them find the way, but she would not leave her warm, cozy house. In some versions of the story, she actually misdirected them. The part of the legend that seems universal is that toward dawn, when the Magi had been gone for some time, Befana had a change of heart and went out to search for them, but was unable to find the Three Kings. Through the centuries, this old woman, carrying gifts in her apron, searches for the caravan of the Wise Men. Her gifts eventually go to good little boys and girls. She also happens to have some bags of ashes for those who weren't quite so good during the year.

In Italy, January 6 is also called Befana Day, and Befana fairs are held all over the country, notably in Rome. Whistles and earthenware images are traditionally sold at them.

Belgium

In Belgium, St. Nicholas pays two visits to each house. On December 4 he comes to check into the behavior of each child, to find out who's "been naughty and nice." Then on December 6 he returns with just rewards for all, either presents or switches, which he leaves in the shoes or small baskets that have been placed inside near the doorway where he will easily find them. Just to get on his good side, there are also snacks of hay, water, and carrots left for his horse or donkey.

Christmas Day itself is reserved for religious celebrations, although Nativity plays sponsored by the churches are a well-loved institution. These are often performed in sixteenth-century costumes, which is what would have been modern dress when the tradition began. In small villages, there are often three virtuous men chosen to portray the three Wise Men and go throughout the town, caroling at each door and receiving small gifts of food. Since these snacks are eaten on the spot, stomach capacity may weigh as heavily as virtue in larger villages' choice of Wise Men.

Bells

The ringing of bells at Christmastime is a holdover from pagan midwinter celebrations. When the earth was cold and the sun was dying, evil spirits were very powerful. One of the ways to drive them off was by making a great deal of noise. As making a great deal of noise was also rather fun, the noisemaking ceremonies were entered into with much good will. Bells were a very useful part of this, since you could play a bell and shout or sing at the same time.

Today, church bells ring throughout the world on Christmas Eve, not to drive away the evil spirits, but to welcome in the spirit of Christmas with a joyful noise. In Scandinavia, bells signal the end of work and the beginning of festivity. In England, the tolling of the devil's knell welcomes the birth of Christ. In Italy and Spain, it signals the Midnight Mass. In America, no sidewalk Santa could hope to function without a hand bell to brighten the sounds of the city with its joyous tinkle. And we all join in lustily to sing "Jingle Bells," while we think of sleigh bells and dashing horses and being bundled under warm furs—a treat which almost none of us have actually experienced but which we all remember vividly in our collective Christmas memory.

Belsnickel

Belsnickel, or Pelznickle, is another name for Knecht Rupprecht to the Pennsylvania Dutch. He is one of the frightening companions of St. Nicholas who is there to see to it that the children who have been bad don't get off lightly. He used to be portrayed by a man wearing a sheet and a mask. Now whole groups of children will dress up in costumes and go "belsnickling," parading through the streets to parties at friends' houses.

Berchta

Berchta, or Frau Freen, or Budelfrau, as she is variously known, is a frightening old woman who watches out for laziness at Christmastime. She appears in the Tyrolean Alps during the twelve days of Christmas, chastising young women who leave unspun thread at their spinning wheels. She has nothing really to do with Christmas. Her concern is for household duties and seeing to it that they don't get neglected at the approach of the holidays by casting bad-luck spells on lazy females. She was probably invented by someone who never had to undergo the drudgery of keeping a house, presumably a man.

Birds' Christmas Tree

This is a custom throughout the Scandinavian countries at Christmastime and is in keeping with the general tendency to try to share the festivities with all animal and even plant life so that the coming year will be a prosperous one. A sheaf of wheat or some other grain, or even just seeds and bread, is placed on a pole and set up outside where the birds are known to congregate. This is done on either Christmas Eve or Christmas Day. The sight and sound of the outdoor festivity at the birds' Christmas tree can add greatly to the zest and warmth of the indoor celebration.

Black Peter

To the medieval Dutch, "Black Peter" was another name for the devil. Somewhere along the way, he was subdued by St. Nicholas and forced to be his servant. This is how he appears now in Dutch folklore, following behind St. Nicholas and carrying the bag containing the presents for children. At St. Nicholas' commands, he drops the gifts down the chimneys and into the children's shoes, thereby saving the saint the difficulty and dirtiness of making the trip down the flue himself, à la Santa Claus. Curiously, Black Peter dresses in sixteenth-century Spanish clothes. This is probably because Holland was then under the control of Spain and understandably didn't like it. Therefore the Dutch version of the devil dressed in Spanish clothes. Today Black Peter carries a bag into which he can pop any children who have been irretrievably bad and carry them off to Spain, which seems a rather mild punishment.

Blowing in the Yule

One of the delightfully noisy traditions of Christmas, this custom probably originated in pagan times when noise was thought to drive off evil spirits. It is today found in areas of Germany and the Scandinavian countries. A group of musicians take their instruments to the belfry of the local church and lustily play four Christmas carols, one in each direction of the compass. They finish with a joyful peal of the bells, which announces that Christmas has arrived.

Boar's Head

The association of the boar's head with Christmas probably dates back to pagan times when the Germanic god Frey, who cared for the fertility of the herds, was symbolized by a boar. Therefore, at mid-winter, to ensure many new calves and lambs in the spring, a boar would be sacrificed to the god. This sacrifice was carried over into Christmas tradition as a nonreligious custom.

A much more amusing explanation of the origin of this traditional Christmas dish concerns a student at Queen's College, Oxford, in

England. He was walking in the nearby forest of Shotover reading a volume of Aristotle when he was charged by a boar. Having found Aristotle's philosophies hard to swallow himself, he cried out "Graecum est" (roughly, "It's Greek to me") and crammed the book down the boar's throat, choking him to death. As he was a poor student, he couldn't afford to lose his textbook, so he cut off the boar's head to get it back. Not wanting to waste anything, he took the head back to his college, where it was roasted and eaten with great festivity. No indication is given in this story of what happened to the rest of the boar.

Whatever its origin, the boar's head was an important part of the medieval English Christmas feast. It took more than a week to properly skin, soak, salt, preserve, prepare, and cook—not to mention the problems of hunting it down in the first place, since the wild boar was a very dangerous animal. The boar's head was brought into the banquet in a procession of cooks, huntsmen and servants, all elaborately dressed to provide as much spectacle as possible. While bringing it in, they would sing the "Boar's Head Carol," which is one of the earliest extant English carols, having appeared in a book printed in 1521. It is partly in Latin as well as English:

The boar's head in hand bear I,
Bedecked with bays and rosemary;
And I pray you, my masters, be merry,

Quot estis in convivio: [Who are in such good spirits:
Caput apri defero,   I bear the head of the boar,
Reddens laudes Domino.   Giving praise to the Lord.]

The ceremony of the bringing in of the boar's head began to die out as early as the thirteenth century, as the wild boar began to become extinct in the British Isles. There are still some places, however, that preserve the custom as a deliberately quaint Christmas tradition, with the one change that a suckling pig must make do for the hard-to-get boar. One such place is Queen's College, Oxford, where a poor student may have started the whole thing with a well-placed tome of indigestible philosophy.

Bonus

A Christmas bonus is the gift given by a business firm to its employees at Christmastime. It probably had its origin in the same tradition as the English Boxing Day, when tradesmen were tipped for good service as an incentive to continue to perform well. Rarely, the Christmas bonus is some kind of merchandise, such as a turkey or ham for the traditional Christmas dinner. More often, it is a sum of money, which may be determined on the basis of a percentage of the company's profits or the number of years of the employee's service. The Christmas bonus began as a freewill gift, but with the increased influence of the labor movement and the rising costs of Christmas festivities, the bonus has become a contractually agreed-upon necessity with some governmental regulation and taxation. The amount of the bonus is hammered out at the negotiating table, and the IRS gets its share, and what's left is usually spent before it's received, but the recognition of service at Christmastime is still a nice idea.

Boxing Day

Boxing Day, December 26, is a legal holiday in England and has nothing to do with prizefighting. The custom of boxing derives from the opening of alms boxes in church on December 26, the Feast of St. Stephen, to distribute the collected money to the poor who have not enjoyed as nice a Christmas as those who are better off. The idea was picked up by apprentices and assistants, who would take a Christmas box around to their employer's customers, asking for tips in return for their service during the year. Eventually children picked up the practice, making it a sort of "trick or treat."

Boy Bishop

One of the most curious figures of the medieval Christmas celebrations was the Boy Bishop. Most churches and cathedrals at that time had a choir school affiliated with them to provide altar boys and the boys' choirs that were extremely popular throughout the Middle Ages. The custom may have begun as early as the tenth century, but definitely by the twelfth century Boy Bishops were being elected in most European countries. A boy elected from among the choristers would be invested with the powers of a bishop on St. Nicholas' Day, December 6. He would then serve until the Feast of the Holy Innocents on December 28. He took up offerings, blessed the people, preached, and led the services except, probably, for the actual saying of the Mass. He wore elaborate and extremely expensive vestments, which were provided by the Church and which, because of their size, were not usable for any other function during the year. He was extremely popular with the people, who gave more to this bishop who entertained them than they might have to a more adult one.

The ceremonies involving the Boy Bishop became more and more elaborate. In a Spanish church, one investment was described thus: "A chorister being placed with some solemnity upon a platform, there descended from the vaulting of the ceiling a cloud, which, stopping midway, opened. Two angels within it carried a miter, which, in their descent, they placed upon the head of the boy."

Anyone who has seen a herd of six-year-olds troop to the front of a modern-day church and attempt to get through one verse of "Jingle Bells" knows that children can be a very charming and not at all sacrilegious part of Christmas festivities. Unfortunately the Boy Bishop, who was probably just as innocent to begin with, did not remain so.

His term of office became an excuse for more boisterous forms of entertainment and he became more closely linked with the Lord of Misrule as a leader of revels with dancing and feasting and singing. His services became, in some instances, a parody of the traditional church service and sometimes included indecent songs and jokes.

The Church outlawed the practice of electing a Boy Bishop. It took a good while for it to die out, though, as it was an extremely popular form of entertainment. In England, it was not until 1542, when Henry VIII forbade the practice in the English Church, that the Boy Bishop was really done for. Yet some private groups still celebrated in a modified form, and vestiges remain today in Italy, where children will preach sermons at Christmas before the image of the infant Jesus in the manger.

Brazil

To Brazilians, Christmas comes at the beginning of their summer season. No sleigh rides for them. It is a time for boating, picnicking, and other summer festivities. The red and green of Christmas decorations are provided not by midwinter holly but by eucalyptus leaves and brilliant red flowers of many sorts.

The *pesebre*, or manger scene, is important, but there is also a Christmas tree decorated with candles. On Christmas Eve the *cena*, or meal, is set out before the family goes to Midnight Mass so that the Holy Family can have some of it if they wish while everyone is out. A popular menu would include turkey, fish, and champagne. Before going to bed, the children set out their shoes for Papa Noël. On Christmas morning, the children fix breakfast, then get their presents from their shoes and look for other gifts that are hidden around the house. Christmas evening can be spent outdoors in the balmy weather and is a great time for fireworks.

Buzebergt

Buzebergt is another unpleasant old woman who is connected with Epiphany. She comes to the Bavarian regions of Germany. Unlike Befana and Babouschka, she does not bring gifts but has a surprise of a different sort for those who cross her path. She carries a pot of starch instead of a bag of goodies or an apronful of presents, and she smears this starch on anyone she can catch.

Candle

Light was an important part of the pagan midwinter festivities, since this was the time when the sun ceased to wane and began to grow stronger and brighter. In imitation, candles and bonfires helped to drive away the forces of cold and darkness. Wax tapers also were given as gifts at the Roman festival of Saturnalia. To the Christian community, the lighting of candles took on the additional symbolic significance of Jesus as the Light of the World. Christmas candles are made in all shapes, colors, and sizes and are very often manufactured with such Christmasy scents as balsam and evergreen. Very often candles are displayed as Christmas motifs on Christmas cards and seals. In 1962 the U. S. Post Office issued its first Christmas stamp, which showed a Christmas wreath and a pair of candles. The beautiful idea of Christmas candles shining from home windows is a custom still practiced in Europe, particularly on Christmas Eve; for, who knows, the stranger who is given light and comfort by the candle in the darkness might be Mary seeking shelter from the night. In Ireland during the years of suppression, Catholics placed candles in the windows of certain homes so priests would know where to celebrate the Midnight Mass. In Sweden, St. Lucy appears wearing a crown of candles. In Victorian England, tradesmen made annual Christmas gifts of candles to their loyal customers. Three hundred thousand candles lend their glow to the Australian custom of Carols by Candlelight. In many parts of the world, the Advent candles or the candles of the Advent wreath reflect the dawning season and remind us of the coming of the Light. And it was the addition of lighted candles to the old paradise tree that marked the birth of our most beloved tradition, the Christmas tree. The Christmas candle, with its brightness, sacredness, and sense of well-being, is an indispensable part of the Christmas season.

Candlemas

Candlemas is the celebration of the ritual purification of Mary, which, as required by Jewish law, took place forty days after the birth of her child. Candlemas is thus February 2. The first celebration of this day took place in the late seventh or early eighth centuries under Pope Sergius I. Later in the century, the custom of blessing the candles that were carried in processions gave the day its popular name of Candlemas.

In many countries, Candlemas has been looked upon as the end of the Christmas season, probably since the purification of Mary would be looked upon as the last chapter in the story of Christ's birth. This was the day when the decorations would be taken down and stored away for another year. The Christmas plants would be burned, with the remnants of the Yule log (always holding back the one piece to light next year's log), and the ashes would be spread over gardens and fields to ensure a good harvest. The Yule log for the next year would be chosen then. Candlemas was also a good day for weather forecasting. If it was a sunny day, there would be forty more days of cold and snow. This belief has carried over into American folk tradition: February 2 is Groundhog Day. That's a far step from Candlemas.

Card

The immediate predecessors of Christmas cards were called Christmas pieces. These were elaborate colored sheets of paper with biblical scenes or pictures of nature at the head and around the borders. In the middle, schoolchildren would put their best sample of penmanship to show their parents how diligent their studies had been. Usually they expressed a wish for happy holidays or promises to be good or something else of dubious sincerity designed to put the parents in a good mood when gift-giving time came.

Two things made the advent of the Christmas card an inevitability. One was the creation of the "penny post" by the British postal system, in 1840. This made it possible and relatively inexpensive to correspond with larger numbers of friends. The other was the great increase in printing in the early nineteenth century because of the invention of the steam press. Printers could turn out more and more and were looking for markets to exploit. The Christmas piece was already an important source of income; the Christmas card would be a landslide.

The first Christmas card was probably designed by John Calcott Horsley at the suggestion of and for his friend Sir Henry Cole in 1846. The card depicted three panels: in the center one was a family enjoying wine; on either side were shown acts of charity, the feeding and clothing of the poor; beneath it all was the sentiment "A Merry Christmas and a Happy New Year to You." The center panel caused a stir and drew much heated criticism because one of the family members offering the toast was a child enjoying his first sip of wine. Temperance adherents accused the creator of the Christmas card of condoning excessive drinking and fostering the moral corruption of children. Nevertheless, a thousand copies of the card were printed and sold for a shilling each.

It is impossible to say definitively that the Horsley-Cole card was the first Christmas card, although it is generally accepted as such. In 1844 W. A. Dobson sent out hand-painted cards to friends rather than Christmas letters. As these were not printed, they are not considered in the running. In the same year, the Rev. Edward Bradley lithographed cards to his friends, again not a printing process for mass production and not sold to the general public. The one card that may possibly lay claim to being older than the Horsley-Cole card was designed by William Egley. This card carries a very clear date—for the first three figures. The last figure is obscure, so the date may be either 1842 or 1849. If it is the former, then William Egley is the Father of the Christmas Card; if the latter, he is just another imitator.

Louis Prang, a German-born printer, working in his shop in Roxbury, Massachusetts, printed his first American cards in 1875. Even more important than his printing was the fact that he did more than anyone else to popularize the cards by instituting nationwide contests for the best Christmas designs, which were awarded cash prizes.

Today Christmas cards are one of the greatest nuisances and greatest pleasures of Christmastime. More than a billion are sold each year in the United States and Britain. Addressing those great stacks of cards produces more writer's cramp than good will. And the mails become impossible because of the huge volume at Christmas. And the postage costs a small fortune. And there's always someone you forgot to write to until you got *his* card in the mail, and by then it's too late to send him one before Christmas. And yet Christmas cards are so nice to receive. The bulging mailbox is filled with happy surprises instead of circulars and junk mail. Many families send reports of what they've done during the year, so you catch up on the doings of old friends. Pictures may let you see how big the kids are getting. And a display of cards around the Christmas tree, or on the table or on the wall, is one of the very loveliest of Christmas decorations, for every card both brightens the room and reminds you of a friend who is there in spirit.

Ceppo

The Italian *ceppo* is closely related to the Christmas pyramid of northern Europe, but has never been replaced by the Christmas tree as its northern equivalent has been. The *ceppo* is a pyramid-shaped framework with several shelves which is decorated all over with greenery, ribbons, candles, and other Christmas ornaments. On its shelves sit gifts and sweets and sometimes the *presepio*, or manger scene. Often it will have a motor in its base so that it will revolve like a merry-go-round.

Cert

Cert is a demon in Czechoslovakian Christmas lore. He accompanies Svaty Mikalas (St. Nicholas) when he descends from heaven on a golden cord on December 6 to give gifts to the children. A good angel makes up the third member of the extremely mixed company. Cert is dressed in black garments and carries a whip and chains as symbols of the punishment for naughty boys and girls.

Chile

Chile's gift-bringer is called Viejo Pascuero, or Old Man Christmas. He strongly resembles Santa Claus and likewise comes drawn by reindeer. However, as chimneys are less than roomy in this warm clime, he contents himself with climbing in a window.

As in all of Latin America, the manger scene is the center of festivities; and following the midnight Mass of the Rooster, the Christmas Eve meal often includes *azuela de ave,* a chicken soup filled with potatoes, onions and corn on the cob; and *pan de pasqua,* a Christmas bread filled with candied fruit.

China

In China, Christmas is called Sheng Dan Jieh, the Holy Birth Festival. China has been exposed to Western influences, including Christianity, for only about four hundred years. Less than one per cent of the population is Christian. Yet these Christian Chinese celebrate Christmas joyfully with customs that they have adapted from the missionaries who brought them the word. They have the Christmas tree, which they call the Tree of Light, and hang up stockings for presents. These gifts are brought by their version of Santa Claus, whom they call Lam Khoong-Khoong ("Nice Old Father") or Dun Che Lao Ren ("Christmas Old Man"). Festive paper lanterns are hung for decorations, and fireworks, which were invented in China, are an important part of the revelry.

Christkind

Christkind (or Christkindli or Christkindlein) means "Christ Child" in German, and originally it applied to the Holy Infant, who was thought to bring the gifts on Christmas Eve. Gradually it evolved, however, into the name given a sort of angelic helper who brought the presents instead of the baby Jesus. Christkind is a veiled, radiant figure who wears a sparkling, jeweled crown, carries a tiny Christmas tree or a wand, wears a flowing white robe, and has golden wings. Often a window is left open for it to enter by. It lets the household know that it has been there by ringing a bell when the presents are all in place beneath the tree. The Christkind is looked for each year in certain areas of Switzerland, Austria, and Germany and in the Pennsylvania Dutch country of America. Just as its appearance and gender have changed over the years, its name has been changed into more of a real name, Kris Kringle. In America, this name has been incorrectly picked up as just another name for Santa Claus. Thus we wrongly think of Kris Kringle as being male, when actually, as an angelic being, Christkind cannot be said to have any gender at all.

Christmas Club

The big problem with Christmas has always been how to pay for it. Gone are the days of Saturnalia when a few twigs of evergreen plucked at the local sacred grove would cover the whole gift list for the season. Today a properly happy Christmas can ruin all the rest of the year's finances.

In its own inimitable way, America provided an answer to this problem. In 1909, Merkel Landis established the first Christmas savings club at the Carlisle Trust Company in Carlisle, Pennsylvania. This was then, as it is now, a bank savings plan that enabled depositors to set money aside for Christmas expenses by making periodic payments during the year. Often these payments begin as early as November of the previous year. The following Christmas, the money can be withdrawn and used to buy all the Christmas accouterments. In the middle of the 1960s, American banks began to offer dividends on Christmas club accounts, and recently other inducements, such as discounts on merchandise, have been added. Basically, the Christmas club is a nice way of hiding your money from yourself so you can squander it all at once instead of gradually through the year.

Not all Christmas clubs are the same. Here are some of the questions an educated consumer should ask before selecting one:

What is the highest interest rate permitted by law?

Is there daily compounding so the account will provide the maximum yield?

What is the amount of interest paid from the day of deposit to the day of withdrawal?

Is there a penalty for missed payments or for a Christmas club that is not completed?

What is the minimum payment you are allowed to make each week?

Will your passbook always give you the current balance?

Will your Christmas club account automatically renew itself every year?

C.M.B.

These are the initials of the three Wise Men, Caspar, Melchior, and Balthazar. They are written over front doors of homes in Poland,

Czechoslovakia, and Sweden by the Star Boys on their Epiphany Day visits. Along with the initials, three crosses are drawn. According to tradition, the homes marked with these holy symbols will experience only good fortune throughout the year.

Costa Rica

Bright, tropical flowers highlight Costa Rican decorations for Christmas. Special trips are made to gather the wild orchids that bloom in the jungle areas. The manger scene is called a *portal* and is decorated with these brilliant flowers and colorful fresh fruit. Wreaths are very popular, not of holly, but of cypress leaves and red coffee berries.

The supper after Midnight Mass will consist of tamales and other local dishes. Children used to leave their shoes out for the Christ Child to fill, but more and more Santa Claus is relieving Him of this pleasant task as American influence continues to gain in strength.

Cradle Rocking

This was a charming custom emphasizing the humanity of the Christ Child. It originated in Germany at the Midnight Mass of Christmas Eve. A manger scene would be set up in the church and the celebrant and altar boys would rock the cradle of the Holy Infant. Lullabylike carols would be sung at the same time to help the infant Jesus sleep. With the Protestant Reformation and its forbidding of images in church, this practice began to die out, but even now there are some vestiges of it left.

Czechoslovakia

Czechoslovakia has found two days necessary to get all the good will out of its system. December 25 and 26 are called "First Christmas" and "Second Christmas" and are both state holidays. The Christmas tree is lighted after the big meal on Christmas Eve, and the gifts are placed under it. There is also a manger scene, which is called a *jesličky* or Bethlehem. Carp is a favorite dish for Christmas. Other dishes of the season are *kuba*, a pudding of peeled barley, boiled in milk, buttered, and baked with mushrooms; and *masika*, a fruit stew of pears, apples, prunes, nuts, and raisins served with a slice of *calta*, the delicious plaited white Christmas bread.

Denmark

Christmas is an especially jolly time in Denmark, where the national sense of humor gets free play at this time of year. Notices appear in the paper three months in advance advising that it is almost the deadline for Christmas packages to Tasmania, Fiji, the Aleutians, and many of those other locales which are sure to be on everyone's mailing lists. The Folketeatret in Copenhagen goes through its annual soul-searching and finally announces that this year's Christmas program will be called "Christmas in Nøddebo Rectory"—a great surprise to everyone, as this program has been given at this theater only every year since 1888. And Christmas is the time when the Nisser can run amok. A Julnisse (plural, -nisser) is a mischievous elf who lives in the lofts of old farmhouses and concerns himself with playing practical jokes on one and all. He wears gray homespun with a red bonnet, long red stockings, and white clogs. He must be left a bowl of rice pudding on Christmas Eve or his jokes will indeed be terrible. If he is properly placated, however, he can be very friendly and will watch over the livestock throughout the year. He is closely associated with the household cat, and there are even those who attribute the disappearance of the Christmas Eve rice pudding to the cat itself rather than to the Nisse, but these are people without proper Christmas spirit.

The big Christmas Eve dinner starts off with rice pudding sprinkled with cinnamon, with a magic almond hidden in it. The child getting the almond in his or her portion will win a surprise, usually a marzipan animal or some other goodie. The main course is roast goose stuffed with apples and prunes, with red cabbage and small caramel-browned potatoes. For dessert there is an astonishing variety of Danish pastries and baked goods.

As Greenland is a Danish possession, that has become the popular home for Santa Claus. Letters written to Santa Claus, Greenland, are answered by the Danish Tourist Association.

A famous Danish Christmas tradition is the Christmas plate. This may have started long ago when the wealthier Danes gave plates of cookies and fruit to their servants for Christmas presents. As the plates would be of a higher quality than anything those servants would have, they would be collected and kept separate from the day-to-day china. The collection of Christmas plates became fashionable, and special plates were issued for the occasion. Today, two leading manufacturers issue different designs each Christmas, often featuring that delightful Christmas symbol the Julnisse.

Dipping in the Kettle

In memory of an ancient famine, the family gathers in Swedish kitchens on Christmas Eve before the midday meal. A great pot is filled wih a broth made of the drippings of pork, sausage, and corned beef. Each family member dips a piece of dark bread on a fork into the broth until the bread is thoroughly saturated and then eats it. This *doppa i grytan,* "dipping in the kettle," is necessary for good luck and a coming year of plenty.

Ecuador

Christmas Day in Ecuador is a day of colorful procession as the Indians who live and work in the highlands and mountains dress in their finest and ride their brightly arrayed llamas down to the ranches where their employers live. They bring gifts of fruit and produce, which they lay before the image of the Christ Child in the *pesebre,* or manger scene, which is set up in the ranch house. Children, too, bring their gifts and make pretty speeches to the Holy Infant, asking blessings for their family and their animals. Then there is a fiesta with much singing and dancing outdoors. The owner of the ranch distributes gifts to all his employees and their families. The huge meal will consist of roast lamb, baked potatoes, and brown sugar bread. There is always entirely too much to eat, so that the processions that wend their way into the mountains at the end of the day are as heavily laden with leftovers as they were with offerings in the morning.

Eisteddfod

In Wales at Christmastime, a Christmas poem is designated each year to be set to music. Choirs all over the country vie for the honor of having their music chosen to be the official Christmas carol. These choirs come together in the marketplaces of every size village and town to sing their version as well as the official carols from many years past. This combination carol sing and contest is called an *eisteddfod*. There is also a National Eisteddfod, held every year since 1860, which determines the final selection and also has contests in drama, prose, and poetry. The custom of choosing a national carol was begun sometime in the tenth century.

England

Ever since Dickens sparked the revival of interest in the old-fashioned Christmas, England has been second to none in the enthusiasm and variety of its Christmas celebrations. Many customs are its own, but many others from all over the world have found their way into the heart and hearth of the English Christmas.

Father Christmas reigns in the place of Santa Claus or Saint Nicholas, although his dimensions, joviality, and dress make him hard to distinguish from his American cousin. Letters are sent to him by children who want to be sure he has got their order straight. These letters are not mailed, though: they are thrown into the fireplace. If they go up the chimney, the wish will be granted; if not, one's wish goes ungranted. This uses up a good deal of paper, but does save on postage to the North Pole. Stockings are hung by the chimney or at the foot of the child's bed to receive small presents, which are opened Christmas morning.

The Christmas tree has occupied a central position in the festivities ever since Prince Albert brought it from his native Germany in the mid-nineteenth century. However, it has never completely replaced the combination of greenery and mistletoe called the kissing bough, probably because it is very awkward to try to kiss under a Christmas tree.

Such venerable customs as the bringing in of the Yule log and the boar's head are not commonplace today, although the ceremonies do still survive in some institutions such as the universities. In the countryside, you can still find some Christmas mummers, amateurs who perform plays of St. George at the drop of a hat, and waits still carol their way through the village streets. In a place in Yorkshire, the tolling of the devil's knell takes place every Christmas Eve. The church bell is rung once for every year since Christ's birth with the last stroke timed exactly for midnight.

Christmas has always been a time of feasting for the English. Once it was good old English roast beef (Sir Loin, as it was dubbed in the Middle Ages) that held pride of place. But now that unlikely bird from America, the turkey, has conquered the British as it has so many countries and occupies the place of honor at most Christmas dinner tables. Dessert, however, is still British: mince pies and flaming plum pudding (called Christmas pudding). Mince pies contain no minced meat and plum pudding has no plums, but the English would never let mere fact stand in the way of tradition.

In Trafalgar Square in the heart of London, a great Christmas tree is set up each year. During World War II, King Haakon of Norway was forced into exile in Britain when the Germans occupied his country. Each year during the war, Norwegian forces would smuggle a tree through the German coast patrols at great risk so that the king could celebrate Christmas before a tree from his beloved homeland. Since the war, Norway has expressed its gratitude to the British people for their help by continuing to send a tree that can be shared by all. Thus the giant tree in Trafalgar Square stands as a symbol both of the child who brought such love with Him into this world and of the love that can exist between peoples. It is sad that it so often requires great hardship to discover that love.

Father Christmas

Although he is the English equivalent of Santa Claus, Father Christmas is rather different from our jolly old elf and even further removed from the original ascetic and holy St. Nicholas. Father Christmas developed from several pagan predecessors. The Roman Saturnalia celebrated the brief return each year of the Golden Age when the god Saturn returned to rule over Italy. Saturn was a giant who came bearing good food and wine, joy and revelry, and equality of all people. When carried into the northern regions of Europe, Saturn probably combined with the wild figure of Odin and his raging host of spirits who would sweep across the land during the winter. Thus Father Christmas was never a Christian religious figure, but symbolized rather the arrival of those secular pleasures which came from elsewhere than the Christian tradition. He was always portrayed as a giant, wearing a scarlet or green robe lined with fur; crowned with holly, ivy, or mistletoe; and carrying the Yule log and a bowl of Christmas punch. The Ghost of Christmas Present in Dickens' *Christmas Carol* is probably meant to be Father Christmas: "The walls and ceiling were so hung with living green, that it looked a perfect grove, from every part of which, bright gleaming berries glistened. The crisp leaves of holly, mistletoe, and ivy reflected back the light, as if so many little mirrors had been scattered there; and such a mighty blaze went roaring up the chimney . . . Heaped up upon the floor, to form a kind of throne, were turkeys, geese, game, poultry, brawn, great joints of meat, sucking-pigs, long wreaths of sausages, mince-pies, plum-puddings, barrels of oysters, red-hot chestnuts, cherry-cheeked apples, juicy oranges, luscious pears, immense twelfth-cakes, and seething bowls of punch, that made the chamber dim with their delicious steam. In easy state upon this couch, there sat a jolly Giant, glorious to see; who bore a glowing torch, in shape not unlike Plenty's horn . . . It was clothed in one simple deep green robe or mantle, bordered with white fur. This garment hung so loosely on the figure, that its capacious breast was bare, as if disdaining to be warded or concealed by any artifice. Its feet, observable beneath the ample folds of the garment, were also bare; and on its head it wore no other covering than a holly wreath set here and there with shining icicles. Its dark brown curls were long and free: free as its genial face, its sparkling eye, its open hand, its cheery voice, its unconstrained demeanour, and its joyful air. Girded round its middle was an antique scabbard; but no sword was in it, and the ancient sheath was eaten up with rust."

Fête des Rois

The Feast of the Kings is the name given by the French to January 6, Epiphany, in honor of the Wise Men. It is, traditionally, a day for dining out for French families, unlike Christmas, which is a day for feasting at home. It is also the day when tradespeople are rewarded with gifts of money for loyal service, much like the English Boxing Day.

First-footing

In some areas of the world, such as Scotland, first-footing takes place at the New Year, but in much of rural England it happens on Christmas Day. The "first-footer" is the first person to enter the house and is said to "let in Christmas." In some areas, he is professionally hired to be sure that all is done properly, because there are many superstitions involved in this custom. He carries an evergreen twig, comes in at the front door, passes through the house, and exits at the rear. He may be given salt or bread or some other small gift as a symbol of hospitality. He should have dark hair, but not red hair, as that is the color associated with Judas Iscariot. To let a woman in first is thought to be disastrous.

And what does a successful first-footing accomplish? This carol, which is sung in some areas where the first-footers move in a group, gives us the answer:

> I wish you a merry Christmas
> And a happy New Year;
> A pocket full of money
> And a cellar full of beer,
> And a great fat pig
> To last you all the year.

71

France

The center of French Christmas celebration is the *crèche*, or manger scene. Every home will have its own nativity setting featuring the tiny clay figures called *santons*, little saints. These brightly colored images are made by local craftsmen throughout the year and are sold at great Christmas fairs at Marseilles and Aix in the South of France where the tradition is strongest. The manger scene, which was created by St. Francis in Italy in 1223 or 1224, was brought to France by Pope John XXII in 1316 when the papacy was moved to Avignon in southern France. About 1800, Italian vendors brought some of the *santi belli* which were popular in Italy and which quickly caught on in France. Soon local figures began to make their appearance at the manger side, since the people were less concerned with historical accuracy than with expressing in their own way their adoration of the Christ Child. Thus it became a perfectly normal sight to see the town mayor be-

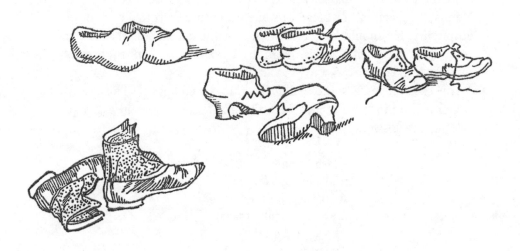

tween the ox and the ass; a knife grinder arriving with the Magi, and a gypsy, the town crier, a hunter, or a gardener being serenaded by the angels' song, all carefully detailed in clay.

The Christmas tree has never gained general acceptance in France. The Yule log was once important, but now it is remembered mostly by the shape it gives to a cake, the *bûche de Noël*, which is traditionally baked at Christmastime.

After Midnight Mass on Christmas Eve comes the *réveillon*, the late supper that is the culinary high point of the season. As might be expected in a country where every region has its own high standard of native cuisine, the menu varies widely. In Alsace, goose is the main dish, and in Brittany, buckwheat cakes with sour cream; Burgundy feasts on turkey and chestnuts, while Paris revels in oysters and pâté de foie gras. After dinner, the children see to it that their shoes are set out by the fireside for presents, which are brought by Père Noël (Father Christmas) or le Petit Noël (Little Christmas, the Christ Child). Once the shoes were the traditional sabots, wooden peasant shoes, but now almost anything will serve. Adults don't exchange presents until New Year's. Puppet shows and nativity plays are popular forms of entertainment on Christmas Day and provide a good place to send the children after they have eaten, broken, or gotten bored with whatever Père Noël brought them.

Frumenty

Traditionally, frumenty was the first food eaten on Christmas morning in many areas of England. It was made of wheat slowly stewed in milk and served with raisins, sugar, and spices.

Germany

So much of our modern Christmas originated in Germany, that to understand the German Christmas fully, you must read this whole book and that might begin to give you the idea. To summarize it briefly, the German Christmas is a tremendously important time to each person and family. Preparations are made for weeks. Advent wreaths, candles, and calendars set the mood. St. Nicholas' Day, December 6, although not actually celebrated by most people, marks the real beginning of the season. Although the crib is often found in German homes, frequently in beautifully carved woodcraft, the tree is the center of attention. The custom began in Germany, and every German home must have a tree. Usually it is the mother who trims the tree on Christmas Eve. No one else is allowed in until it is finished, usually about 6:00 P.M. on Christmas Eve. Church services are held Christmas Eve, and many famous Christmas carols dating back as far as Martin Luther are sung. It is the Christkind who brings the presents, accompanied by one of its many devilish companions, Knecht Rupprecht, Pelznickle, Ru-Klas, or one of the other monstrous playmates created by this nation, which is known for its fairy tales. The highlight of the Christmas food is the cookies. There are dozens of different German Christmas cookies, shaped like figures of

74

Christmas or stamped with familiar designs. Edible trees and tiny baked brown gnomes fill the warm kitchens for a week before the festivities, but disappear afterward like a flash to turn into happy smiles and round tummies.

Gift

Gift-giving at the winter solstice goes back to the Roman festivals of Saturnalia and Kalends. At first the gifts consisted simply of twigs from a sacred grove as good luck emblems. That soon escalated, however, and food, candles, statues of gods, and small pieces of jewelry became the standard gifts. These presents were called *strenae* and survive still in France, where gifts called *étrennes* are exchanged in January. To the early Church, gift-giving at this time was a pagan holdover and therefore severely frowned upon. However, the people would not part with it, and some justification was found in the gift-giving of the Magi and later figures such as St. Nicholas. So by the Middle Ages, gift-giving was accepted. This was especially true in the courts of kings, where a formal exchange of gifts was often very carefully regulated as to the correct amount to be spent. Today, gift-giving is such an important part of our festivities that the whole year's budget has to be carefully planned to allow for the expense of Christmas presents, often with the help of a Christmas club, and retail firms count on December as their biggest sales month of the year. That's a far step from passing out a few evergreen twigs for good luck.

Grandfather Frost

Before the Communist Revolution, Russia had several legendary figures who brought gifts at Christmastime. Father Christmas or Kolyáda came on Christmas Eve, while Babouschka came on Epiphany Eve. Today, with the official regime atheistic, these semireligious characters are not tolerated. In their place has appeared the character of Grandfather Frost, who brings presents on the nonreligious holiday of New Year's. He is always an old man who is dressed in winter furs like Santa Claus, or sometimes in bishop's robes like St. Nicholas, although he is not allowed any religious function.

Great Supper

This is the name given to the meal taken after Midnight Mass in many parts of France. It is a banquet consisting of thirteen different foods, many of them rich desserts. The number thirteen is symbolic of Christ and his twelve Apostles.

Greece

As in many other areas of the East, Easter is a more important feast day than Christmas for the Greeks. Christmas is more a time of religious observance. Still, there are some customs associated specifically with Christmas.

As December is a time of storms in the seas around Greece, St. Nicholas is important not as a bringer of gifts but as the patron of sailors. Thinking ahead to the rough seas to come, many seamen are especially religious on December 6, the feast day of the good saint who stilled the waters.

At dawn on Christmas, the children go from house to house singing carols called *kalanda* and accompanying themselves on tiny metal triangles and clay drums. The pig that has been fattening since harvesttime is slaughtered so that pork is the main course at Christmas dinner, although in some areas chicken is also enjoyed. A special loaf of bread has been baked for the occasion, called *christopsomo*, "Christ-bread." It is decorated elaborately with frosting, usually in some way that indicates the family occupation, such as a plow for a farmer. In some areas, it is traditional to give the first slice to a beggar; others put an olive sprig into the loaf, decorate it with dried figs, apples, and oranges, and don't eat it until Epiphany. Another loaf is often baked for the livestock in the shape of a harness or something similar and crumbled into their food to bring good luck in the coming year.

A great log called the *skarkantzalos* is often burned during the entire twelve days of Christmas. This is not just for Christmas cheer, but specifically to frighten away the Kallikantzaroi, the evil spirits that slip down the chimney at Christmastime and cause all sorts of devilment.

Greek Cross Day

An important part of the Christmas festivities in the Eastern Church takes place on January 6, the day long considered Christ's birthday before the final acceptance of December 25. On this day, which is known as Greek Cross Day, the Blessing of the Waters takes place when a crucifix is dipped into the sea, lake, or river by the local priest. The practice dates back to the second century and is connected by many with Christ's first miracle, when He changed the water into wine at the wedding at Cana. Others believe the Blessing of the Waters has its origins in Christ's baptism, which is said to have taken place on January 6. Whatever its origin, the blessed water, called "Baptismal Water," is taken home by the faithful, who believe its application will cure spiritual and bodily ailments. In some areas, the crucifix is thrown into the water and young men of the parish plunge in to retrieve it. The one who brings up the cross from the water receives special blessings and gifts and is hailed as a hero for the day. The Blessing of the Waters is common in the Greek, Syrian, and Coptic churches and is also carried out in Greek and Russian communities all over the world, including American cities such as Tarpon Springs, Florida.

Guatemala

For nine days before Christmas, *posada* processions pass through the streets of Guatemala. The beat of drums and the crackle of fireworks provide lively accompaniment as the figures of Mary and Joseph are carried to a friend's house, where a carol is sung asking for lodging for the Holy Family. After ritual questions and answers, the doors are opened and Mary and Joseph are taken to the *nacimiento*, or manger scene, where they will remain until the next night, when they will once again go out seeking shelter. Everyone who accompanied the figures on their quest makes a great party with punch and hot tamales and dancing once the goal is accomplished. On Christmas Eve, the figure of the Christ Child is added to the *nacimiento* at the last of the nine houses to receive the Holy Family. This is the signal for the biggest party of all, and the house selected had better be a large one, since everyone who was involved over the last nine days will show up on this night.

The Christmas tree has joined the *nacimiento* as a popular Christmas ornament because of the large German population in Guatemala. Gifts are left under the tree on Christmas morning by the Christ Child for the children. Parents and adults do not exchange gifts until New Year's Day. As in all of Latin America, Midnight Mass on Christmas Eve follows the *posada* and is in turn followed by a full supper.

Hans Trapp

In many areas of Germany, Hans Trapp is the demon who accompanies Christkind on its gift-giving rounds. He has a blackened face and wears a bearskin. He often arrives first and threatens the children with a stick until the Christkind arrives and banishes him.

Heaven

In Finland, a heaven is a type of Christmas ornament. It is not one that is hung on the tree, however; it is hung in the center of the dining room ceiling. It is made up of brightly colored paper stars, paper baubles, little silver bells, flags, and other ornaments that will reflect the candlelight to form a festive setting for the Christmas banqueting.

Holland

To the Dutch, St. Nicholas' Day is the time of greatest revelry in the Christmas season. Even the chilly, drizzly weather of December can do nothing to dampen their spirits.

Much as Santa first appears in America at Thanksgiving parades, St. Nicholas comes to the Netherlands on the last Saturday of November. No flying sleigh for him—he arrives by steamer. As he comes into the port of Amsterdam (and his double into other harbor towns), all business and traffic stop as the people pour out to greet him. He disembarks with his servant Black Peter and riding his white horse. He is dressed in traditional bishop's robes while Black Peter wears picturesque sixteenth-century Spanish attire. They are greeted by the mayor and lead a great parade through the streets to the royal palace. Here all the royal children are waiting and must give accounts of their behavior over the past year, just as all Dutch children must do. After the princes and princesses have proved their worth, the parade continues to a major hotel, where St. Nicholas will establish his headquarters for the season.

December 5, St. Nicholas' Eve, is when the presents are exchanged. The presents are called "surprises" because they are disguised as much as possible to make the final discovery more delightful. A small gift may be wrapped inside a huge box, or hidden inside a vegetable, or sunk in a pudding. A large gift may lurk in the cellar with clues to its location elaborately gift-wrapped. All surprises must be accompanied by a bit of verse.

It would cause quite a shock in our Senate, but it is no surprise to the Dutch in the midst of their gaiety when a distinguished Dutch legislator rises in Parliament on St. Nicholas' Eve and addresses his colleagues in verse. His respondents compound the fun by answering him in rhyme. All are lighthearted when St. Nicholas comes.

On Christmas itself, there are no presents. There are church services both Christmas Eve and morning and a big dinner in the evening. The Christmas tree is the center of the home celebration, which consists of carols and story-telling in the afternoon. December 26 is also a holiday, called Second Christmas Day, and is a time to take it easy and probably go out to eat.

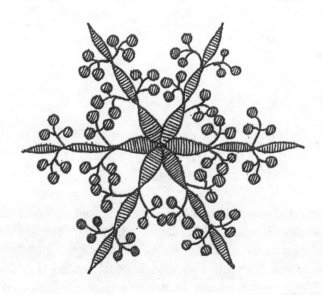

Holly

Holly is a familiar green shrub, usually thought of as having red berries and dark glossy green leaves with thorny tips, although there are many other varieties whose leaves and berries may vary in color. The bright colors of the holly made it a natural symbol of rebirth and life in the winter whiteness of northern Europe. In late December, the Teutonic peoples traditionally placed holly and other evergreens around the interior of dwellings to ward off winter bad weather and unwanted spirits. Holly flourishes in almost any kind of soil and extreme temperatures, but does not do well in the shade. The berries are poisonous to human beings.

Traditionally in England, the prickly holly is called "he" and the nonprickly "she." Which type of holly is first brought into the house at Christmas determines who will rule the household for the coming year.

Hunting the Wren

This odd and somewhat violent custom is common only in the more rural areas of England and Ireland. It may have had its origins in the ancient custom of sacrificing an animal as a symbol of the death and rebirth of the old year. The wren is widely called the "King of the Birds," and it is normally illegal to kill one, which may be what makes it appropriate for this sacrifice the day after Christmas.

After the bird was killed by the village boys on the morning of St. Stephen's Day, it would be placed on a pole or on a bundle of evergreens and carried from house to house. Traditional carols were sung, such as:

> The Wren, the Wren, the King of All Birds,
> St. Stephen's Day was caught in the furze,
> Although he is small, his family is great,
> Open up, lady, and give us a "trate."

or,

> We hunted the wren for Robin the Bobbin,
> We hunted the wren for Jack of the Can,
> We hunted the wren for Robin the Bobbin,
> We hunted the wren for everyone.

The owner of the home thus serenaded would give a treat to the carolers and would receive a feather in return for good luck. Today, happily, a stuffed wren or one made out of straw has largely replaced the real thing.

India

Because India is overwhelmingly Hindu and Moslem, there is no official celebration of Christmas. However, because of the British influence which was so strong before India gained her independence, this is looked upon as an appropriate time for gift-giving and tipping or giving "baksheesh," charitable handouts to the many impoverished people of the country.

Iran

In Iran, Christmas is called the "Little Feast," reflecting its secondary importance to Easter, which is called the "Big Feast." The whole month of December leading up to Christmas is a period of fasting during which no meat, eggs, milk, or cheese may be eaten. This lasts until after the Communion at Mass on Christmas Day. Then the day is given over to feasting. There is no exchanging of presents, but this is considered an appropriate time to give the children new clothes, just as Easter is the time for a new outfit in America.

Ireland

To the Irish, Christmas is a time for religious celebration rather than revelry. The manger scene is in most houses and there are few Christmas trees.

The best-known Irish Christmas custom is that of putting a candle in the window, often decorated with some greenery, on Christmas Eve. The idea is to help light the way of the Holy Family or any other poor travelers out on such a night. After the evening meal, the table is also set with bread and milk and the door left unlatched as a symbol of the hospitality that the family is offering to Mary and Joseph and the little one to come.

The only festive note that is struck is in the pudding that caps the meal. Three puddings are made early in December, one each for Christmas, New Year's, and Twelfth Night. The day after Christmas, St. Stephen's Day, witnesses the rowdy old custom of hunting the wren, when boys go from door to door with a wren on a stick (usually, today, the wren is not a real one), singing the traditional song and begging for treats.

Israel

Christmas comes three times each year to the village of Bethlehem. The Western Church celebrates on December 25. The Russian Orthodox Church celebrates on December 25, too, but it is December

25 by the old Julian calendar, which means that it comes on January 7 by our reckoning. The Armenian Church celebrates on January 6 by the old Julian calendar, which means January 19 to us. What makes it even more confusing is that Epiphany is celebrated twelve days after Christmas by the Western and Eastern churches, so while the Russian Orthodox are welcoming Christmas, the Roman Catholics are celebrating Epiphany. All of this overlaps and comes together in the Church of the Nativity.

The Church of the Nativity was built in the sixth century by the Emperor Justinian on the ruins of the original church built by the Emperor Constantine and his mother, St. Helena. That church, in its turn, had been built to replace a temple to the Greek god Adonis. All of these structures were built in Bethlehem over a series of caves that were considered to be the location of Christ's birth. The church was almost destroyed in 614 by Persian invaders, but they were stopped by a mural of the Magi that showed the Kings in Persian dress, since that was assumed to be their home country.

The Church of the Nativity does not belong to any one religious group, but is carefully administered and looked after by a combination of bodies. The rights and responsibilities of each group are carefully spelled out and watched over by civil authorities to prevent conflict. Certain areas are allotted to each group. For instance, in the Grotto of the Nativity, the traditional spot of Jesus' birth, the Catholics control the manger set up there while the Greeks and Armenians split the altar and are strictly limited as to what pictures or vessels they may place on it.

In the nineteenth century, the French were pushing the interests of the Roman Catholics in the church; the Russians were on the side of the Eastern Church. There was considerable conflict between them. Then the star marking the exact location of the original manger disappeared. This unfortunate incident caused accusations and counteraccusations and was finally one of the contributing causes of the Crimean War. A new star was finally placed in the Grotto—by the Turkish Sultan, of all people. It is this fourteen-pointed star which is there still, made of silver. The floor around it is marked in Latin, *"Hic De Virgine Maria Jesus Christus Natus Est,"* "Here of the Virgin Mary, Jesus Christ was born."

Christmas Eve festivities traditionally begin at Shepherds' Field, where the shepherds heard the song of the angels. Here again, rivalry is apparent, as there are three different Shepherds' Fields, one Greek Orthodox, one Roman Catholic, and one controlled by the YMCA. The Greek field dates from the fourth century and so may have a prior claim, but the YMCA field features a carol sing in the early evening.

The only Protestant service is an Anglican one, which takes place in the Greek monastery attached to the church. Even the Catholic services are not in the church itself but in one of the attached buildings. They begin about 10:30 P.M., under the supervision of the Patriarch of Jerusalem, and last until two in the morning, when a procession carries the image of the Christ Child to the Grotto to be laid in the manger. There it will remain until just after the Greek Christmas Eve service on January 6, when it will be removed as part of the Catholic Epiphany service.

There is room for only a few hundred people at the service itself, and they are there by invitation only, but Manger Square outside the church is decorated and the service is broadcast on a large television screen on the wall of the police station. Thousands of people crowd into the square to be close to the great mystery of this night.

Italy

Italy was the birthplace of the manger scene, which is still the primary element of Italian Christmas decoration. Craftsmen called *figurari* make the world-famous figures called *pastori* that enliven the Italian manger scene or *presepio*, found in every home and church.

Special care is taken with the Bambino, the figure of the infant Jesus. A particularly famous Bambino is displayed each year at the Church of Santa Maria in Aracoeli in Rome. It is said to have performed miracles and to have come home by itself when it was kidnapped. Children often stand before the manger scene in the church and preach sermons, which they have been carefully taught by their parents complete with gestures and declamatory style. This custom, symbolic of the child who came to show the world the truth, is strongly reminiscent of the medieval custom of preaching by the Boy Bishop without the sacrilegious excesses of that custom.

There used to be a very charming tradition in Italy and Sicily, but it has fallen into neglect. Ten days before Christmas the *pifferari*, shepherds from the Calabrian region, would come to Rome and play their bagpipes, the *zampogne*, before the many shrines to the Virgin both in the streets and in private homes. Similarly, the local shepherds would come to Naples and Sicily. Although they had no songs for him, they would also be sure to stop in at carpenters' shops to pay their respects to Joseph.

The main Christmas meals vary from region to region in Italy, but a general menu would feature *capitone*, roasted, baked, or fried female eel for the meatless Christmas Eve supper, the *pranzo della vigilia*; Christmas dinner might consist of *tortellini*, a capon, and a variety of home-baked cakes. On Christmas Eve the children would present their parents with their Christmas letter, best wishes and promises to be good printed in their best hand on ornate stationery and strongly reminiscent of the English Christmas piece, which may have been the forerunner of the Christmas card.

Gift-giving is saved for Epiphany. On January 6 it is Befana, the old woman who foolishly refused to help the Wise Men, who brings gifts or bags of ashes for the children.

Jack Horner Pie

Obviously, this is named for the Christmas or mince pie from which the famous nursery rhyme character abstracted a plum. The term applies to a type of Christmas gift in modern England. It is a container in the shape of a pie, although it is not to be eaten. Its actual function is to contain a variety of small gifts and goodies, like a grab bag.

Jamaica

Jamaican Christmas festivities reached their height in the late eighteenth and early nineteenth centuries with feasts and processions featuring strolling singers and performers. In this century, the celebration came under more regulation so that performers had to be licensed. This has added to a general decline, although all the customs can still be found in various parts of the island.

The women were called "set-girls," because they worked together in a set of a specific number. They danced to the accompaniment of gourd rattles, fifes, triangles, and tambourines. The men were called "actor boys" or "koo-koo boys." They wore masks and elaborate headdress and would sometimes perform plays or skits. The name "koo-koo boys" derived from a song in one of the plays which begged for food. "Koo-koo" was the sound used to imitate the rumbling of an empty stomach.

The most colorful figure in these bright festivities was the "John Canoe" dancer. He wore a mask, a wig, and a military jacket. On his head was a pasteboard houseboat with puppets of sailors, soldiers, or plantation workers. Often this was of great size, and the most skilled dancer had to be chosen to wear it. The name John Canoe is obscure. It may be a corruption of the French *gens inconnu*, which means "unknown people," or it may come from *cornu*, "horned," since early dancers wore animal masks. The origins of all these festivities are lost in antiquity, but they seem to derive equally from African and European customs.

The following discription of the lively Jamaican festivities was published in 1874:

At the Christmas carnival the younger women adorned themselves with all the finery they could procure. . . . Gaily adorned, the damsels paraded the streets in parties, known as the Reds and Blues, or the Yellows and Blues, each seeking to outshine the other. . . .

. . . Their frocks were usually of fine muslin, with satin bodices of the colors named above. In Kingston and Montego Bay, groups of twenty, thirty, or even more, passed through the streets, singing and dancing as they went. Each party had its queen, dressed far more gorgeously than the rest, and selected for much the same reasons as the May Queen of an English village.

Sometimes the "setts" as these companies were termed were all of the same height. Others varied greatly in this respect, but were carefully arranged, the line tapering down from the portly, majestic woman who led the procession, to quite little children in the rear. But every one in the sett was dressed exactly alike, even in the most minute particulars, not excepting the parasol and the shoes, the latter frequently of white kid, then costing nine or ten shillings sterling a pair. There was another rule from which departure was unknown—blacks and browns never mingled in the same sett. The creole distinction of brown lady, black woman, was in those days of slavery and social distinctions strictly observed; and, except in the smaller towns, different shades of color did not readily mingle.

While these setts were parading in the streets, John Canoe parties also displayed themselves. . . . The different trades and occupations formed separate parties, each with its John Canoe man, or some quaint device. In some cases a resemblance might be traced to the English mummers of olden time. Now and then these people were dressed up to represent characters they had seen on the stage. Shakespeare was sadly parodied on such occasions. Richard III, for example, after shouting vociferously for a horse, would kill an opponent, who, however, again revived, and performed a sword dance with the monarch.

Bermuda was the home of similar Christmas festivities, as were parts of the American South.

Japan

As in China, less than one per cent of the population of Japan is Christian. Japan was a closed country even longer than China, becoming really open to Western influence only about a hundred years ago. There is no official celebration of Christmas, yet two factors have helped to create an unofficial widespread secular observance of Christmas. The first was the influence of Americans after the war. The second may be seen stamped on the bottom of innumerable toys and trinkets that we purchase at Christmastime: "Made in Japan." As a whole industry grew up in Japan for supplying our insatiable demand for trinkets and ornaments at Christmas, it was natural for the Japanese to become interested in our celebration and to absorb some of the customs into their own society.

Non-Christian Japanese often celebrate Christmas with all our trappings: a Christmas tree and a dinner of turkey and trimmings. Gifts are brought by Hoteiosho, one of the gods from the Japanese pantheon. He is especially appropriate as an overseer of the behavior of boys and girls since he has eyes in the back of his head.

Julbock

Julbock means "Yule goat" in Swedish and is the name of one of the popular symbols of Christmas. In pagan times, Thor, the god of thunder, was supposed to ride on a goat. This picturesque means of travel has been adapted in our time to more Christian ends. It is the Julbock, a goat made of straw, who provides transportation for the Jultomten when he makes his rounds on Julafton, Christmas Eve, to deliver presents and get his offering of porridge.

Julebaal

Julebaal is the Danish name for the Christmas fire. The fire is always started with a remnant of last year's Yule log and is meant to dispel any evil spirits that might be lurking about the house.

Julebukk

This is the Norwegian version of trick or treat. It is named for Thor's goat, which was a popular costume in pagan festivities. Any type of costume is considered appropriate today as the children go door to door after Christmas asking for treats.

Julesvenn

Norway's answer to Santa Claus. America's worldwide influence has introduced Santa to many countries that did not have a tradition of Christmas gift-giving. Many of these countries adopted Santa Claus without any change. Norway, however, looked back to its national mythology to find a similar figure. They found it in Julesvenn, who used to come during the midwinter festivities of Jul to hide lucky barley stalks around the house as a symbol of good harvests to come. The timing was right, and slipping into the house to leave happy surprises fitted the image as well, so Julesvenn was a natural to play Santa Claus and bring presents on Christmas Eve.

Julklapp

Julklapp means "Christmas box" and is a delightful custom in northern Germany, Denmark, and Sweden. There will be a knock or a ring at the door, and a present will be thrown in. The giver hurries away before he or she can be discovered. The present itself attempts to be as mysterious as the giver, since it is wrapped in many layers of paper or several different-sized boxes or may merely contain directions for finding where the real present is hidden. The longer it takes to find what the present is and who gave it, the more successful the Julklapp.

Julnisse

A Julnisse is a Danish Christmas elf. One lives in every barn and is attached to the household. He is known for playing practical jokes. Thus, as with the World War II gremlin, which was created as an "explanation" for inexplicable mechanical failures, any accident around the house can be blamed on the Nisse. He is described as being very small and wearing gray homespun with a red bonnet, long red stockings, and white clogs, although no one but the family cat ever actually sees him. Every Christmas Eve he must be left a bowl of rice pudding to placate him and ensure that he will watch over the family and the farm animals for another year. The Julnisse is as popular in Danish advertising and decoration as Santa Claus is in America.

Jultomten

The Jultomten of Sweden is similar to the Danish Julnisse in that he is an elf who lives in the hayloft and is a guardian of the household, but he is also the one who brings the Christmas gifts. He sports a red cap and a long white beard and rides in a sleigh pulled by the Julbock when he comes on Christmas Eve to deliver the presents which will be found under the Christmas tree.

Kallikantzaroi

In Greek superstition, the Kallikantzaroi are evil, half-human monsters who, during most of the year, chop away beneath the ground at the tree that supports the earth. At Christmastime, that tree is renewed by the birth of Christ and the enraged demons come to the surface to vent their fury in malicious practical joking. They slip down chimneys and put out the fire in a particularly indelicate manner or ride on people's backs and force them to dance until they are exhausted. There are several ways of guarding against them. One is to keep the *skarkantzalos*, the Christmas log, burning brightly all twelve days of Christmas so they can't get down the chimney. Another is to burn salt or an old shoe, the smell of which will keep them away. Also, the lower jaw of a pig hung behind the door or inside the chimney will keep them out for reasons lost in antiquity. The kallikantzaroi roam the earth until Epiphany, or Greek Cross Day, when the Blessing of the Waters drives them underground again.

Any child born on Christmas or during the twelve days is in danger of becoming a Kallikantzaroi, in opposition to other national traditions that usually hold a Christmas child to be lucky. In Greece, the child must be bound in tresses of garlic or straw or have his toenails singed to protect him from his terrible fate. Similarly, in Poland and parts of Germany, folk traditions hold that werewolves are active during the twelve nights of Christmas and that a child born then faces the danger of becoming one.

Kettle

In the United States and Europe, sidewalk Santas use a kettle for receiving donations. The idea is said to have begun at the turn of the century in California, when the Salvation Army used a soup kettle from one of its mission kitchens to collect donations for survivors of a shipwreck to buy food and clothing. Today the coins thrown in by the passing throngs are turned into Christmas dinners and happy Christmases for the poor.

Kissing Bough

Until the introduction of the Christmas tree in the middle of the nineteenth century, the kissing bough was the primary piece of decorative greenery in the English Christmas. It was in the shape of a double hoop with streamers going up to a central point, like a Maypole with two circles of garlands. It was made up of evergreen boughs, holly, and ivy and hung with apples and pears or ribbons and ornaments, with lighted candles and a bunch of mistletoe hanging from the center. As its name implies, the woman who "accidentally" wandered under the kissing bough had to pay the ancient penalty and allow herself to be kissed. Other names for this decorative and useful ornament were the kissing ring, the kissing bunch, and the kissing ball. As these names demonstrate, the exact shape may have varied, but what went on under it remained the same.

Klapparbock

The name of this Danish creature means "Goat with Yule gifts." As with the Swedish Julbock, he probably derives from the goat Thor rode on, but unlike his Swedish counterpart, he is not a pleasant character. He is often represented by a man in a goatskin, and his job is to frighten children who have not been quite as good as they should have been.

Klaubauf

Klaubauf is a demonic page who accompanies St. Nicholas on December 5 when he visits Austria on the eve of his name day. Dressed in rags, Klaubauf has a shaggy hide, a coal-black face, goatlike horns, fiery eyes, and a long red tongue. Clanking chains are attached about his feet. He serves as a very effective warning to naughty children.

Knecht Rupprecht

The Christmas demon Knecht Rupprecht first appeared in a play in 1668 and was condemned by the Roman Catholic Church as being a devil in 1680. That did not dim his popularity or notoriety, depending on how you looked at it. Today he still shows up in much of central and northern Europe, especially parts of Germany and Austria. To the Pennsylvania Dutch, he is known as Belsnickel. Other names for the same character are Pelznickle, "Furry Nicholas," and Ru-Klas, "Rough Nicholas." From these names, it is easy to see that he is looked upon as being, not merely a companion to St. Nicholas, but almost another version of him. There is some speculation that Knecht Rupprecht derives from the pagan god Odin and represents the darker side of St. Nicholas' character, that of the punishment which must be meted out to the wicked. Knecht Rupprecht's job is to examine children in their knowledge of prayers and punish those who are deficient.

Krampus

Another Christmas demon from lower Austria, Krampus or Grampus, accompanies St. Nicholas on December 6. He carries a rod or whip for children who are badly behaved or who don't know their school lessons. However, Krampus does not get to test his rod, for St. Nicholas intercedes on a child's behalf when the child promises to be good and to study hard.

Krippe

This is the German word for "crib" and is used to apply to manger scenes set up in church or home. The Krippe has never been as important to the Germans as the Christmas tree, but it was once very popular for the custom of cradle rocking, which took place on Christmas Eve. Germany has a rich tradition of wood carving and has produced many beautiful examples of hand-carved Krippen.

Kris Kringle

Kris Kringle is a popular corruption of the name of the Christkind, the Christ Child originally, later the gift-bringing angelic figure in much of northern Europe. When the Pennsylvania Dutch brought this figure with them to America, it mingled with the notions of other immigrants and became, by the middle of the nineteenth century, a figure very much like Santa Claus, who was himself rather new at the time. The idea that Kris Kringle was just another name for Santa Claus became part of the tradition and was solidified in the popular mind by the movie *Miracle on 34th Street*.

Lamb's Wool

This was one of the traditional hot drinks that would have gone into the wassail bowl of England; it was the toast floating on the top that made it look like lamb's wool. The drink itself was made up of hot ale, sugar, nutmeg, cinnamon, cloves, eggs, and roasted apples.

Lights

One of the greatest sources of danger in the old Christmas celebration was the burning candles on the Christmas tree. They were lovely, but they were a fire hazard of the first order. Often buckets of water were kept standing around the living room to douse the blazes that happened all too easily.

The idea of electric Christmas tree lights first occurred to Ralph E. Morris, an employee of New England Telephone, in 1895. The actual strings of lights had already been manufactured for use in telephone switchboards. Morris looked at the tiny bulbs and had the idea of using them on his tree. When the idea was introduced commercially, it caught on immediately and led to a great proliferation of sizes, shapes, and colors in Christmas tree lights as well as to vastly increased safety.

Lord of Misrule

The Lord of Misrule was the leader of the Christmas revelries in medieval England. In the court, he was appointed by the king or members of the nobility and was in charge of arranging all the feasting, masquing, and mumming to take place during the Twelve Days of Christmas. He was also given a very real power, in that all, even the king, had to submit to his whims during the period of his reign. Obviously there had to be some exceptions, and a wise Lord of Misrule did not overstep the bounds if he wished to retain the favor he had been shown in being appointed. But within those bounds, he was king for the day.

Among the commoners, the Lord of Misrule presided over less orderly proceedings as the people frolicked through the streets. This description of a fifteenth-century Lord of Misrule in Norfolk, England, calls him by the name King of Christmas, but gives a good picture of his typical doings:

> John Hadman, a wealthy citizen, made disport with his neighbours and friends, and was crowned King of Christmas. He rode in state through the city, dressed forth in silks and tinsel, and preceded by twelve persons habited as the twelve months of the year. After King Christmas followed Lent, clothed in white garments trimmed with herring skins, on horseback, the horse being decorated with trappings of oyster-shells, being indicative that sadness and a holy time should follow Christmas revelling. In this way they rode through the city, accompanied by numbers in various grotesque dresses, making disport and merriment; some clothed in armour; others, dressed as devils, chased the people, and sorely affrighted the women and children; others wearing skin dresses, and counterfeiting bears, wolves, lions, and other animals, and endeavouring to imitate the animals they represented, in roaring and raving, alarming the cowardly and appalling the stoutest hearts.

The Lord of Misrule and his merry mummers probably derive from ancient Roman times, when dressing up as animals or women or just in fantastic costumes was associated with the Saturnalia. It was also a time when servants were made equal to or even higher than their masters. The Romans also had the Magister Ludi, the Master of the Games, who was appointed to handle all festivities and celebrations on special occasions.

The Lord of Misrule died out after the Restoration of the British kings in 1660 for a number of reasons. He had been a very rowdy figure, and the upsurge of Puritan feelings had made him very unpopular. He was also no longer welcome to the king. Royalty had thought itself secure until the Commonwealth temporarily abolished the monarchy. Now the king was back in power, but never again would a king be so confident that he could readily give up even the semblance of rule to that madcap monarch the Lord of Misrule.

Mari Llwyd

Only the Welsh could produce such an unpronounceable-looking name for a Christmas creature. It is a half-man, half-animal fantasy creature whose origin is unknown. It wears a white sheet on which hang such holiday ornaments as bells, Christmas balls, baubles, holly, and tinsel, while a huge headpiece resembling the head of a horse covers the upper torso. Making queer shrill noises, prancing like a hobby horse, dancing, and darting at the children, the Mari Llwyd stirs up laughter and mirth as it parades about the countryside. In former times the head was actually made up of the skull of a horse wired so that the jaws could be worked. If someone was bitten by the Mari Llwyd, he or she had to pay a fine.

Mass of the Carols

This Puerto Rican tradition begins each year on December 16. At 5:30 A.M. on that day and each successive day until Christmas Eve, all the people attend the Mass of the Carols. It is so called because of the happy carols that are sung at the mass rather than the usual hymns. Quite frequently, this caroling will be continued after the mass by many people on their way home or to work, helping to carry the joy of the season into everyday life.

Mass of the Rooster

According to tradition, the rooster has crowed only once at midnight, at the moment when Christ was born. Hence, Spanish and Latin American countries call their midnight mass on Christmas Eve Misa del Gallo, the Mass of the Rooster.

Mass of the Shepherds

In honor of the shepherds who first heard the good tidings on the first Christmas, the people of Poland call their Christmas Eve Midnight Mass Pasterka, the Mass of the Shepherds.

Mexico

South of the border, Christmas color is provided by the brilliant red of the "Flower of the Holy Night," which we call poinsettia. The Spanish name derives from the time the flower's bright red leaves appear, which is usually around Christmas Eve.

The *posada* is popular in Mexico. For nine days before Christmas, processions go from house to house, or on a smaller scale from room to room within a single house, carrying the images of Joseph and Mary and looking for shelter. Also for days before Christmas, one can see the colorful *puestos* in the marketplaces. These are booths set up especially to sell the handicrafts, food, and toys brought down from the mountains by the Indians who have labored all year in preparation for this time.

After the Christ Child has been added to the manger scene on Christmas Eve, it is time for the *piñata*, Mexico's special contribution to the world of Christmas. The *piñata* is an earthenware jar in the shape of an animal or person or some fantastic figure that is filled with small toys and candy and hung from the ceiling. One child at a time is blindfolded and turned around and given a stick to take a few swings at the hard-to-crack clay figure. When it is finally broken open, everyone scrambles for the goodies that shower down all over the room. At midnight, it is time for the Mass of the Rooster.

Although the children may get small trinkets from the *piñata*, they must wait until Epiphany for their major presents. As in so many Spanish countries, it is the Wise Men who bring the gifts on their day, January 6.

Midnight Mass

In the Roman Catholic Church, the first mass of the Feast of Christmas takes place at midnight, Christmas Eve, that being traditionally the time of Christ's birth. No one knows for sure when the first Midnight Mass occurred, but it is believed that the custom may go as far back as the early part of the fifth century. Certainly the custom was taken into account in the sixteenth century, when the Council of Trent passed new legislation concerning the hours of masses. Priests are allowed the special privilege of celebrating three masses on Christmas Day. Today, television allows many people to visit some of the famous Midnight Masses without leaving their homes. One such is broadcast from the Church of the Nativity in Bethlehem, the traditional site of Christ's birth. Another comes from St. Peter's Basilica in Rome. In 1975 Pope Paul VI celebrated an unprecedented open-air Midnight Mass before 100,000 people filling St. Peter's Square, while the mass was seen on television by an estimated 330 million viewers in forty-one countries throughout the world.

Many other churches have late services on Christmas Eve, often at 11:00 P.M. rather than midnight. Usually they are candle-lit and feature a great deal of singing of the traditional carols that set the mood for the Christmas celebration to come. The Episcopalian Service of Lessons and Carols is typical of this kind of service. Prophecies of Christ's birth and the Gospel stories are read, interspersed with the singing of ancient carols.

Mince Pie

It seems hard to imagine that a religious controversy could rage over a piece of baked goods, but such was the case with the mince pie. Meat pies become popular in England following the Crusades, when the many eastern spices were introduced to England for the first time by the returning knights. The pies were made of minced bits of venison, pheasant, partridge, peacock, rabbit, apples, sugar, suet, molasses, raisins, currants, and spices in differing combinations. At Christmas a special pie was baked. The spices and sweetmeats were looked upon as symbolic of the Wise Men's gifts to the Christ Child, so the pie was baked in the rough shape of a manger and an image of the baby Jesus was put on top of it. Later, this image outraged the Puritans, who looked upon it as idolatry. Mince pies were outlawed along with Christmas under the strict Puritan Commonwealth and in the early American New England settlements. All through the seventeenth and eighteenth centuries, the making of mince pies was looked upon as a sign of Roman Catholic leanings. This probably resulted in the change of shape to a normal circular one and the replacement of the Christ Child with sprigs of greenery.

Today the mince pie has lost its religious nature along with its meat. It is usually made with apples, raisins, currants, suet, molasses, lemon peel, spices, sugar, and salt.

Mince pie was also known as "Christmas pie" in medieval England. Thus it is a mince pie that plays an all-important role in a familiar nursery rhyme and the startling story that inspired it.

> Little Jack Horner
> Sat in a corner
> Eating a Christmas pie;
> He put in his thumb
> And pulled out a plum
> And said, "What a good boy am I!"

The real Jack Horner was Thomas Horner, a servant to Richard Whiting, who was a church official at Glastonbury in the time of Henry VIII. That greedy monarch was engaged at the time in seizing as much of the Church's lands as he could get away with. In an effort to appease him, Whiting sent him an unusual Christmas present, a mince pie with the deeds to a dozen rich estates hidden inside it. He hoped that the king would be satisfied and not take any more of his lands. Horner was entrusted with the secret mission. On the way, it is said, he opened the pie and stole one of the deeds for himself. With this "plum" he made his fortune. Little did he know that he would be remembered in a bit of nonsense verse hundreds of years after his death.

Mistletoe

In Norse mythology, Balder was the best loved of all the gods, both by all living creatures and by the gods themselves. But one night he had a dream that indicated danger was approaching. When he told this to his mother, Frigga, she resolved to protect him. She went throughout the world asking and receiving a promise from every-thing, even the rocks and the trees, that they would not harm Balder. When this was known, it became a great sport to throw deadly ob-jects at Balder, since they would always fall short or turn aside be-cause of their promise. All were happy for Balder's safety except the sly Loki, who was jealous of him. He found out craftily from Frigga that there was one plant so insignificant that she had overlooked it when she was getting the promises: the mistletoe. Taking a sharp sprig of the plant, Loki went to Hoder, Balder's brother, who was blind, and asked why he did not join in the jolly game of throwing objects harmlessly at Balder. Hoder pointed out that he was blind and had nothing to throw. Loki gave him the mistletoe and guided his hand. The dart went straight to Balder's heart and he fell dead. All wept, and Loki was severely punished, but Frigga blessed the plant that had, through no fault of its own, caused Balder's death. She made it a symbol of love and promised to bestow a kiss on all who passed beneath it.

Mistletoe was a holy plant to the ancient Celtic priests called the Druids. Around the New Year, a priest would cut the mistletoe from the holy oak tree with a golden sickle and catch it in a white cloth, so that it would not touch the ground. It would then be offered in sacrifice to the gods along with two white bulls. There were also ceremonies in which kisses beneath the mistletoe symbolized the end-ing of old grievances. Sprigs of mistletoe were hung over doors for the same symbolic reasons.

The hanging of mistletoe at Christmas and New Year's was one of many pagan customs carried over into the Christian era, in this case without any specific justification, but simply as a charming custom. The kissing beneath it died out in most areas except England. (Austria has a related custom in which Sylvester kisses anyone beneath the greenery, but this is not specifically mistletoe and only Sylvester is allowed to do it.) The British are known today for their lack of emotional display, but this was not always so, which may explain why kissing beneath the mistletoe survived there. In the sixteenth century, kissing was widespread in England as a form of greeting without requiring close relationship between the kissers. The great continental scholar Erasmus wrote at this time of a visit to England: "Wherever you go, everyone welcomes you with a kiss, and the same on bidding farewell . . . in short, turn where you will, there are kisses, kisses everywhere." It may just be because they were so inclined to kissing anyway that the English preserved the ancient mistletoe tradition when others let it fade.

Mistletoe is a parasitic plant that grows hanging from the limbs of various nonevergreen trees. It has leathery evergreen leaves, yellow-green flowers, and waxy white berries. One old English custom required the plucking of one berry for each girl kissed until the sprig was bare or the man ran out of girls.

The pleasures and harmless frivolity of mistletoe have been delightfully detailed in Dickens' *Pickwick Papers:*

From the centre of the ceiling of this kitchen, old Wardle had just suspended with his own hands a huge branch of mistletoe, and this same branch of mistletoe instantaneously gave rise to a scene of general and most delightful struggling and confusion; in the midst of which, Mr. Pickwick, with a gallantry that would have done honour to a descendant of Lady Tollimglower herself, took the old lady by the hand, led her beneath the mystic branch, and saluted her in all courtesy and decorum. The old lady submitted to this piece of practical politeness with all the dignity which befitted so important and serious a solemnity, but the younger ladies, not being so thoroughly imbued with a superstitious veneration for the custom—or imagining that the value of a salute is very much enhanced if it cost a little trouble to obtain it—screamed and struggled, and ran into corners, and threatened and remonstrated, and did everything but leave the room until some of the less adventurous gentlemen were on the point of desisting when they all at once found it useless to resist any longer and submitted to be kissed with a good grace. Mr. Winkle kissed the young lady with the black eyes, and Mr. Snodgrass kissed Emily, and Mr. Weller, not being particular about the form of being under the mistletoe, kissed Emma and the other female servants just as he caught them. As to the poor relations, they kissed everybody, not even excepting the plainer portions of the young-lady visitors, who, in their excessive confusion, ran right under the mistletoe, as soon as it was hung up, without knowing it! Wardle stood with his back to the fire, surveying the whole scene with the utmost satisfaction; and the fat boy took the opportunity of appropriating to his own use, and summarily devouring, a particularly fine mince-pie that had been carefully put by for somebody else.

Now, the screaming had subsided, and faces were in a glow, and curls in a tangle, and Mr. Pickwick, after kissing the old lady, as before mentioned, was standing under the mistletoe, looking with a very pleased countenance on all that was passing around him, when the young lady with the black eyes, after a little whispering with the other young ladies, made a sudden dart forward and, putting her arm round Mr. Pickwick's neck, saluted him affectionately on the left cheek; and before Mr. Pickwick distinctly knew what was the matter, he was surrounded by the whole body and kissed by every one of them.

It was a pleasant thing to see Mr. Pickwick in the centre of the group, now pulled this way, and then that, and first kissed on the chin, and then on the nose, and then on the spectacles, and to hear the peals of laughter which were raised on every side. . . .

Mumming

Mumming is difficult to define exactly since it includes every kind of dressing up and acting out or dancing or performing that people choose to do at Christmastime. The annual Christmas pageant is a form of mummery in our own country.

Mumming can be traced back to the rowdy bands that roamed pre-Christian Rome at the time of the Saturnalia dressed as animals or women and carousing in the streets. In the Middle Ages these activities remained popular, sometimes carried on for the entertainment of homeowners who would then be expected to provide a treat, but just as often for the entertainment of only the performers themselves. Sometimes bands would break into church services and disrupt the proceedings with their "geese dancing" (a corruption of the word "disguise" or "guise dancing"). There were many legends of such sacrilegious revelers who were cursed by a priest and compelled to dance without interruption for a full year until the following Christmas.

In the royal courts, there was usually appointed a Lord of Misrule who governed the mumming. He would set up masques, processions, and other entertainments, as well as leading in spontaneous outbursts. Frequently court personages would disguise themselves and indulge in the unusual license that was allowed the Christmas mummers. Henry VIII himself was known to mask his face, as when, with a band of fellow revelers, he broke into a supper party given by Cardinal Wolsey.

Gradually the official court mumming and the rowdy masquerades of the street died out. But mumming took on a new form as the disguised figures devoted themselves to acting out exotic plays and skits. As these were short performances, they could be done several times a night around a village, in return for the traditional handout. Sometimes the mummers were vagabonds just looking for the money or food; often they were village groups who would perform the same play every year. One of the most widespread Christmas plays was the *Play of St. George,* which existed in many versions, all of them rather naïve to the modern playgoer. Thomas Hardy features this play in his famous novel *The Return of the Native.* The story of the play has nothing to do with Christmas, but as St. George was the patron saint of England, his exploits against the Turks were considered patriotic and a suitable spectacle for Christmas or anytime. Max Beerbohm, in a parody of the style of George Bernard Shaw, described one of these St. George plays:

> Entered, first of all, the English knight, announcing his determination to fight and vanquish the Turkish knight, a vastly superior swordsman, who promptly made mincemeat of him. After the Saracen had cele-

brated his victory in verse, and proclaimed himself the world champion, entered Snt George, who, after some preliminary patriotic flourishes, promptly made mincemeat of the Saracen—to the blank amazement of an audience which included several retired army officers. Snt George, however, saved his face by the usual expedient of the victorious British general, attributing to Providence a result which by no polite stretch of casuistry could have been traced to the operations of his own brain. But here the dramatist was confronted by another difficulty: there being no curtain to ring down, how were the two corpses to be got gracefully rid of? Entered therefore the Physician, and brought them both to life.

Traditionally, after this successful resurrection, a devil would go about with a large frying pan collecting donations. There was obviously very little serious drama here but a very great deal of fun.

America has one very large-scale remnant of mumming in the annual Philadelphia Mummers' Parade. Over a hundred years old, this event still offers a great opportunity for much dressing up, music-making, and satirical reminders of the past year's events.

Nacimiento

As in most of southern Europe, in Spain the manger scene is a more important image of Christmas than the Christmas tree. *Nacimiento* is the Spanish term for a manger scene and is used both in Spain and in most of the Latin American countries. The Magi are very popular in Spain, so they figure prominently in the *nacimiento*. Often in Spanish communities, men dressed as the Three Kings will visit the large outdoor manger scenes during the festivities of Epiphany Eve.

Nativity Scene

St. Francis of Assisi was responsible for the popularization of the nativity scene. It probably existed before him, but only as a decorative element. St. Francis was a very gentle man, known for his love of animals. He wanted to bring home to the people the humanity and humility of the Christ Child. The Church at this time was a very rigid institution, emphasizing that this life was a place of sin and sorrow. St. Francis wanted to add the hope and joy of God's love to this disheartening message. So, in 1223 or 1224, in Greccio, Italy, he constructed a life-sized manger scene with live animals. The gospel was sung around this scene, and this may very well have been the start of caroling, since the church songs of the time were Latin hymns not known for being joyous. The people were charmed and captivated and immediately embraced the nativity scene as a means of making the Christmas message more real.

The nativity scene has always been most important to southern Europe, where the symbol of the first tree amid the winter snows has less meaning because of the warmer climate. The scenes range from the simplest little cutout figures to whole roomfuls or even village squarefuls of elaborately decorated scenery. Naples is especially famous for its manger scenes. In the beginning of the eighteenth century, the king of Naples began making his own manger scenes. He was not known for much else, but he was very good at working with his hands. He would carve the figures and his wife would help outfit them. It became very fashionable at the court for the nobility to emulate the king and vie with each other to produce ever more spectacular effects. Very often the stable would be set amid elaborate architectural ruins, which had little to do with biblical times, but offered great opportunity for picturesqueness.

The nativity scene has many names in many countries. In Italy, it is the *presepio*; in France, it is the *crèche*, a name often used in America as well; some areas of Germany have the *Krippe* as well as the tree; Czechoslovakia builds the *jesličky*; Spain and much of Latin America call it a *nacimiento*; Brazil has a *pesebre*, in Costa Rico, it is a *portal*. In all countries, it is a way of bringing home the message that Christ was made a little child and lay lowly in a manger for the sake of humankind.

Noche-Buena

The "Good Night" is the Spanish name for Christmas Eve. Noche-Buena is a time for singing and dancing, both in the streets and around the *nacimiento* at home before it is time to attend the midnight Mass of the Rooster.

North Pole

The North Pole first appeared as Santa's home in the cartoons of Thomas Nast. In 1882 Nast drew a cartoon showing Santa sitting on a box addressed "Christmas Box 1882, St. Nicholas, North Pole." In 1885 another cartoon traced Santa's route on a map, showing him coming home to the North Pole. Nast never gave his reasons for settling on Santa's home territory; presumably he just felt Santa's costume was best suited to a cool climate and he knew that Santa would never do anything by half measures.

Norway

At 4:00 P.M. all work comes to a halt on Christmas Eve in Norway. Everyone bathes and puts on new clothes to greet the season. The largest sheaf of grain is hung out for the birds to make their Christmas merry, too. Christmas dinner begins with rice pudding with a lucky almond hidden in it for someone, and a bowl is also set out for the barn elf so that he will continue to watch over the animals and not turn mischievous. A Christmas pig provides most of the meat dishes.

Traditionally the Norwegians kept the season bright with a Yule log. It literally formed the center of the celebration since it was frequently an entire tree that could only partly fit into the fireplace and so extended well out into the middle of the living room. As it burned, it would be pushed farther and farther into the fire to provide continuous light and warmth through the whole Christmas season. More and more, though, the Christmas tree, introduced from Germany in the 1830s, has taken the place of the Yule log. The celebration may have lost some warmth thereby, but it has gained a great deal in spaciousness.

The worldwide popularity of Santa Claus has caused in recent years the resurrection of an ancient Norse figure called Julesvenn. In ancient times he would come during the feast of Jul to hide lucky barley stalks around the house. Now he comes on Christmas Eve to bring gifts to good children.

114

After Christmas Day is past, Norwegian children indulge in a custom much like the American trick or treat. It is called Julebukk after the goat that drew the cart of Thor, the god of thunder in Norse mythology. In pre-Christian festivities, Thor's goat was popular as a costume for the Jul festivities. Today children wear costumes and go door to door asking for goodies in a much more innocent version of those ancient revelries.

Old Christmas Day

This is a term still sometimes used in England for January 6, Epiphany. In 1752 Britain finally adopted the Gregorian calendar, which was already current in most other European countries. This calendar was created to correct an error in calculation in the old Julian calendar which was very small, but which over the centuries had accumulated a total error of eleven days. Thus in 1752 September 3 became September 14 in Britain. This caused considerable confusion, especially when it came time for an important holiday such as Christmas. Many people refused to follow the new calendar, but consulted such portents as the famous Glastonbury thorn, which always blossomed on Christmas Eve. When it blossomed on Old Christmas Eve, they followed its example and celebrated by the old calendar.

While the calendar is now completely accepted, the old date is still remembered in folklore.

Old Hob

This old English custom is very rare today. Old Hob is a horse who may have had his origin in pre-Christian representations of Odin's eight-footed horse. Like the Welsh Mari Llwyd, the English Old Hob is represented by a horse's head on a pole carried by a man under a sheet. It was accompanied by groups of waits who sang Christmas ditties and rang hand bells for coins. The Old Hob festivities would begin as early as All Souls' Day, November 2, and usually ended by Boxing Day, December 26. There was similar tradition in northern Germany, where the horse was called Schimmel.

Ornaments

The first Christmas trees had real fruit and flowers as their only ornaments. Cookies, nuts, and other kinds of food were later added. Lighted candles were placed on the trees. All of this was understandably heavy, and it took a sturdy tree to stand up without drooping to the ground. Perhaps as a remedy for this problem, German glass blowers began producing featherweight glass balls to replace the fruit and other heavy ornaments. This was the beginning of the highly specialized industry that today produces the myriad Christmas tree ornaments ranging from simple colored balls and tinsel to elaborate stars and blinking Santa Clauses.

Other countries have some very lovely forms of traditional ornaments. Painted eggshells are a favorite in Czechoslovakia. In Sweden, straw figures of animals and little wooden ornaments adorn the tree. The Danish like bells and paper hearts. In Japan, pastel-colored paper fans and delicately cut paper butterflies are popular.

Pantomime

The Christmas Pantomime is to the British what the Christmas show at Radio City Music Hall is to Americans, except that it is found all over, not just in one place. Pantomimes are presented most often during the twelve days after Christmas and are a treat for the whole family.

The pantomime may have started in the seventeenth century in the form we understand to be pantomime in America, that is, the wordless acting out of a story. But by the early eighteenth century it had come into full flower and refused to be silent. The stories combined as many emotions as possible, serious, comic, and highly adventurous. Elaborate stage transformations were always a main feature.

Today the stories are almost always traditional subjects, such as fairy tales or *Robinson Crusoe*, and exist largely as an excuse to string together a great variety of performers and scenic effects into a giant vaudeville. It is not unusual for a pantomime to include dancers, singers, comedians, acrobats, magicians, and ventriloquists—possibly even swimmers or ice skaters.

Papa Noël

Papa Noël is the Brazilian name for Santa Claus. He comes on Christmas Eve to fill children's shoes with Christmas gifts and sweets.

Pastori

This Italian word for shepherds applies to all the figures made for the *presepio*, the Italian manger scenes. First made in Naples in the eighteenth century, the *pastori* were elaborate figures fashioned out of wood or clay and costumed in silk finery with exquisite detail by the *figurari*, the figure makers. Since the townspeople would worship and celebrate before the *presepio*, it did not seem unreasonable for them to appear as figures in the setting. Thus the mayor, local businessmen, and other townspeople began to appear as carved figures beside the shepherds and Wise Men of the original Christmas. Other popular *pastori* still include animals, birds, bagpipe-playing local shepherds, minstrels, Franciscan monks, angels, and stars.

Père Fouettard

Also known as Père Fouchette, this French Christmas figure takes his name from the French word *fouet*, which means a birch rod. Father

Birch Rod comes with Père Noël, Father Christmas, to deal out punishments to those who haven't been good enough to earn a reward from the jolly old man. Père Fouettard carries the birch rod he is named for and also a basket into which irretrievably naughty children can be bundled and carried off.

Père Noël

Père Noël is French for Father Christmas. He is one of the two gift-bringers who come to different areas of France to fill the children's shoes on Christmas Eve. The Christ Child is the other and is called le Petit Noël, "Little Christmas."

Peru

Many Peruvian manger scenes will feature the quaintly beautiful figures carved from wood by the Quechua Indians. The techniques they used date back to the sixteenth century, and many of the traditional images and forms of dress also come from that time of the *conquistadores*.

On Christmas Eve, the meal after Midnight Mass features tamales. Christmas Day festivities in Lima, the capital, are highlighted by a bullfight and a procession with the statue of the Virgin Mary.

Petit Noël

Petit Noël is the name given the Christ Child by the French when he comes in the role of gift-bringer to the children on Christmas Eve. His name means "Little Christmas," and he comes to the areas not taken care of by Père Noël, Father Christmas.

Piñata

This is a joyful custom of Mexico and some other areas of Latin America. The *piñata* is a clay or earthenware jar in the shape of an animal or person which is filled with toys, candy, and cookies and suspended from the ceiling. One at a time, children are blindfolded and given a stick. After being turned around until his or her sense of direction is gone, the child is set free to flail wildly in every direction, trying to find the *piñata*. Even if the child hits it, he or she may have trouble cracking the tough jar. When it finally is broken, everyone scrambles for the goodies. To spare the feelings of easily frustrated modern youth, some *piñatas* are now made of easy-to-break papier-mâché.

Plum Pudding

Plum pudding is one of the famous traditional English Christmas dishes. Even for Americans, it conjures up images of a Dickensian Christmas, although most of us have not tasted a plum pudding.

That is probably just as well, since this Christmas dish is a bit tricky and a poorly prepared one is a very hard tradition to swallow.

The first plum puddings were made around 1670. They were a stiffened form of the earlier plum porridge, which was made of similar ingredients but was served semiliquid. Interestingly, plum pudding does not contain any plums. "Plum" may refer to the raisins in it, or to the fact that the ingredients swelled during baking, "To plum" once meant to rise or swell as we see in the modern "to plump." To the early mild porridge or frumenty were added lumps of meat, dried fruits such as raisins and currants, rum and brandy, butter, sugar, eggs, and many spices. These first plum puddings were made in large copper kettles and were prepared several weeks before Christmas. The making of the pudding was attended with much ceremony. The entire household was present and each family member took turns at stirring the thick steaming stew and each made a wish. A coin, a thimble, a button, and a ring were mixed into the pudding. Later when it was eaten, each object would have significance for the finder. The coin would mean "wealth," in the new year; the button, "bachelorhood"; the thimble, "spinsterhood"; and the ring was "marriage."

At the Christmas Feast, the pudding came to the table amid great anticipation. If eyes could consume, the pudding would have been gone in an instant. The arrival of the plum pudding was the capstone of the Christmas dinner, and there was always room, no matter how full the stomach. What was not eaten was saved, sometimes lasting into mid-January, for the pudding was very rich and filling.

Today plum pudding is not made as it once was, but it still requires time and patience. It takes about five or six hours to prepare. This is mainly because all the suet (hard fat from beef or mutton) must dissolve before the flour particles burst. If the fat is not allowed to melt, the pudding will not cook properly, and the results will be a compressed hard pudding, impossible to digest. Plum pudding is usually served decorated with holly and with hard sauce on the side.

The champion of all plum puddings was created in the village of Paignton in Devon, England, in 1819. This village had a custom of making a gigantic plum pudding for the entire community once every fifty years. The custom has since been discontinued, but in 1819 the pudding used four hundredweights of flour and 120 pounds each of suet and raisins. The finished concoction weighed 900 pounds and had to be pulled by three horses. With great celebration, the pudding was sliced up and served. There was great dismay among the villagers when they discovered that the pudding wasn't properly cooked.

Poinsettia

In Mexican legend, a small boy knelt at the altar of his village church on Christmas Eve. He had nothing to offer the Christ Child on his birthday because he had no money, but his prayers were sincere and a miracle gave him the present that could be bought by no one: the first Flower of the Holy Night sprang up at his feet in brilliant red and green homage to the holy birth. Thus was born the flower we know as the Poinsettia.

Dr. Joel Roberts Poinsett was the American ambassador to Mexico from 1825 to 1829. His keen interest in botany made him very interested in the Flower of the Holy Night and he brought it back to his home in South Carolina. It became very popular as a Christmas plant and was named after him.

The red part of the poinsettia is not a flower, but is made up of bracts, inner leaves that are small in most flowers. The actual flowers of the poinsettia are the small yellow buds in the center of the red clusters. Besides the familiar red poinsettia, other varieties can also be found with white and pink flowers, and a yellow variety is found in Guatemala.

There are some areas of our country where the poinsettias are so abundant they turn whole towns into Christmas decorations. The town of Encinitas, California, is known as the poinsettia capital of the world because of the superabundance of the flower there. Each Christmas the chamber of commerce organizes special poinsettia tours to view nature's Christmas offering in its most picturesque locales.

Poland

The lucky children of Poland receive presents twice. On St. Nicholas' Day, the good saint himself brings presents. On Christmas Eve, it is the Star Man.

The Star of Bethlehem is the most popular image in the Polish Christmas. It is the first star of Christmas Eve, which marks the end of the Advent fast and ushers in the time of Christmas feasting. The Christmas Eve supper must have an odd number of dishes, from five to thirteen, for luck, and there must be an even number of diners. Empty places are left for absent family members and for the Christ Child. *Oplatki*, small white wafers, are served with the meal. These are symbolic of the Sacred Host that is received at Mass and make the Christmas Eve dinner a secular version of Communion for the family circle.

After supper the Star Man arrives, attended by the Star Boys. They are dressed fantastically, as Wise Men or animals or other figures from the nativity. The Star Man examines the children in their catechism and rewards them with small presents if they do well, even if they need a bit of coaching. The Star Boys sing carols and are given a treat for their help. After the fun, all go to Pasterka, the midnight Mass of the Shepherds.

Polaznik

This is a custom of the Eastern European Slavic regions that is similar to the English and Scottish first-footing. Polaznik is usually a young man who visits a family at the dawn of Christmas Eve, holding a handful of wheat which he throws over the members of the household before wishing them a Merry Christmas. After enjoying a large pre-Christmas feast with the family, Polaznik is given a gift and departs at evening. His visit is looked upon as a sign that the family will enjoy prosperity throughout the coming year.

Posada

The *posada* is a beloved custom of Mexico and other Latin American countries. *Posada* means "inn" in Spanish, and the custom derives from plays that were once performed depicting the wandering of Mary and Joseph looking for shelter. Tradition says their search lasted for nine days. So on December 16 a procession sets out with the figures of Mary and Joseph to find shelter for them. This procession may pass through the streets to prearranged houses, or it may take place entirely inside one house, going from room to room. When the "inn" is reached, there is a ritualistic series of questions and answers to be gone through. One such is called the Litany of Loretto:

Who knocks at my door, so late in the night?
We are pilgrims, without shelter, and we want only a place to rest.
Go somewhere else and disturb me not again.

But the night is very cold. We have come from afar and we are very tired.

But who are you? I know you not.

I am Joseph of Nazareth, a carpenter, and with me is Mary, my wife, who will be the mother of the Son of God.

Then come into my humble home, and welcome! And may the Lord give shelter to my soul when I leave this world!

The innkeeper always shows himself to be more hospitable than the original one at Bethlehem. When they are allowed to enter, the figures of Mary and Joseph are taken to the manger scene, where they are set among the animals by the crib. This is done for each of eight nights. On the ninth, Christmas Eve, the figure of the Christ Child is also added to the scene. Each evening the *posada* procession finishes with much singing and dancing.

Presepio

For Italians, the *presepio*, or manger scene, is the absolute center of all festivities. On Christmas Eve, it is set up without the Christ Child, since it is not yet time for his birth. Then on Christmas morning, in a simple ceremony witnessed by the entire family, the mother of the household places the Bambino in the *presepio*. All then repeat their prayers in the presence of this very physical reminder of the real meaning of Christmas.

Puerto Rico

Early in the Christmas season, carolers begin going from house to house or farm to farm. They wear homemade fantastic versions of what the Magi might have worn and sing bright, rhythmic Spanish carols called *aguinaldos* and *villancicos*. They are rewarded with food and drink, and many from each house will join them, so that eventually there are great crowds going singing from place to place. Sometimes, this goes on till dawn.

Nine days before Christmas, the Mass of the Carols begins. This takes place each morning at 5:30 A.M. It is filled with music and usually the carolling continues on the way to work or home after it is over.

The manger scenes are peopled with *santos*, hand-carved figures that represent some of Puerto Rico's oldest works of art, dating back to the sixteenth century. The tree and Santa Claus are also popular in Puerto Rico, largely because of American influence and that of the large Puerto Rican population which has settled in the United States. Gifts, therefore, arrive on Christmas morning; but also, following Spanish tradition, on Epiphany. On January 5 in the evening, children leave water, grass, and grain under their beds for the camels of the Wise Men, and the next day they find presents in their place.

Putz

The name *putz* comes from the German *putzen*, which means "to decorate." The putz is the Pennsylvania Dutch form of the manger scene. It differs from almost all others in the elaborateness of the winter scene, which includes the stable and the Holy Family as only one element in the whole. The putz may take up an entire room and be landscaped with earth, rocks, and water. There may be mill wheels, waterfalls, bridges, fountains, villages, log cabins, and other natural and man-made features.

At Bethlehem, Pennsylvania, which was founded by Moravian missionaries, there is a community putz that is different each year and unveiled only on Christmas Eve. This is an extremely elaborate setting. One year it required 800 pounds of sand, 12 bushels of moss, 64 tree stumps, 40 Christmas trees, 48 angels, 200 animals, 16 lighting effects, 29 lamps, 700 feet of rockearth, 400 feet of other materials, and several oil paintings.

Pyramid

Before the development of the Christmas tree in the fifteenth or sixteenth century, the Christmas pyramid was the most important decoration to Germany and much of northern Europe. It was a wooden
framework in the shape of a pyramid, decorated with greenery and ornaments. Gifts or food, or a manger scene, could be placed on its
shelves. As the tree became more popular, more and more of the
functions of the pyramid were shifted over to the tree. By the early
part of this century, the pyramid was virtually nonexistent as a
Christmas decoration outside Italy, which imported the idea of the
ceppo but never took up the Christmas tree.

Red and Green

Red and green are looked upon as the official colors of Christmastime, yet no one can say definitely why that is. The best guess is that
they are the colors of the holly. The bright red and green of leaf and
berry seen against the cold whiteness of snow would stand as a prom-

ise of the winter's end and the spring to come. This promise of life in the midst of death is a fitting symbol for the birth of Christ.

Réveillon

Réveillon is from the same French word that provides a name for one of the Army's most annoying habits, reveille, and which means "to awaken." The *réveillon* is the happy meal and celebration that take place in French homes after Christmas Eve Midnight Mass.

Ringing In Christmas

At four in the afternoon of Christmas Eve, all work must stop in Norway so that the Christmas celebrations can begin. The signal is given by church bells all across the land, putting an end to work and ringing in Christmas.

Russia

Under the atheistic Communist regime of Russia, there is no official celebration of Christmas. Yet nothing can completely subdue the spirit of Christmas and there are still some vestiges of the old celebration left. Father Christmas was the name of the old Russian Santa Claus; he disappeared with the revolution. But there is a new figure symbolic of winter named Grandfather Frost, and he bears a suspicious resemblance to the officially banned Father Christmas. There's no Christmas tree any more, but a New Year's tree brings the same spirit of rebirth in the midst of hardship.

In the past, it was Babouschka who brought presents to good children on the eve of Epiphany. She was just like the Italian Befana, an old woman who failed to help the Wise Men on their way. There was also a white-robed girl named Kolyáda (which also means Christmas) who would go house to house in a sled on Christmas Eve with attendants who would sing *Kolyadkiad*, Christmas carols, and be given small gifts and treats. These customs do not officially exist any more, but no one so far has succeeded in completely suppressing the spirit of Christmas. Time alone will measure the success of the Russian effort.

Santa Claus

THE HISTORICAL ST. NICHOLAS

To twentieth-century America, St. Nicholas is just another name for Santa Claus, bearded, round, and rosy, and dressed in red and white. To most of Europe, he is a thin figure dressed in bishop's robes who comes riding a white horse on St. Nicholas' Day, December 6. What was the real St. Nicholas like?

Unfortunately, very little is known about the real St. Nicholas. Countless legends have grown up around this very popular saint, but very little historical evidence is available. He was born around A.D. 280 in Asia Minor and became bishop of Myra, now Demre, in Turkey. The only definite historical evidence of his life is in the records of the First Council of Nicaea in 325, which was responsible for creating the Nicene Creed, a famous statement of doctrine still widely in use. He was definitely in attendance, although what role he might have played is shrouded in mystery. He probably suffered in the persecution of Christians under the emperor Diocletian, which lasted until about 311, at which time Nicholas would have been about thirty-one. The new emperor Constantine at first tolerated, then encouraged, and finally established Christianity as the state religion. St. Nicholas died about 343.

It was not long after his death that the legends began and the popularity of his cult began to spread. In 1003 Vladimir of Russia came to Constantinople to be baptized and brought back relics and stories of St. Nicholas, who became the patron saint of Russia. It was not much later that the sailors of southern Italy, who also regarded him as their patron, introduced the cult to western Europe. By the height of the Middle Ages, St. Nicholas was probably invoked in prayer more than any other figure except the Virgin Mary and Christ Himself. He was the patron saint of children, students, Russia, bankers, sailors, pawnbrokers, vagabonds, and thieves.

An event that contributed strangely to the growth of St. Nicholas' popularity in Europe was the fact that his body was stolen from Asia Minor and taken to Italy. In 1087, ostensibly to protect the remains from infidels, sailors from Bari in Italy broke into his tomb and carried the body from Myra to their own home. A great basilica, one of the most impressive still in existence, was built to house the saint's new resting place. This new home gave a focus and impetus to the growing cult of St. Nicholas.

Ironically, the church built to house the remains stolen from Myra to protect them from possible desecration by Moslem invaders carries an Islamic message. Skilled Moslem craftsmen from North Africa or the Near East were brought in to help in the construction, and they included disguised Arabic calligraphy as part of a design on the building. It was years before it was realized that the message read "There is no God but Allah, and Mohammed is His Prophet." Church officials decided not to destroy the beauty of the building by effacing the message, and so it remains.

What might have proved a setback to the popularity of St. Nicholas occurred in 1969 when the Roman Catholic Church demoted the saint in the universal calendar of the saints. However, this has had very little effect on celebrations of the saint's day.

The mortal remains of St. Nicholas made their last journey in 1972 when, as a gesture of ecumenicism, the Roman Catholic Church donated some of the relics to the Greek Orthodox Shrine of Saint Nicholas in Flushing, New York. It had taken nine hundred years and a journey to a continent he had never heard of, but at last the mortal remains of the good saint had returned to the Greek Church that he had known in life.

PATRON SAINT OF CHILDREN

From the very beginning, St. Nicholas was closely connected with children. Stories relating to his birth are very similar to those of Samuel in the Old Testament. Nicholas' mother, Nonna, had been sterile until the conception of Nicholas, who immediately devoted himself to the service of God, just as with Samuel. He was precocious both physically and religiously. He was said to be able to stand in his bath at an' incredibly early age. As an infant, he would observe fast days by refusing his mother's breast until after sunset. Because of these miracles, he was looked upon as an important intercessor both for children and for sterile women.

One of the oldest and most enduring St. Nicholas' stories concerns his role as benefactor of children. It happened after his death, on the eve of his name day, December 6. The people of Myra, where he had been bishop, were celebrating in his memory when pirates from Crete fell upon them. A great deal of booty was seized, and a young boy named Basilios was carried off into slavery. He was chosen by the emir of Crete to be his personal cupbearer, and for a year he served in that position. On the eve of the next St. Nicholas' Day, Basilios' parents were in no mood to celebrate with the rest of the town, but as they were devout people they made a quiet celebration at home. Suddenly the dogs began to bark, and they rushed to the courtyard to find what the matter was. Had the pirates returned to complete their devastation? Consider their surprise and amazement when there were no pirates, just their son wearing Arab dress and carrying a full goblet of wine. As in all real miracles, they felt as much terror as joy in that first moment. Then Basilios explained that he had just been about to serve his master a cup of wine when a power had lifted him up and carried him off. He had been filled with fear, but then St. Nicholas appeared to him, calmed him, and brought him to his home. St. Nicholas' Day had once again become a cause for rejoicing.

This story took different forms during the centuries to follow, but one element did not change in artwork or story. This touch still brings the miracle home in such a precise way: the full goblet of wine didn't spill a drop during that miraculous, headlong flight across the Mediterranean Sea.

PATRON OF SAILORS

Almost as early as St. Nicholas' protection of children was his patronage of sailors. He decided to make a pilgrimage to Jerusalem and made the trip by boat without letting anyone know who he was. One night on board, he dreamed that the devil was cutting the ropes of the main mast, which he interpreted to mean that a bad storm was brewing. He warned the ship's crew, but also told them that God would protect them, so they shouldn't fear.

The storm blew up quickly, and the ship was out of control. St. Nicholas prayed for their deliverance. One of the sailors climbed to the main mast to tighten the rigging. When he finished, he lost his hold and fell to his death on the deck far below. The storm soon responded to the saint's prayers and lessened. All were grateful for their deliverance, but upset over the death of the sailor. St. Nicholas prayed for him, and suddenly he was restored to life with no injuries at all. St. Nicholas' fame as a healer would later spread wide, but to sailors the saint was always their special protector.

Having a patron involves responsibility as well as benefits. St. Nicholas is no exception. In another story he showed sailors their right duty. His visit to the Holy Land was cut short when an angel appeared to tell him to return home with haste. He went to the port and sought for a ship. He finally found one that had just been loaded and whose master agreed for a fee to take him to Patara, his birthplace. But the captain and crew believed that he wouldn't know enough to object when they went first to their home port, which was out of the way. So they set off in the wrong direction. It was not long before a violent storm blew up, and in the heavy seas that it produced the rudder was damaged beyond repair. The storm died as quickly as it had come, and it looked as though they would drift until they died of starvation. But the boat drifted in a very specific direction, and the crew began to hope that they might encounter land somewhere. Indeed, that was what happened and all the sailors were very thankful. When they learned that they had come to land at Patara, the very spot that St. Nicholas had wanted to reach, they were first amazed and then contrite. St. Nicholas forgave them their deception, but cautioned them to be more honest in the future. Thus St. Nicholas not only protected sailors but taught them their responsibilities as well.

PATRON OF STUDENTS AND OTHER VAGABONDS

St. Nicholas probably became the patron saint of students in a roundabout manner: it is more likely that the story relating how he protected three students was created after he had already become the patron of students. It all happened in the Middle Ages. Students did not have a patron, so they probably settled on St. Nicholas since he was already the patron of children and a very popular figure, and as young men they would find him very suitable. Then this story grew up, probably in northern France in the twelfth century.

Three young theology students were traveling and stopped at a roadside inn for the night. While they slept, the less-than-hospitable innkeeper went through their belongings and was delighted to discover a large sum of money. He not only killed the students but, in a nicely melodramatic touch, cut them up, preserved the flesh with salt, and hid it in pickle barrels. St. Nicholas passed that way some time

later and sensed what had happened. He miraculously restored the three students to their original forms and brought them back to life.

This story was immensely popular in the Middle Ages. Many pictures show it, and it was the subject of a large number of plays. The scene in which the three students rise up out of the barrels was always a sensation.

As a result of this story, St. Nicholas found himself in unusual company. All travelers began to look to St. Nicholas for protection, including those who might have identified more with the innkeeper than with the students. Vagabonds, thieves, and even murderers took Nicholas as their patron saint. By the time of Shakespeare, such traveling brigands and highwaymen were known as "St. Nicholas clerks" and one of Shakespeare's characters in *Henry IV, Part I* tells of just such a rascal: "I know thou worshippest Saint Nicholas as truly as a man of falsehood may."

HOW ST. NICHOLAS SAVED THREE UNFORTUNATE GIRLS AND BECAME THE PATRON SAINT OF PAWNBROKERS

This is the most famous story of St. Nicholas. In his hometown there lived a man with three daughters who had fallen upon particularly hard times. As he could not afford a dowry for any of the three girls, there was no possibility that they would marry, and if they stayed home the whole family would starve. Regretfully, he began to face the necessity of selling his girls into slavery or prostitution—an awful choice, but his only hope in this hard time. St. Nicholas learned of his plight. There is some question as to Nicholas' background: his family may have been wealthy or middle-class, but they were never poor. The saint, however, never used his money for his own purposes, but only to help others. He resolved to do so in this case. Being a humble man, he did not want any recognition or thanks, so he stole to the house in the dead of night and threw a bag of gold through the window. (In some versions of the story, he throws it down the chimney, thus providing a possible background for Santa Claus' favorite means of dropping in.) The gold saved the eldest girl by providing a dowry so that she could be honorably wed. In the same way, as each girl reached marrying age, St. Nicholas was the guardian angel who secretly provided the means to their happiness. The last time he was discovered by the father, who began to express his extreme gratitude, but St. Nicholas would have none of it. He begged the father to accept the gifts humbly and silently as they were given and to repent of the immoral choice he had almost made. Also, he was asked not to tell the story until after St. Nicholas' death.

It is easy to see from this tale how St. Nicholas became associated with gift-giving and children. It is a little more difficult to see how he ended up in the company of pawnbrokers. Because Nicholas was the patron saint of sailors, he became very important to merchants who depended for their livelihood on the safe arrival of shipments. He also was known as a protector of oaths and guarantor of financial integrity, largely on the basis of the following story.

Long after St. Nicholas' death, a Christian borrowed a large sum of money from a Jew and swore by St. Nicholas to return it on a certain date. When the date came, the Christian wickedly decided to cheat the moneylender. So he put the exact amount of money into a hollow cane and, in the course of walking to the court where he was to be sued for the money, he asked the Jew to hold his cane for a moment. Then when he came before the court he was able to swear by all that was holy that he had put the exact amount of money into the Jew's hands and that he was being charged twice. The Jew had no choice but to allow himself to be cheated. But St. Nicholas had other ideas. On the way home, the Christian was struck down dead by a runaway cart and his cane was split open, revealing the trick. The Jew refused to accept the money under such circumstances, saying that if the saint were as humane as he was supposed to be, he should not let the Christian die. Immediately the Christian was restored to life. He repented his sin and paid the Jew what was owed him. The Jew, in his turn, was so impressed that he converted.

This combination of giving money and protecting oaths on financial matters made St. Nicholas a logical choice for bankers and pawnbrokers. There was also the symbolism from the story of the three dowries of redeeming something of value.

The three bags of gold underwent a metamorphosis. The story was so popular that St. Nicholas was always depicted in paintings with the three bags of gold somewhere about him, even when that was not the story being told. Eventually they were simplified into three gold balls. These gold balls first took on a financial bent when they appeared on the coat of arms of the great Florentine bankers the Medici family, as a symbol of St. Nicholas. After that they became a common symbol for a pawnbroker's establishment. And that is why three gold balls above the doorway are still the traditional sign for a pawnbroker, although few of us would associate him with the jolly gift-giver St. Nick.

THE REFORM OF ST. NICHOLAS

The Protestant Reformation raised several problems for St. Nicholas. He had become well established as a gift-bringer and the opener of the Christmas season on his name day, December 6. With the Reformation, though, it became improper to celebrate anything having to do with Catholic saints. But St. Nicholas was far too popular just to be done away with. Something had to give.

In a few countries, St. Nicholas just changed his name and kept right on going. Thus there developed Father Christmas in England, Weihnachtsmann in Germany, and Père Noël in France. Germany also established the figure of the Christkindlein or Christ Child, who would come with the Pennsylvania Dutch to America, where his name would gradually be corrupted by popular pronunciation until he became Kris Kringle. All these figures were jolly, venerable gift-givers, dressed in clothes appropriate to the season, except for the Christ Child, and even he changed with time so that Kris Kringle looked like all the rest.

At least one country, Holland, did not change the name of St. Nicholas, but did change his religious aspects into purely secular ones. He became just like Father Christmas or Père Noël but kept his old name. When the Dutch settled in New Amsterdam, later to become New York, they brought St. Nicholas with them. But as in so many cases, popular pronunciation had its effect: St. Nicholas became Sinta Claes. The stage was almost set for the arrival of Santa Claus.

SANTA CLAUS AND THE THREE MEN
WHO GAVE HIM BIRTH

Although the Dutch brought Sinta Claes with them to the New World in the seventeenth century, Santa Claus was not born until the nineteenth century and was an American, not a Dutch, creation. Having sprung from a Puritan beginning, America did not have much to do with saints or Christmas celebration in its earlier years. It was not until after the Revolution that the Christmas customs of such groups as the Pennsylvania Dutch began to filter out into the general population. And the first great interest in St. Nicholas was stirred up by the writings of Washington Irving.

Irving published a book called *Diedrich Knickerbocker's A History of New York from the Beginning of the World to the End of the Dutch Dynasty*. This was an extremely satirical book, with at least as much fantasy as fact in it. One of the things that Irving did was make St. Nicholas a sort of patron saint for the Dutch and throw him into the story whenever possible, including one appearance as the figure-head of a ship. Fictitious celebrations were included, and St. Nicholas flew about in a wagon to bring children presents. One passage will serve both to show Irving's lively satirical style and to illustrate the picture he drew of St. Nicholas. Oloffe Van Kortlandt, who arrived at a new development named Communipaw too late to get any land, dreams a dream in which St. Nicholas tells the people to settle elsewhere.

And the sage Oloffe dreamed a dream—and lo, the good St. Nicholas came riding over the tops of the trees, in that selfsame wagon wherein he brings his yearly presents to children, and he descended hard by where the heroes of Communipaw had made their late repast. And he lit his pipe by the fire, and sat himself down and smoked; and as he smoked the smoke from his pipe ascended into the air and spread like a cloud overhead. And Oloffe bethought him, and he hastened and climbed up to the top of one of the tallest trees, and saw that the smoke spread over a great extent of country—and as he considered it more attentively, he fancied that the great volume of smoke assumed a variety of marvelous forms, where in dim obscurity he saw shadowed out palaces and domes and lofty spires, all of which lasted but a moment, and then faded away, until the whole rolled off, and nothing but the green woods were left. And when St. Nicholas had smoked his pipe, he twisted it in his hat-band, and laying his finger beside his nose, gave the astonished Van Kortlandt a very significant look, then mounting his wagon, he returned over the tree-tops and disappeared.

And Van Kortlandt awoke from his sleep greatly instructed, and he aroused his companions, and related to them his dream, and interpreted it, that it was the will of St. Nicholas that they should settle down and build the city here. And that the smoke of the pipe was a type how vast would be the extent of the city; inasmuch as the volumes of its smoke would spread over a wide extent of country. And they all with one voice assented to this interpretation excepting Mynheer Ten Broeck, who declared the meaning to be that it would be a city wherein a little fire would occasion a great smoke, or in other words, a very vaporing little city—both which interpretations have strangely come to pass! . . .

And the people lifted up their voices and blessed the good St. Nicholas, and from that time forth the sage Van Kortlandt was held in more honor than ever, for his great talent at dreaming, and was pronounced a most useful citizen and a right good man—when he was asleep.

One phrase in that passage probably rang a bell for you: "Laying his finger beside his nose, gave . . . a very significant look, then mounting his wagon, he returned over the tree-tops and disappeared." If that sounds suspiciously reminiscent of "And laying his finger aside of his nose,/And giving a nod, up the chimney he rose" there is good reason for it. Irving's book was very popular and was still in current circulation and people's thoughts twenty years later when Dr. Clement Clarke Moore wrote the little poem *A Visit from St. Nicholas* for his children. He was the second of the three men most responsible for Santa Claus. His description of the jolly elf solidified Irving's, in whose work, after all, St. Nicholas had not been the central figure. A children's book of the time, *A New Year's Present to the Little Ones from Five to Twelve*, had shown St. Nicholas' sleigh being drawn by one reindeer. That was the first time he had appeared without a wagon and horse. It may have been the idea of snow in winter and St. Nicholas as patron of Russia and other Arctic areas that inspired the sleigh and reindeer. Whatever it was, Moore seized upon it, increased the team to eight reindeer with fanciful names, and froze our image of St. Nick and his coursers until a popular song came along and added the much more prosaic name Rudolph to the crew list.

Moore's poem served in its turn as the inspiration for the man who finally drew a picture of Santa Claus for us. By the 1860s the old Dutch mispronunciation of "St. Nicholas" had gained popular acceptance and "Santa Claus" had replaced the saint's name as Americans cheerfully mispronounced the Dutch mispronunciation. Santa appeared frequently in children's books, but his appearance varied widely, sometimes tall and thin, sometimes dressed in buckskins. The great political cartoonist Thomas Nast finally popularized a single image of the jolly old elf, based on the description in Moore's poem. He did a whole series of pen-and-ink drawings over a period of years for *Harper's Weekly* which completed the birth of Santa Claus.

The last small touch in our image of Santa Claus came from an unlikely source, the Coca-Cola Company. This was his passage from black and white to color. Haddon Sundblom did a series of ads for Coca-Cola beginning in the 1920s which depicted the full-blown Santa we now know with the rosy cheeks that had only been described before in the age of pen and ink. Santa had also grown from the elf size of Moore and Nast to the more-than-human proportions that contribute so much to his jollity.

If Nicholas, the ascetic bishop of fourth-century Asia Minor, could see Santa Claus, he would not know who he was. But it's a safe guess that the saintly patron of children, even if he didn't know who Santa was, would still love him for the joy he brings the world.

Santos

Santos are the hand-carved figures that appear in the Puerto Rican *nacimientos*, or manger scenes, at Christmastime. These figures of wood and clay offer examples of one of the earliest native art forms, dating back to the sixteenth century.

Scotland

Scotland never fully recovered from the Puritan ban on Christmas celebration in the seventeenth century. Even after the Restoration, the innate Scottish Puritanism kept festivities to a minimum. The Scots save most of their energies for Hogmanay, as they call New Year's. Still, there are some customs and observances connected with Christmas. For instance, it is bad luck to let the fire go out on Christmas Eve, since that is the time when the elves are abroad and only a good, roaring fire will keep them from slipping down the chimney. On Christmas Day itself, it is not unusual to have a bonfire and dance to the sound of bagpipes before settling down to a hearty dinner.

Seals

Christmas seals are the decorative paper stamps sent out each year by the American Lung Association to raise funds. People wishing to use the stamps to close Christmas cards and packages return a contribution for the seals.

Christmas seals were originated by a Danish postmaster, Einar Holboll, in 1903. Since he handled stamps all the time, he had the idea of selling a special decorative stamp at Christmastime and giving the proceeds to a worthy cause. The first seals were printed in 1904 with a portrait of Queen Louise of Denmark. More than four million of these were sold in the Danish Post Office that year.

The European success of Christmas seals led Jacob Riis, a friend of Teddy Roosevelt, to write an article advocating their sale in America.

This was the inspiration for Emily Bissell, a Red Cross worker, to introduce Christmas seals for the benefit of the Red Cross in Wilmington, Delaware, in December of 1907. By 1908 the seals were issued coast to coast and were a huge success for a number of charitable organizations. In 1919 the National Tuberculosis Association (now the American Lung Association) became the sole sponsor, and in 1920 the familiar Red Cross symbol was replaced by the double-barred cross, an adaptation of the Lorraine Cross, the emblem of the Eastern branch of the Christian Church since the ninth century.

Shooting In Christmas

This is one of the noisiest of Christmas traditions and is found in parts of Norway. It derives from the old pagan beliefs that noise would drive away evil spirits, which was especially needed at midwinter when the forces of death and cold seemed to have such a strong grip on all of nature. Today young men travel from farm to farm on Christmas Eve filling the air with gunshot blasts. After the evil spirits have been properly frightened off, the marksmen are rewarded with refreshments for shooting in Christmas.

Shopping Days

Shopping days are the invention of retailers who are concerned that Christmas Day would arrive and we would still have some odd change left in our pockets. Radio, newspapers, and TV all remind us how many shopping days are left until Christmas. There are never enough.

There are two kinds of Christmas shoppers. The first has all of his Christmas shopping done by December 2. He can be recognized by his smug expression and the fact that (like someone who has just quit smoking) he seems unable to carry on a conversation without mentioning at least once that he has finished all his shopping. More often it is the sole topic of conversation. He can also be recognized because very few people will talk to him. The second kind of Christmas shopper does his shopping a little bit later. He can be recognized around the middle of December by his well-intentioned look and his neat appearance; about the twentieth, he has become disheveled and his expression is increasingly haunted. On the twenty-fourth he can be spotted in great flocks inside every store, where he buys any and everything.

On the day after Christmas, some store or other will always take out an ad saying there are only 364 shopping days to Christmas. No one is amused.

Snapdragon

This was once a very popular game played most at Christmas in England. Raisins were placed in a bowl and covered with brandy, which was set ablaze. The object was to snatch the raisins out of the fire and pop them into your mouth before the flames did too much damage. There was probably very little flavor left in the burned and shriveled raisins, but danger and daring make a great sauce, and snapdragon was popular for many years before dying out in our own practical century.

Spain

The Spanish Christmas season begins December 8 with the feast of the Immaculate Conception, which lasts a week. There is a fascinating custom at this time, which dates back into antiquity, called Los Seises, or "the Dance of the Six." While this dance may originally have been performed by six, it is now done by ten boys, who are carefully trained in the tradition. They dance before the altar at the cathedral in Seville in a series of stately poses and movements that symbolize many of the mysteries of the incarnation and birth of Jesus.

As in most of southern Europe, the manger scene is more important than the Christmas tree, which is very rare. Here the manger scene is called a *nacimiento*. These scenes are set up both in homes and on a grander scale in village squares. It is a delight for the children to sing and dance before the image of the tiny Christ Child in the family home.

Christmas Eve is called Noche-Buena, the "Good Night." There will be singing and dancing in the streets to the sounds of guitars and castanets. At midnight everyone attends the Misa del Gallo, the "Mass of the Rooster," so named because of the legend that the only time the rooster has crowed at midnight was the night when Jesus was born. After mass the dinner, or *cena*, is served, usually featuring turkey and the Christmas favorite *turrón*, a candy loaf of roasted almonds in caramel syrup.

Christmas Day is a time for family reunions and exchange of gifts among the adults. The urn of fate is brought out for fun. This is a large bowl with the names of all present in it on slips of paper, which are drawn out two at a time. Officially this is to wish only that the people whose names are so joined will endeavor to be good friends during the coming year, but there is often some finagling of fate to help Cupid do some matchmaking. In some rural areas the Yule log is still part of the festivities.

The Wise Men are very popular in Spain, and it is they who bring presents to the children. On Epiphany Eve, January 5, shoes filled with straw are set out for the camels that carry the Magi. In the morning, of course, the straw has been replaced by presents. Also on Epiphany Eve, it is common for three villagers richly dressed as the Wise Men to pay a visit to the village *nacimiento*, to the delight of the whole village, which gathers to watch them pay homage to the Christ Child.

Stamp

In 1898 Canada instituted its Penny Postal System on Christmas Day. To commemorate the occasion, it issued a stamp with a Christmas motif. Since that time many other countries have printed special postage stamps at Christmastime with either secular or religious themes. These have proved to be very popular, especially in the mailing of Christmas cards, which are made more decorative by the substitution of bright Christmas scenes for stamps with portraits of presidents or monarchs.

The United States issued its first Christmas stamp in 1962. The most popular one ever was produced in 1971. It was a reproduction of the Adoration of the Shepherds by the early Renaissance Italian painter Giorgione. The stamp was the largest printing order in the history of the postage stamp; over a billion copies were printed.

Star Boys

On January 6, the traditional date for the visit of the Wise Men, groups of children in Norway, Sweden, and Poland dress up as the

Magi or other biblical figures. Carrying a paper star with a candle inside on a long pole, they go house to house singing carols, performing short plays, or narrating the story of the Three Kings. In return, they are given presents of candy and coins.

Stocking

The custom of hanging up a stocking to receive gifts from Santa Claus probably originates with a variant on the St. Nicholas' legend of the three dowryless girls. In that version, each time that St. Nicholas threw the bag of gold down the chimney, it landed in a stocking that happened to be hanging up there to dry.

Sugarplums

Sugarplums still exist, although we don't call them that any more. Quite simply, they are round or oval candies made of very rich fruit preserves, cream fillings, and other sweet concoctions, often covered with chocolate. Thus our familiar boxes of Christmas chocolates contain many candies that could be called sugarplums. The name would have died out completely long ago but for its immortalization in two sources, A Visit from St. Nicholas, where "visions of sugarplums danced" in the children's heads, and the Sugarplum Fairy, a famous dancing character in Tchaikovsky's ballet The Nutcracker.

Sweden

The Christmas season lasts a whole month in Sweden, from December 13 to January 13. December 13 is St. Lucia's Day and a very special one for the children. St. Lucia was a young girl who was put to death in Sicily in A.D. 304 for professing Christianity. She is honored in Sweden because legend has it that she brought food to that country during a terrible famine, appearing with her head all circled with light. So before dawn on St. Lucia's Day the eldest daughter of the family dresses herself in a white robe, with a green wreath on her head with lighted candles on it. She wakes her parents by singing the familiar Italian song "Santa Lucia" and brings coffee, buns, and cookies to everyone while they are still in bed. The younger children often wear a conelike hat with a star on top and accompany her on her rounds. There is also an official popular election to choose a Lucia who will preside at the big parade in Stockholm.

Before the midday meal on Christmas Eve, the family gathers in the kitchen for a custom called *doppa i grytan*, "dipping in the kettle." All gather around a pot filled with drippings of pork, sausage, and corned beef and dip dark bread into it, which they eat when it is completely soaked with the drippings. This specifically recalls an ancient famine when there was nothing else to eat, but symbolically it calls to mind in the midst of thanksgiving and plenty all those who are in need and hunger.

The traditional Christmas Eve dinner would start off with smorgasbord with a sip of akvavit; then *lutfisk*, a sun-cured cod served in cream sauce, and ham; finally, the traditional rice pudding with an almond in it. The finder of the almond, it is sometimes said, will marry in the next year. No provision is made in this tradition for the already wed or those just out of diapers. Presumably there is some hanky-panky to see to it that the almond ends up in the right serving.

147

After dinner all gather around the Christmas tree to open the presents. These gifts were brought by the Jultomten, a gnome who lives in the barn, if there is one, and is very similar to the Danish Nisse. He, too, has to have his portion of rice pudding if he is to behave in the coming year. The Julbock is a goat of straw, modeled after Thor's goat, which serves as a steed for the Jultomten in making his rounds. All the presents are accompanied by humorous verses hinting at what the package contains while actually making it as obscure as possible.

On Christmas Day there is a service at five in the morning. After that the day is devoted to rest and to religious observance.

December 26 is called the Second Day of Christmas. The men of the village ride through the streets waking all the people early on this day. It is also a day when extra food is given to the animals.

On January 6, Twelfth Night, the Star Boys come out. These are the children dressed in nativity costumes or other fantastic attire and carrying paper stars on poles with candles inside the stars to make them shine. They sing from house to house and are given treats.

Christmas finally ends on January 13. When King Canute was king of Sweden a thousand years ago he decreed that the Christmas feasting should last twenty days. Therefore, instead of ending after twelve days on January 6 (which is actually the thirteenth day if you count both December 25 and January 6), another week is added to the celebration of Christmas in Sweden.

Switzerland

In terms of its traditions, Switzerland is basically four different countries. The language and customs are determined at any given point by who is the closest neighbor in that area. Thus there are predominantly German, French, and Italian areas, as well as the remaining pockets of the Swiss dialect, Romanche. There is therefore no way to pin down specific customs, since they draw upon four distinct traditions and then combine them according to local usage. Gifts may be given on either Christmas Eve or New Year's, and they are brought by the Christkindli or St. Nicholas, or even Father Christmas with his wife, Lucy. Both the manger and the Christmas tree hold sway. Carols drift on the air in four languages. Switzerland has maintained its careful neutrality by absorbing the best of all nations.

Sylvester

Sylvester is a charmingly grotesque custom found in certain parts of Austria. He usually appears on New Year's Eve, although he is associated with Christmas greenery. A standard decoration is a bunch of green pine twigs hung from the ceiling. When a girl passes beneath it, she becomes fair game for Sylvester. He is old and ugly (or wears a mask to that effect) and sports a wreath of mistletoe, and he kisses whoever he can catch under the greenery. At midnight, he is driven out like the old year.

Syria

On Christmas Eve, the outer gates of the homes of Syrian Christians are locked as a reminder of the years of persecution when all worship had to be hidden behind closed doors. The whole family gathers in the courtyard with lighted candles, around a pile of wood that will become a bonfire. The youngest son reads the Gospel story of the Nativity, and the father lights the fire. All observe the fire carefully, because the particular way that it spreads through the wood will determine the luck of the household for the coming year. All sing psalms while the fire burns, and when it dies down, they make a wish and jump over the embers. Early on Christmas morning, there is a mass before dawn, and there is a bonfire in the center of the church as well. The image of the Christ Child is carried around the church in a joyous procession.

Syrian children receive their gifts at Epiphany from a very original source, the Smallest Camel of the Wise Men. On their way to see Jesus, the Wise Men traveled in a caravan with many camels. The smallest was exhausted by the long journey but refused to give up, his desire to see the Christ Child was so great. When the infant Jesus saw the faith and resolve of this loving creature, he blessed it with renewed strength and immortality. Every year he comes bearing the gifts for the good boys and girls, who learn the importance of even the most insignificant of us from his example.

Tolling the Devil's Knell

This is an old English custom still practiced in Dewsbury, Yorkshire. A death knell is the ringing of the bells to signify that someone has died. On Christmas Eve the devil's knell must be tolled because, according to folklore, the devil died when Christ was born. Therefore the church bell is rung slowly, once for each year since the birth of Christ, with the last ring timed to come exactly at midnight, the traditional moment of Christ's birth.

Tree

ST. BONIFACE AND THE CHRISTMAS TREE

One very popular legend of the origin of the Christmas tree involves the early Christian missionary St. Boniface. In the eighth century he was attempting to win the pagan Germans over to the worship of Christ. One Christmas Eve in the great forest, he was shocked to come upon a ceremony of human sacrifice taking place at the foot of the sacred oak tree of Odin at Geismar. Seizing an ax, he struck one great blow at the tree, which was then toppled by a great wind. The people were awe-struck and won over to Christianity, but they felt lost without the symbol of their giant tree. St. Boniface pointed to a tiny fir tree that had nestled among the roots of the now fallen oak, and told them to take that as their sign. Christ was a bringer of life "ever green," and the fir tree became his symbol.

THE FIRST CHRISTMAS TREE

Popular legend often attributes to Martin Luther the creation of the first decorated Christmas tree. Walking one night and looking up at the starry sky through the branches of trees, he was struck with the idea and hurried home to place candles on the branches of a tree.

The predecessors of the Christmas tree can be seen in the many pagan customs involving tree worship. These especially involved evergreens during the cold of winter when sacrificing to or decorating with greenery was looked upon as a good way to ensure good crops the following year.

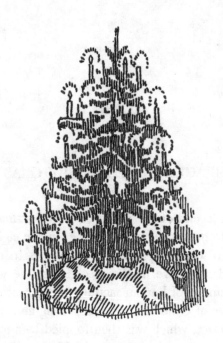

The immediate ancestor of the Christmas tree was the paradise tree. In the medieval Church calendar, December 24 was Adam and Eve Day. Many plays would act out the fall of the first two human beings to make clear the meaning of Christ's birth the next day, the coming of the "second Adam" to redeem the failure of the original. A main set piece of this play was the paradise tree, the tree from which Adam and Eve ate against God's command. It being winter, the tree consisted of a fir tree hung with apples. The custom became popular in homes as well as on the stage, and many German households began to set up their own paradise trees on Christmas Eve. In keeping with the legend that trees bloom at midnight on Christmas Eve, paper flowers and other fruits were hung on the trees. Wafers were added as a symbol of the body of Christ, as in the Communion wafer. These wafers gradually were replaced by cookies.

The first reference in print to Christmas trees is a forest ordinance from Ammerschweier in Alsace, Germany, in 1561. This statute says that no burgher "shall have for Christmas more than one bush of more than eight shoes' length." The custom had become so popular that too many trees were being taken from the forest. In 1605 the first description of fully decorated trees came from Strasbourg. "At

Christmas they set up fir-trees in the parlours at Strasbourg and hang thereon roses cut out of many-colored paper, apples, wafers, gold-foil, sweets, etc." In 1737 a writer at Wittenberg made the first reference to trees with candles on them. Many of the decorations came from the Christmas pyramid, the wooden structure that probably existed before the Christmas tree. Gradually it became less popular, and its decorations were moved over to the tree that took its place. By the end of the eighteenth century, the Christmas tree was to be found everywhere in Germany.

The Christmas tree was known in England as early as 1789, though it did not become generally accepted until the 1840s. At that time the ruling family, which had come from Germany, sometimes had a Christmas tree. Specifically Prince Albert, Queen Victoria's consort, set up a tree in 1844 and started the fad that would later become tradition.

The first Christmas trees in America were probably introduced by Germans also, but under less pleasant circumstances. During the Revolutionary War, Hessians, who were German mercenaries, fought on the British side. These less-than-welcome visitors probably set up the first American Christmas trees.

One of the first Christmas trees set up by an American citizen was in 1847 outside the home of August Imgard in Wooster, Ohio. Americans are quick to realize business opportunities, and so, just four years later, we find record of one Mark Carr, a Catskill farmer, who became the first Christmas tree salesman in New York City. In 1856 Franklin Pierce decorated the first Christmas tree at the White House, and the custom has become a national tradition.

COMMUNITY CHRISTMAS TREES

The idea of a Christmas tree set up out of doors to be decorated and enjoyed by the entire community first occurred in twentieth-century America. Pasadena, California, had the first community tree in 1909. The year 1912 saw New York City's first tree at Madison Square Garden, and also Boston's first on the Common, while 1914 was the first year for a tree in Philadelphia's Independence Square. The first

Christmas tree on the White House lawn was set up under Warren G. Harding in the early 1920s. Also in the 1920s, Altadena, California, developed its mile-long stretch of lighted cedars called "Christmas Tree Lane." In 1926 the Nation's Christmas Tree was dedicated. This was the giant sequoia known as the General Grant Tree in Kings Canyon National Park, California. The tree is 40 feet thick at the base, 267 feet tall, and thousands of years old.

Although the community Christmas tree has been largely an American institution, there is one English tree which embodies admirably the combination of Christmas and national spirit that has inspired the many American trees. This is the tree sent to the British people each year by the people of Oslo, Norway, and set up in Trafalgar Square in the heart of London. It is sent in memory of the time during World War II when the Norwegian king was in exile from his German-occupied land. Each year a tree from his own country was brought to him in England, even though smuggling it past the Germans was very dangerous. Since 1947 Norway has thanked Britain for its help with a yearly Christmas tree.

Ukko

Unlikely as it may sound, Ukko is the name of the jolly steed who brings Santa Claus to Finland. He is a goat made of straw, like the

Julbock elsewhere in Scandinavia. The Finns don't seem to find anything odd about his name, although it would be difficult for Americans to imagine a sleigh drawn by Dasher, Dancer, Prancer, and Ukko.

United States

Christmas in America embraces almost all of the customs of the entire world. Every ethnic group has its place in our society and they all bring their own traditions. The great diversity of climate also makes a difference. Southern California enjoys its sunshine and makes beach outings part of the festivities; Alaska never has to worry about a white Christmas because it's sure to come, and Christmas Day is only a brief twilight in the midst of the months-long night in the farthest north. For most people, turkey is the feast, and the presents are placed beneath a Christmas tree. Families try to gather for the holidays. Gifts come from Santa Claus. Those are some of the basics, but every part of the country and every type of people celebrate differently. Let us just present some of these varied pleasures.

In New York City, Christmas is the time to stroll down Fifth Avenue and see the huge tree at Rockefeller Center and the store decorations. The *Nutcracker* ballet is playing. There are half a dozen different performances of Handel's *Messiah*, even some where you can bring your own score and sing along if you fancy yourself a singer. The holiday spirit of charity is exemplified by the appeals in the New York *Times* for the annual "100 Neediest Cases" drive which has raised millions of dollars for the needy since its inception in 1912.

The South has a long Christmas tradition. The first American Christmases were celebrated in Florida by the Spanish. The first English Christmas in America took place at Jamestown, Virginia, in 1607. Captain John Smith wrote, "The extreame winde, rayne, frost and snow caused us to keep Christmas among the salvages where we were never more merry, nor fed on more plenty of good Oysters, Fish,

Flesh, Wildfowl and good Bread." In later times, Christmas was a season in the South for riding to the hounds and for great open houses in the plantations and mansions. Today in New Orleans, seven thousand carolers gather spontaneously every year in Jackson Square on December 22 for a great community sing. In the French Quarter, the Cabildo Bazaar offers handicrafts, food, and homemade quilts to thousands of tourists doing their Christmas shopping.

In San Francisco the Great Dickens Christmas Fair reproduces an old English street scene with stores offering craftsmen's wares, food, and Victorian melodramas. In the street, costumed singers stroll and play while Punch and Judy shows delight the children.

The Chicago Museum of Science and Industry began a tradition in 1945. Attempting to preserve local ethnic customs, they invited two old Lithuanian women to decorate a tree with the nearly forgotten craft of straw ornaments, thereby saving the custom. Other groups were invited to participate, and the custom caught on. Today the trees are decorated the day after Christmas by dozens of nationalities. Appropriate food is served in the cafeteria and folk dances and songs entertain the visitors.

In Washington, D.C., a high point is always the lighting of the Christmas tree on the Ellipse. Smaller trees are decorated for each state, with one large one symbolizing the nation. Uusually the President himself throws the switch to turn on the dazzling lights. Also on the White House grounds are usually some reindeer for the children to see. A recent custom that may become an annual tradition is the enacting on the grounds of the Washington Monument of the nativity story by a co-operative group of seven local churches of different denominations. Each church provides a different cast for each night it is performed in a series of narrated tableaux, complete with camels and donkeys.

Williamsburg, Virginia, shows each year how a colonial Christmas might have been celebrated. Bruton Parish Church, where the likes of Thomas Jefferson and George Washington worshiped, is beautifully decorated and holds special Christmas services as it has done annually since 1715.

In Boston the caroling festivities on Beacon Hill are famous. All houses are decorated and illuminated, while singers and hand-bell players raise the joyous music.

156

In St. Louis the Christmas Carols Association has a membership of over 30,000 singers to make its community sing a roaring success.

In America's Southwest, Spanish customs such as the *piñata* and *posada* can be found.

In Kings Canyon National Park every year, a Christmas service is held at the base of the Nation's Christmas Tree, which towers 267 feet above the proceedings.

In Hawaii the season is ushered in by the arrival of the Christmas Tree Ship, a steamship bringing a great shipment of the seasonal symbols. Santa also comes by boat.

Bethlehem, Pennsylvania, was founded by Moravian missionaries on Christmas Eve, 1741. Every year there is the great community putz and there is a giant electric star atop South Mountain visible for twenty miles.

Thousands of tourists flock to Altadena, California, to see the mile-long stretch of decorated trees that make up Christmas Tree Lane.

In Salt Lake City the greatest classical music of Christmas is presented by the 420-voice Mormon Tabernacle Choir and the Youth Songfest of 6,000. For those whose tastes are more modern, St. Peter's Lutheran Church in New York City has a special Pastor to the Jazz Community, and every year a Jazz Cantata Service at Christmas proves that there is more than one way to make a joyful noise to the Lord.

Venezuela

The night before Christmas is a lively time in Caracas, because the streets are filled with young people roller-skating their way to a special late mass. A great deal of music and revelry takes place en route, so the Venezuelan Mass of the Rooster is usually a little later than the Midnight Masses in other Latin American countries. After the service, they all roller-skate home to an early breakfast of *hallacas*, meat pies with cornmeal crusts, wrapped in banana leaves and boiled in water.

In Mérida, in the western part of Venezuela, there is a lively custom known as *La Paradura del Niño*, or the Standing Up of the Christ Child. On the first day of the new year, the Christ Child in the traditional *nacimiento* or manger scene must be stood up in his crib as a symbol of the infant's growing maturity. If this is not done, the consequences are delightful. A friend who finds the child lying down will kidnap it and carry it off to his own home, where it is kept in a position of honor. The only way that the original owners can get it back is to throw a *Paradura* party. Godparents are chosen, and there is a procession of friends and family to the hiding place. There the godparents carefully take up the image and bring it back to its home with much caroling and festivity along the way. When it is safely returned to its home (and carefully stood up so the same thing won't happen again), the children offer presents and sing verses of a traditional carol which describe the various gifts. Then there is much dancing and a great deal of refreshments, all provided at the expense of the original malefactors.

Waits

Waits are the old English Christmas carolers. Originally the term applied to the medieval watchmen who would patrol the street and call out the hours of the night, together with comments on the weather and sometimes blessings on the householders. Later the term was applied to the official town musicians who played for civic occasions and were hired to play at private parties and weddings. At Christmastime they would walk through the streets playing music on their instruments in return for small treats. By the end of the eighteenth century, most official waits had been abolished and the name was applied to any carolers at Christmastime.

Wales

The Welsh are known as a musical people, both in the making of poetry and in the singing of songs. At no time is it more evident than at Christmas. The best singers of whole towns gather in great *eisteddfods*, "carol sings." Every village has its own choir of trained singers and everyone else joins in. Each year an official set of words is distributed to all the towns, and all vie with each other in producing the best music, which is judged in national competition. The selected music will be sung the following year by all the choirs and will become part of the great body of carols produced since the custom started in the tenth century.

Christmas is also the time when the Mari Llwyd appears. This grotesque creature, whose origins are lost in antiquity, is played by a man wearing a sheet and carrying a horse's skull or wearing an artificial horse's head. He capers and dances in the streets to the delight of all and tries to bite people with the workable jaw of the horse, in which case they must pay him a small fine.

The main Christmas service is called Plygain and lasts from 4:00 A.M. until the rising of the sun on Christmas morning. Taffy-pulling is a popular way to spend the afternoon.

Wassail

When the cloth was removed, the butler brought in a huge silver vessel of rare and curious workmanship, which he placed before the Squire. Its appearance was hailed with acclamation; being the Wassail Bowl, so renowned in Christmas festivity. The contents had been prepared by the Squire himself; for it was a beverage in the skillful mixture of which he particularly prided himself; alleging that it was too abstruse and complex for the comprehension of an ordinary servant. It was a potation, indeed, that might well make the heart of a toper leap within him; being composed of the richest and raciest wines, highly spiced and sweetened, with roasted apples bobbing about the surface.

Washington Irving, "Bracebridge Hall"

The word *wassail* evolved from the old Anglo-Saxon term *waes hael*, which means "be well" or "hale." The custom originated as a pagan agricultural festival. To help increase the yield of apple orchards, the trees must be saluted in the dead of winter. So at varying times during the twelve days of Christmas, a procession would visit selected trees from the various orchards and either sprinkle the wassail mixture on the roots or break a bottle of it against the trunk as if at a ship's christening. There would be a good luck recitation, such as:

> Here's to thee old apple tree,
> Hats full, sacks full,
> Great bushel bags full,
> Hurrah!

Everyone would make as much noise as possible, partly to frighten evil spirits and partly for the pleasure of making a great deal of noise. This procedure would be repeated until all the major trees had been toasted.

The mixture used on the trees was not exact. It could be mulled ale or cider or wine with apples or eggs in it. Just so, the wassail bowl has never been turned into a recipe, but is usually left to the inspiration of the mixer.

The wassail procession eventually left the orchards and became a sort of progressive Christmas party with caroling. Groups would stroll about the town, singing and being invited in for a glass of punch. This punch bowl became a fixture on Christmas occasions, and can still be detected in the popularity of eggnog and other common punches in modern Christmas festivities.

Aside from the punch bowl, wassailing is primarily known to us today through many familiar carols, such as this one, which may date from the seventeenth century:

> Here we come awassailing
> Among the leaves so green,
> Here we come awand'ring,
> So fair to be seen:
> Love and joy come to you,
> And to you your wassail too,
> And God bless you, and send you
> A happy New Year,
> And God send you
> A happy New Year.

Wigilia

Wigilia, the Vigil, is the name given to Christmas Eve in Poland. A fast is observed all day until the first star appears in the sky; then the big supper is served. Straw or hay is placed under the white tablecloth in memory of the stable where Christ was born. Often a sheaf of wheat will stand in each corner of the room, to be taken later into the fields or orchards to feed the birds and bring good luck in the coming year. The food of the supper has been blessed by the village priest, and an empty chair is placed at the table, reserved for the Christ Child who is there in spirit. The evening ends with the midnight Mass of the Shepherds.

Xmas

Xmas is simply an abbreviation of *Christmas*. There are some who have taken offense at the term, considering it a secular attempt to take Christ out of Christmas. That misconception arises out of the modern use of the letter X as a means of crossing out unwanted information. The X in Xmas, however, is actually the Greek letter Chi. Chi is the first letter of Christ's name written in Greek and has always stood in that language as a symbol for Christ without any bad connotations at all. The use of "Xmas" as a simple abbreviation for Christmas dates back to at least the twelfth century and has been in continuous usage ever since.

Yule Log

At the winter solstice, the ancient Mesopotamians made wooden images of the monsters who struggled with the great god Marduk to destroy the world. These images were burned in imitative magic to help the god conquer the evil forces. These images may be the origin of the Yule log, which came many hundreds of years later.

Whether the Mesopotamian theory is valid or not, it is obvious that light and warmth would be natural sources of comfort in the face of the cold darkness of winter. Thus the burning of bonfires was always an important part of the northern European winter Jul or Yule festivals.

When Yule became Christmas, the Yule log was divested of its religious connotations but of none of its superstitions. The log must be obtained by the family itself, not bought from someone else. It had to be lighted with a piece of last year's log. It must burn continuously for the twelve days of Christmas. If your shadow cast by the light of the Yule log fire seemed to be headless, you would die within one year. The log's ashes could cure ailments and avert lightning.

In medieval times, the log for the coming year was selected on Candlemas Day, February 2, and set out of doors in the late spring or summer sun to dry out. In some areas the log had to come from an ash tree and was called the ashen faggot. In other areas it was oak. In medieval England a tenant could eat at his lord's expense for as long as the log he had given his lord kept burning.

With the general disappearance of fireplaces, the Yule log has gradually disappeared, too. Some communities kept the tradition as recently as a century ago on a major scale, but now it survives only very rarely as an archaic spectacle with little real tradition about it. In France the Yule log survives only as the shape of a traditional Christmas cake, the *bûche de Noël*.

CHRISTMAS MUSIC

❧ Carols ❧

We all know a carol when we hear one. Yet what exactly *is* a carol? Is it a song exclusively connected with Christmas or religion? How is it distinct from a Christmas hymn?

The word "carol" probably derives from the Greek word *choros*, which means a dance. Thus the idea of dancing seems to be at the heart of the carol. The early medieval carols were on any subject, religious or nonreligious, even downright unreligious, and were suitable for dancing. They had great popularity among the common people, for whom the plainsong chanting and Latin hymns of the Church held little interest.

It was St. Francis who reconciled the people's love of music with the needs of the Church and may have invented the first Christmas carols as we would call them today. In 1223 or 1224 St. Francis set up the first manger scene at Greccio in central Italy, complete with living animals and statues of the Holy Family. There was also singing of the Gospel message. This was probably done by setting new religious words to the popular carols of the time. Both the manger scene and the carols were a tremendous success, and the thirteenth century saw a great wave of songs at the same time popular and sacred. Some of these songs were specifically composed; many others grew in the way that folk songs have always grown, being passed down orally from one generation to another with many changes along the way.

The greatest of the early carol composers who followed in St. Francis' steps was Jacopone da Todi. He was born into an aristocratic family about four years after St. Francis' death. He was a wealthy lawyer and little given to thoughts of religion or the plight of the poor. But then, at the age of twenty-eight, his life changed. His wife, who was also of the nobility, collapsed and died in the middle of a festive dance. When trying to help her, he discovered that she wore a hair shirt under her splendid robes. This symbol of penitence haunted him. He devoted his life to asceticism and poverty, wandering the roads of Italy and begging. And most important, he sang. His noble background stood him in good stead when it came to composing and writing. His verse was sophisticated, yet it was concerned with humility and poverty. He sang of the great humanity of the little Christ Child. These carols were famous all over Europe for several centuries.

The popularity of the carols in continental Europe continued unabated down to the present time; but in England the coming to power of the Puritans almost ended the tradition of carols. These songs were looked upon as frivolous and impious, as the celebration of Christmas itself was regarded. Even after the end of Puritan rule and the Restoration, carols were overlooked. They were regarded as unsophisticated and unimportant and suffered, even more than most Christmas customs, the general neglect that set in at this time. The Christmas hymn became important. This was a song composed specifically to instruct in doctrine. Often it was unsingable and didactic in the extreme, sharing none of the natural joyous impulse that had inspired the earlier carols. Yet even in the midst of this uninspired outpouring, there were some compositions such as "O Come, All Ye Faithful" and "Hark, the Herald Angels Sing" that transcended their limited goals and became true carols.

At the beginning of the nineteenth century, it appeared that the old carols would die out. They existed only in rural regions where they were passed down within families or occasionally printed up as broadsheets for Christmas favors. Several collections of carols were printed by men such as Davies Gilbert and William Sandys. They believed they were recording a form that would very soon be extinct. These collections were instrumental in preserving such songs as "The First Nowell," "God Rest You Merry, Gentlemen" and "I Saw Three Ships." With the new emphasis on Christmas that had sprung largely from the influence of Charles Dickens, the carol was rescued and returned to its former state of popularity. Moreover, composers sought to return to the simplicity and directness of the old carol and thereby added greatly to those songs which we would today consider to be true carols.

What is a carol? It is joyous, as was the dance from which it sprang; it is religious, although its religion is usually that of simple people, concerned more with the wonders of that great birth than with doctrine; perhaps most important, it is popular. The great carols endure for centuries, as do the feelings that inspire them.

"All My Heart This Night Rejoices"

Horatio William Parker began his career as an organist and choir-master. His skill as a composer soon brought him greater fame and he was known for his numerous operas and oratorios. Eventually he held the chair of music at Yale University from 1894 until his death in 1919. But of all his compositions, only his simple tune for this carol remains current today. The original words were in German. They were written by Paul Gerhardt, a seventeenth-century minister, who ranks with Martin Luther in popularity as a hymn writer among the German people. The English translation is by Catherine Winkworth, a nineteenth-century writer best known for her translations of German hymns, including another Christmas carol, "From Heaven High."

> All my heart this night rejoices,
> As I hear,
> Far and near,
> Sweetest angel voices;
> "Christ is born," their choirs are singing,
> Till the air,
> Ev'rywhere,
> Now with joy is ringing.
>
> Hark! a voice from yonder manger,
> Soft and sweet,
> Doth entreat:
> "Flee from woe and danger;
> Brethren, come; from all that grieves you,
> You are freed;
> All you need
> I will surely give you."

Come, then, let us hasten yonder;
Here let all,
Great and small,
Kneel in awe and wonder;
Love Him who with love is yearning;
Hail the Star,
That from far
Bright with hope is burning!

"Angels, from the Realms of Glory"

The words of this well-known carol were written by James Mont-gomery and published in his newspaper on Christmas Eve 1816. He was the orphaned son of Moravian missionary parents and had spent some years in finding his vocation. When he became the publisher of *The Iris*, in Sheffield, England, he almost immediately landed in trouble by championing causes unpopular with the local authorities. He was sent to jail several times and discovered that his popularity and fame increased with each visit. Besides being a rabble-rousing journalist, he was a devout Christian. He wrote nearly four hundred hymns in his life, including "Hail to the Lord's Anointed."

The tune that is generally sung with the words of "Angels, from the Realms of Glory" is called "Regent Square." It was named for the most prominent Presbyterian Church in London at the time of its publication, 1867. It was composed by the professional church musician Henry Smart. There is certainly nothing in this tune's spirit of devout joy to indicate that its composer had gone blind two years before its composition.

The original poem had the following five stanzas, although the fifth is usually omitted from the carol books:

Angels, from the realms of glory,
Wing your flight o'er all the earth;
Ye, who sang creation's story,

Now proclaim Messiah's birth:
Come and worship, come and worship,
Worship Christ the new-born King.

Shepherds in the field abiding,
Watching o'er your flocks by night,
God with man is now residing;
Yonder shines the infant Light:
Come and worship, come and worship,
Worship Christ, the new-born King.

Sages, leave your contemplations,
Brighter visions beam afar;
Seek the great Desire of nations;
Ye have seen His natal star:
Come and worship, come and worship,
Worship Christ, the new-born King.

Saints, before the altar bending,
Watching long in hope and fear,
Suddenly the Lord, descending,
In His temple shall appear:
Come and worship, come and worship,
Worship Christ, the new-born King.

Sinners, wrung with true repentance,
Doomed for guilt to endless pains,
Justice now revokes the sentence,
Mercy calls you—break your chains:
Come and worship, come and worship,
Worship Christ, the new-born King!

"Angels We Have Heard on High"

By its style, musicologists have determined that this anonymous
French tune was probably created around the eighteenth century, al-
though some legends place its origins as early as the second century.
This tune is often sung in England with the carol words "Angels

from the Realms of Glory" by James Montgomery. The Sheffield *Iris* was the paper that Montgomery edited when he wrote the hymn which has given the tune the name of "Iris." It is a challenge to a congregation to fit the words of the refrain, "Come and worship," into the florid vocal line to which we sing "*Gloria in excelsis Deo.*" The English translation of the original French is anonymous.

Angels we have heard on high,
Sweetly singing o'er the plains,
And the mountains in reply,
Echoing their joyous strains.

REFRAIN

Gloria in excelsis Deo,
Gloria in excelsis Deo.

Shepherds, why this jubilee?
Why your joyous strains prolong?
What the gladsome tidings be
Which inspire your heav'nly song?

REFRAIN

Come to Bethlehem and see
Him whose birth the angels sing;
Come, adore on bended knee,
Christ the Lord, the newborn King.

REFRAIN

See Him in a manger laid,
Whom the choir of angels praise;
Mary, Joseph, lend your aid,
While our hearts in love we raise.

REFRAIN

"As with Gladness Men of Old"

The poem of this popular Christmas song was written on Epiphany Day, 1859. On that January 6, William Chatterton Dix, the son of a doctor in Bristol, England, and just twenty-one years old, was sick in bed. He was passing the time by reading the Scriptures, and the story of the Wise Men in Matthew 2:1–12, which was the lesson for the day, caught his imagination. Dix was careful not to call his characters Kings or Magi, since they are not so called in the Bible. Nor is their number given. Yet, in spite of this care, Dix made the error of having them come to "that lowly manger bed," when the Wise Men are specified in Matthew as having come to the house where Mary and Joseph were then staying, not to the stable. Some versions of the carol have attempted to correct that mistake, but usually the original is sung today.

Dix wrote one other great carol, "What Child Is This?" which was set to the traditional English folk tune "Greensleeves."

The tune that is always used for "As with Gladness Men of Old" was originally published in Germany in 1838 by Conrad Kocher. It was adapted in 1861 by W. H. Monk specifically for Dix's words, which he published in a collection called *Hymns Ancient and Modern*. The tune was given the title "Dix" and has been used for this hymn ever since. Dix himself did not like it.

There are five stanzas in the original poem, of which four are usually used with the carol:

> As with gladness men of old
> Did the guiding star behold;
> As with joy they hailed its light,
> Leading onward, beaming bright;
> So, most gracious Lord, may we
> Evermore be led to Thee.

As with joyous steps they sped
To that lowly manger bed,
There to bend the knee before
Him whom heaven and earth adore;
So may we with willing feet
Ever seek Thy mercy seat.

As they offered gifts most rare
At that manger rude and bare,
So may we with holy joy,
Pure, and free from sin's alloy,
All our costliest treasures bring,
Christ, to Thee, our heavenly King.

Holy Jesus, every day
Keep us in the narrow way;
And, when earthly things are past,
Bring our ransomed souls at last
Where they need no star to guide,
Where no clouds Thy glory hide.

In the heavenly country bright,
Need they no created light;
Thou its light, its joy, its crown,
Thou its sun which goes not down;
There forever may we sing
Alleluias to our King.

"Away in a Manger"

There has been a great deal of confusion about this hymn. The words
to the first two verses first appeared anonymously in an 1885 American collection of Lutheran hymns. Two years later, James R. Murray,
a music editor with a company in Cincinnati, set the text to his own
tune and published it in *Dainty Songs for Little Lads and Lasses, for
Use in the Kindergarten, School and Home.* No one knows if he was

merely mistaken or if he wished to create more interest in the song, but he headed it "Luther's Cradle Hymn (Composed by Martin Luther for his children and still sung by German mothers to their little ones)." Thus, for some sixty years it was universally believed that Martin Luther had written the lullaby. Moreover, some anonymous publisher credited the tune to a "Carl Mueller." No one knows where this name came from, but it added to the confusion. Only in the 1940s was Murray's composition given its correct credit, and the song is still popularly attributed to Martin Luther. A third verse was added sometime before 1892, but again the author is unknown. In Britain, these words are sung to a different tune, which was composed in 1895 by William J. Kirkpatrick, the American composer of "'Tis So Sweet to Trust in Jesus," and "We Have Heard the Joyful Sound."

> Away in a manger, no crib for a bed,
> The little Lord Jesus laid down His sweet head;
> The stars in the sky looked down where He lay,
> The little Lord Jesus, asleep on the hay.
>
> The cattle are lowing, the Baby awakes,
> But little Lord Jesus, no crying He makes;
> I love Thee, Lord Jesus! look down from the sky,
> And stay by my cradle till morning is nigh.
>
> Be near me, Lord Jesus, I ask Thee to stay
> Close by me forever, and love me, I pray;
> Bless all the dear children in Thy tender care,
> And fit us for heaven to live with Thee there.

"The Boar's Head Carol"

This may be the oldest carol we have. Its author is unknown, although it may have been written at Queen's College, Oxford, where the tradition of bringing in the boar's head is said to have originated.

The carol was first printed in 1521 by Jan van Wynken de Worde in a collection that may have been the first printed music in England. Like the original of "Good Christian Men, Rejoice," this carol is macaronic, that is, it mixes English and Latin freely.

The boar's head in hand bear I,
Bedecked with bays and rosemary;
And I pray you, my masters, be merry,
Quot estis in convivio: [Who are in such good spirits:

REFRAIN
   Caput apri defero,   I bear the head of the boar,
   Reddens laudes Domino.   Giving praise to the Lord.]

The boar's head, as I understand,
Is the rarest dish in all this land,
Which thus bedecked with a gay garland
Let us *servire cantico*:   [serve it with a song:]

Our steward hath provided this,
In honor of the King of bliss,
Which on this day to be servèd is,
In Reginensi atrio: [In the Queen's hall:]

"Brightest and Best of the Sons of the Morning"

This song is really an Epiphany carol, although most of us do not make that fine a distinction. Reginald Heber won prizes at Oxford for his poetry before going on to take Holy Orders in the Church of England. He was very interested in producing a large enough body of hymns to provide an appropriate text for each Sunday of the liturgical year. His efforts include "Holy, Holy, Holy!" "The Son of God Goes Forth to War," and "From Greenland's Icy Mountains." He died in 1826, three years after being made bishop of Calcutta in India.

"Brightest and Best" was written in 1811 while Heber was village vicar in Hodnet, a little village in western England. The poem shows the influence of the new Romantic style of poetry. It is written in dactyls—that is, long-short-short—rather than the traditional, more stately iambs—long-short. This gives it a more flowing style. Also, it abounds in florid images: the star is not simply the Star of the east but the "brightest and best of the sons of the morning"; gold, frankincense, and myrrh are "odours of Edom . . . gems of the mountain and pearls of the ocean," and so on. This caused some delay in the complete acceptance of this hymn, but by the start of the twentieth century it had achieved a regular place in the ranks of the Christmas carols. It has been set to almost twenty different tunes, none of which has gained enough general acceptance to override the others.

Brightest and best of the sons of the morning,
Dawn on our darkness and lend us thine aid;
Star of the east, the horizon adorning,
Guide where our infant Redeemer is laid.

Cold on His cradle the dewdrops are shining,
Low lies His head with the beasts of the stall;
Angels adore Him in slumber reclining,
Maker and Monarch and Saviour of all.

Say, shall we yield Him, in costly devotion,
Odours of Edom and offerings divine;
Gems of the mountain, and pearls of the ocean,
Myrrh from the forest, and gold from the mine?

Vainly we offer each ample oblation,
Vainly with gifts would His favor secure;
Richer by far is the heart's adoration,
Dearer to God are the prayers of the poor.

In the original, the first stanza is repeated as the fifth stanza.

"Bring a Torch, Jeannette, Isabella"

This delightful seventeenth-century carol came from Provence, the southeastern region of France. The song suggests the custom of acting out a scene by the side of the manger, a charming way of making the nativity scene come to life. The English version, which is a very close translation, is by British composer and organist Edward Cuthbert Nunn.

Bring a torch, Jeannette, Isabella!
Bring a torch, to the cradle run!
It is Jesus, good folk of the village;
Christ is born and Mary's calling:
Ah! ah! beautiful is the Mother!
Ah! ah! beautiful is her Son!

It is wrong when the Child is sleeping,
It is wrong to talk so loud;
Silence, all, as you gather around,
Lest your noise should waken Jesus:
Hush! hush! see how fast He slumbers;
Hush! hush! see how fast He sleeps!

Softly to the little stable,
Softly for a moment come;
Look and see how charming is Jesus,
How He is white, His cheeks are rosy!
Hush! hush! see how the Child is sleeping;
Hush! hush! see how He smiles in dreams.

"The Cherry Tree Carol"

This traditional carol originated in medieval England and achieved widespread popularity. The carol collectors in the nineteenth century found it in many parts of England. The original story is a popular apocryphal legend of one of Christ's prenatal miracles. Like so many folk songs, this one had verses added to it in the course of its passage through many hands. Thus it starts as a pre-Christmas carol but continues with predictions of Christ's birth and crucifixion.

Joseph was an old man,
And an old man was he,
When he wedded Mary
In the land of Galilee.

Joseph and Mary
Walked through an orchard good,
Where was cherries and berries
So red as any blood.

Joseph and Mary
Walked through an orchard green,
Where was berries and cherries
As thick as might be seen.

O then bespoke Mary
With words so meek and mild,
"Pluck me one cherry, Joseph,
For I am with child."

O then bespoke Joseph
With answer most unkind,
"Let him pluck thee a cherry
That brought thee now with child."

O then bespoke the baby
Within his mother's womb—
"Bow down then the tallest tree
For my mother to have some."

Then bowed down the highest tree,
Unto his mother's hand.
Then she cried, "See, Joseph,
I have cherries at command."

O then bespoke Joseph—
"I have done Mary wrong;
But now cheer up, my dearest,
And do not be cast down.

"O eat your cherries, Mary,
O eat your cherries now,
O eat your cherries, Mary,
That grow upon the bough."

Then Mary plucked a cherry,
As red as any blood;
Then Mary she went homewards
All with her heavy load.

As Joseph was awalking,
He heard an angel sing:
"This night there shall be born
On earth our heav'nly King;

"He neither shall be born,
In housen nor in hall,
Nor in the place of Paradise,
But in an ox's stall.

"He neither shall be clothed
In purple nor in pall,
But all in fair linen
As wear the babies all.

"He neither shall be rocked
In silver nor in gold,
But in a wooden cradle
That rocks upon the mould.

"He neither shall be christened
In white wine nor red,
But with fair spring water
As we were christenèd."

Then Mary took her young son,
And set him on her knee:
Saying, "My dear son, tell me,
Tell how this world shall be."

"O I shall be as dead, mother,
As stones are in the wall;
O the stones in the streets, mother,
Shall sorrow for me all.

"On Easter-day, dear mother,
My rising up shall be;
O the sun and the moon, mother,
Shall both arise with me."

"Deck the Halls with Boughs of Holly"

This is one of the most familiar of the purely secular carols of Christmas. It has nothing to do with the birth at Bethlehem, but is concerned entirely with the decoration and festivities attendant upon Christmas and New Year's. The carol is of Welsh origin, but no one has been able to put a definite age to it. It was well known enough by the eighteenth century to appear in a composition by Mozart. The repeated nonsense word was a very popular feature of medieval ballads and madrigals.

Deck the halls with boughs of holly,
Fa-la-la-la-la, la-la-la-la;
'Tis the season to be jolly,
Fa-la-la-la-la, la-la-la-la.

Don we now our gay apparel,
Fa-la-la, fa-la-la, la-la-la.
Troll the ancient Yuletide carol,
Fa-la-la-la-la, la-la-la-la!

See the blazing yule before us,
Fa-la-la-la-la, la-la-la-la;
Strike the harp and join the chorus,
Fa-la-la-la-la, la-la-la-la.
Follow me in merry measure,
Fa-la-la, fa-la-la, la-la-la,
While I tell of Christmas treasure,
Fa-la-la-la-la, la-la-la-la!

Fast away the old year passes,
Fa-la-la-la-la, la-la-la-la;
Hail the new, ye lads and lasses,
Fa-la-la-la-la, la-la-la-la.
Sing we joyous songs together,
Fa-la-la, fa-la-la, la-la-la,
Heedless of the wind and weather,
Fa-la-la-la-la, la-la-la-la!

"The First Nowell"

The author and composer of this great carol are unknown. It is believed to have been written some time before the eighteenth century. The words were first published in Davies Gilbert's *Some Ancient Christmas Carols* in 1823. The tune was first published by William Sandys in his *Christmas Carols, Ancient and Modern* in 1833. The second stanza mistakenly refers to the shepherds seeing the star of Bethlehem, an occurrence not recorded in the Bible. This error has not affected the popularity of the song one bit. The original nine stanzas are given here.

The first Nowell the angel did say
Was to certain poor shepherds in fields as they lay;
In fields where they lay, keeping their sheep,
On a cold winter's night that was so deep.

REFRAIN

Nowell, Nowell, Nowell, Nowell,
Born is the King of Israel!

They lookèd up and saw a star,
Shining in the east, beyond them far;
And to the earth it gave great light,
And so it continued both day and night.

REFRAIN

And by the light of that same star,
Three Wise Men came from country far.
To seek for a king was their intent,
And to follow the star wheresoever it went.

REFRAIN

This star drew nigh to the northwest;
O'er Bethlehem it took its rest,
And there it did both stop and stay
Right over the place where Jesus lay.

REFRAIN

Then did they know assuredly
Within that house the King did lie:
One entered in then for to see,
And found the babe in poverty.

REFRAIN

Then entered in those Wise Men three,
Full reverently upon their knee,
And offered there in His presence
Both gold and myrrh and frankincense.

REFRAIN

Between an ox-stall and an ass
This child truly there born He was;
For want of clothing they did Him lay
All in the manger, among the hay.

REFRAIN

Then let us all with one accord
Sing praises to our heavenly Lord,
That hath made heaven and earth of naught,
And with His blood mankind hath bought:

REFRAIN

If we in our time shall do well,
We shall be free from death and hell;
For God hath preparèd for us all
A resting place in general.

REFRAIN

There has been some speculation regarding the tune that has been passed down for this carol, because of its repetitiveness. Why in the singing of the verse and refrain is the exact same tune sung three times in a row with the only variation on the final words, "Born is the King of Israel"? Also, the melody line touches the keynote only once in each repetition. These facts have given rise to the theory that what we have is only a part of the original tune, perhaps even a descant written to harmonize with the original tune, and that this was all the singer whom Sandys interviewed for his collection could remember. We will probably never know the truth of the matter.

"From Heaven High"

This is one of the very favorite carols in Germany, the land where it was composed. The original words, "Von Himmel hoch" and the music are attributed to Martin Luther, who did indeed publish them in 1539, although his composition may have been based on earlier sources. J. S. Bach uses this tune in his *Christmas Oratorio*, where it appears in three different harmonizations. The English translation was done in the last century by Catherine Winkworth.

From heaven high I come to you,
To bring you tidings strange and true.
Glad tidings of great joy I bring,
Whereof I now will say and sing.

To you this night is born a Child
Of Mary, chosen Mother mild;
This little Child, of lowly birth,
Shall be the joy of all the earth.

Glory to God in highest heaven,
Who unto us His Son hath given!
While angels sing with pious mirth,
A glad New Year to all the earth.

"God Rest You Merry, Gentlemen"

This carol is of unknown authorship and probably dates from the sixteenth century or earlier. It was first published in 1846 by E. F. Rimbault, who had collected the tune in the London area. Other tunes have since been found elsewhere, but the one we know today seems most likely to be the original. One of the reasons for its popularity is the general feeling of the tune: it sounds old and exotic. The reason for this is that it was not composed in our modern idea of major and minor keys, but in one of the medieval forms called modes. The word "rest" in the first line is used in the old English sense of "keep": thus, "God keep you merry, gentlemen."

God rest you merry, Gentlemen,
Let nothing you dismay,
For Jesus Christ our Saviour
Was born on Christmas Day;

To save us all from Satan's pow'r,
When we were gone astray:
O tidings of comfort and joy.

In Bethlehem, in Jewry,
This blessed Babe was born,
And laid within a manger
Upon this blessed morn;
The which His mother, Mary,
Did nothing take in scorn:
O tidings of comfort and joy.

From God our heav'nly Father
A blessed angel came,
And unto certain shepherds
Brought tidings of the same,
How that in Bethlehem was born
The Son of God by name:
O tidings of comfort and joy.

"Fear not," then said the angel,
"Let nothing you affright,
This day is born a Saviour,
Of virtue, power, and might;
So frequently to vanquish all
The friends of Satan quite":
O tidings of comfort and joy.

The shepherds at those tidings
Rejoicèd much in mind,
And left their flocks afeeding,
In tempest, storm, and wind;
And went to Bethlehem straightway
This blessed Babe to find:
O tidings of comfort and joy.

But when to Bethlehem they came,
Whereat this infant lay,
They found Him in a manger,
Where oxen feed on hay;
His mother Mary kneeling,
Unto the Lord did pray:
O tidings of comfort and joy.

185

Now to the Lord sing praises,
All you within this place,
And with true love and brotherhood
Each other now embrace;
This holy tide of Christmas
All others doth efface:
O tidings of comfort and joy.

"Good Christian Men, Rejoice"

This carol comes originally from Germany. It was written in a style
called "macaronic," that is, it alternated lines in the native language
with lines in Latin. Thus, although largely in German, the original
had as its first line and title "In Dulci Jubilo," which means "In sweet
jubilation." Legend has it that it was written by the German mystic
Henry Suso in the fourteenth century after dreaming that he was invited by angels to join in a dance. The first manuscript copies date
from about 1400, and it began appearing in English translations by
1540. The version we know today was a very free translation made
from a Swedish manuscript by J. M. Neale in 1853. In singing this
song, we often wonder at the two sustained notes in the middle of
the stanza (in some versions, they are even left out). This was the result of a misreading of the Swedish manuscript. Two short notes
seemed to be written as long notes, so Neale provided the words
"News! news!" which have nothing to do with the original lyrics at
all.

Good Christian men, rejoice,
With heart, and soul, and voice;
Give ye heed to what we say:
News! news!

186

Jesus Christ is born today:
Ox and ass before Him bow,
And He is in the manger now.
Christ is born today! Christ is born today!

Good Christian men, rejoice,
With heart, and soul, and voice;
Now ye hear of endless bliss;
Joy! joy!
Jesus Christ was born for this!
He hath opened the heavenly door,
And man is blessed evermore.
Christ was born for this! Christ was born for this!

Good Christian men, rejoice,
With heart, and soul, and voice;
Now ye need not fear the grave:
Peace! peace!
Jesus Christ was born to save!
Calls you one and calls you all,
To gain His everlasting hall.
Christ was born to save! Christ was born to save!

"Good King Wenceslas"

Wenceslas was actually a duke, the ruler of Bohemia in the tenth
century, before kings were in fashion. He was murdered by his
brother in a court intrigue, but was later canonized because of his
good deeds. The story of the page who was kept from freezing by
walking in his footsteps was a standard and popular legend by the
nineteenth century. The Reverend John Mason Neale, the warden of
Sackville College in East Grinstead, Sussex, England, thought this
story would make a good carol for St. Stephen's Day, December 26.
So he took the anonymous melody from the *Piae Cantiones*, the
same Swedish carol collection that gave him the tune and inspiration

for "Good Christian Men, Rejoice." As it happened, the tune he chose was not a Christmas carol at all but a carol welcoming the coming of the flowers at springtime. Undaunted, the good Reverend smothered the flowers in snow and wrote one of our most delightful Christmas carols, even though snow and good will are all it has in common with Christmas.

Good King Wenceslas looked out,
On the feast of Stephen,
When the snow lay round about,
Deep and crisp and even.
Brightly shone the moon that night,
Though the frost was cruel,
When a poor man came in sight,
Gath'ring winter fuel.

"Hither, page, and stand by me,
If thou knows't it telling,
Yonder peasant, who is he?
Where and what his dwelling?"
"Sire, he lives a good league hence,
Underneath the mountain,
Right against the forest fence,
By Saint Agnes' fountain."

"Bring me flesh, and bring me wine,
Bring me pine logs hither:
Thou and I will see him dine,
When we bear them thither."
Page and monarch, forth they went,
Forth they went together;
Through the rude wind's wild lament
And the bitter weather.

"Sire, the night is darker now,
And the wind blows stronger;
Fails my heart, I know not how;
I can go no longer."
"Mark my footsteps, good my page,
Tread thou in them boldly;
Thou shalt find the winter's rage
Freeze thy blood less coldly."

In his master's steps he trod,
Where the snow lay dinted;
Heat was in the very sod
Which the Saint had printed.
Therefore, Christian men, be sure,
Wealth or rank possessing,
Ye who now will bless the poor,
Shall yourselves find blessing.

"Hark! the Herald Angels Sing"

The Reverend Charles Wesley was the brother of John Wesley, the founder of Methodism. Charles Wesley wrote the astonishing total of more than six thousand hymns. In the year 1739 alone, he wrote, among many others, three hymns still loved today. "O for a Thousand Tongues to Sing," "Christ the Lord Is Risen Today," and the beloved Christmas carol "Hark, How All the Welkin Rings." (If you aren't familiar with that last one, it's because the first line was changed in 1753 by George Whitefield who published it in a collection and apparently didn't like the word "welkin," which means "the vault of heaven" and so changed it to "Hark! the Herald Angels Sing.") The carol was originally published in ten four-line stanzas, as follow:

Hark, how all the welkin rings
"Glory to the King of Kings,
Peace on earth and mercy mild,
God and sinners reconciled."

[Later changed to: "Hark the herald angels sing,/'Glory to the newborn King! etc.'"]

Joyful all ye nations, rise,
Join the triumph of the skies,
Universal nature say
"Christ the Lord is born today."

[Later changed to: "With the angelic hosts proclaim,/'Christ is born in Bethlehem!'"]

Christ, by highest heaven adored,
Christ, the everlasting Lord:
Late in time behold Him come,
Offspring of a Virgin's womb.

Veil'd in flesh, the Godhead see,
Hail the incarnate Deity!
Pleased as man with men to
  appear
Jesus, our Immanuel here!

[Later changed to: "with men to
dwell,/Jesus, our Immanuel."]

Hail the heavenly Prince of
  Peace!
Hail the Sun of Righteousness,
Light and life to all He brings,
Risen with healing in His wings.

Mild He lays His glory by,
Born—that man no more may
  die,
Born—to raise the sons of earth,
Born—to give them second birth.

Come, Desire of Nations, come,
Fix in us Thy Humble home;
Rise, the woman's conquering
  seed,
Bruise in us the serpent's head.

Now display Thy saving power,
Ruin'd nature now restore;
Now in mystic union join
Thine to ours and ours to Thine.

[This whole stanza omitted from
the carol.]

Adam's likeness, Lord, efface;
Stamp Thy image in its place;
Second Adam from above,
Reinstate us in Thy love.

Let us Thee, though lost, regain,
Then the Life, the Inner Man;
O! to all Thyself impart,
Form'd in each believing heart.

[This whole stanza omitted from
the carol.]

190

For the first hundred years after the poem was written, it was sung to various tunes, one of them being "Hendon," which is still sung today with the words "Ask Ye What Great Things I Know" and "Take My Life, and Let It Be." The tune that finally became inseparably linked with Wesley's words has an interesting story.

In 1840 the great German composer Felix Mendelssohn wrote his *Festgesang* no. 7 in honor of the anniversary of Gutenberg's invention of the printing press. The music of the second section of the work seemed to be especially appropriate to be set to words and published separately. But Mendelssohn worried about the correct text to use. He wrote: "If the right [words] are hit at, I am sure that piece will be liked very much by the singers and the hearers, but it will *never* do to sacred words. There must be a national and merry subject found out, something to which the soldier-like and buxom motion of the piece has some relation, and the words must express something gay and popular, as the music tries to do." It just goes to show that great composers can be wrong, too. In 1857, ten years after Mendelssohn's early death, the English church musician William H. Cummings discovered that Wesley's words fit Mendelssohn's music perfectly by doubling up the four-line stanzas and repeating the first two lines as a refrain. Thus the carol in the form we know it today was finally completed almost 120 years after its words were first written.

"Here We Come Awassailing"

The words and music of this bright wassail song probably date from the seventeenth century in northern England. Unlike some other wassail carols the singers are obviously children asking for goodies.

> Here we come awassailing
> Among the leaves so green,

Here we come awand'ring,
So fair to be seen:

REFRAIN

Love and joy come to you,
And to you your wassail too,
And God bless you, and send you
A happy new year,
And God send you
A happy new year.

We are not daily beggars
That beg from door to door,
But we are neighbors' children
Whom you have seen before:

REFRAIN

Call up the butler of this house,
Put on his golden ring;
Let him bring us up a glass of beer,
And better we shall sing:

REFRAIN

We have got a little purse
Of stretching leather skin;
We want a little money
To line it well within:

REFRAIN

Bring us out a table,
And spread it with a cloth;
Bring us out a moldy cheese,
And some of your Christmas loaf:

REFRAIN

God bless the master of this house,
Likewise the mistress too;
And all the little children
That round the table go:

REFRAIN

Good Master and good Mistress,
While you're sitting by the fire,
Pray think of us poor children
Awandering in the mire:

REFRAIN

"The Holly and the Ivy"

There is a whole series of popular medieval English carols on the subject of the rivalry between these two plants. The most familiar, which
is given below, merely uses the various parts of the holly plant as symbols of different aspects of Christ's life and does not discuss the ivy at
all. In other holly and ivy songs of the period, the holly and ivy
symbolized male and female respectively, and the songs detailed their
often rowdy vying for mastery in the forest or in the house.

The holly and the ivy,
Now they are full well grown,
Of all the trees that are in the wood,
The holly bears the crown:

REFRAIN

*The rising of the sun
And the running of the deer,
The playing of the merry organ,
Sweet singing in the choir.*

The holly bears a blossom,
As white as the lily flower,
And Mary bore sweet Jesus Christ
To be our sweet Saviour:

REFRAIN

The holly bears a berry,
As red as any blood,

And Mary bore sweet Jesus Christ
To do poor sinners good:

REFRAIN

The holly bears a prickle,
As sharp as any thorn,
And Mary bore sweet Jesus Christ
On Christmas Day in the morn:

REFRAIN

The holly bears a bark,
As bitter as any gall,
And Mary bore sweet Jesus Christ
For to redeem us all:

REFRAIN

The holly and the ivy,
Now both are full well grown,
Of all the trees that are in the wood,
The holly bears the crown:

REFRAIN

"I Heard the Bells on Christmas Day"

The poem "Christmas Bells" by the great American poet Henry
Wadsworth Longfellow has been set to a number of hymn tunes, but
it was originally intended only as a poem and he would probably have
been surprised that it became a carol. It was written in 1863 while the
Civil War was raging and at a time when his son had been seriously
wounded in the fighting. The poem is not really about Christmas but
is a description of the feelings that run through the author's mind
upon hearing the Christmas bells. His thoughts are of peace and war
and keep returning to the words of the angels' song. The fourth and
fifth stanzas, which refer specifically to the Civil War, were left out
of the carol; and the third stanza was moved to the end to give a
more joyous ending.

I heard the bells on Christmas Day
Their old, familiar carols play,
And wild and sweet
The words repeat
Of peace on earth, good-will to men!

And thought how, as the day had come,
The belfries of all Christendom
Had rolled along
Th'unbroken song
Of peace on earth, good-will to men!

Till, ringing, singing on its way,
The world revolved from night to day,
A voice, a chime,
A chant sublime,
Of peace on earth good-will to men!

Then from each black, accursed mouth
The cannon thundered in the South,
And with the sound
The carols drowned
Of peace on earth, good-will to men!

It was as if an earthquake rent
The hearth-stones of a continent,
And made forlorn
The household born
Of peace on earth, good-will to men!

And in despair I bowed my head:
"There is no peace on earth," I said,
"For hate is strong,
And mocks the song
Of peace on earth, good-will to men!"

Then pealed the bells more loud and deep:
"God is not dead, nor doth He sleep!
The Wrong shall fail,
The Right prevail,
With peace on earth, good-will to men!"

"I Saw Three Ships"

The words and music of this traditional English carol may be more than five hundred years old. The legend of three mysterious ships that are seen on Christmas morning has been traced to the ships that brought the relics of the Wise Men to Cologne in 1162. Thus the three ships originally were thought to carry the Wise Men, but later the emphasis was shifted to the Holy Family itself. The question-and-answer format of this carol make it a lively one when divided between two groups that alternate the verses.

I saw three ships come sailing in,
On Christmas Day, on Christmas Day;
I saw three ships come sailing in,
On Christmas Day in the morning.

And what was in those ships all three,
On Christmas Day, on Christmas Day?
And what was in those ships all three,
On Christmas Day in the morning?

The Virgin Mary and Christ were there,
On Christmas Day, on Christmas Day;
The Virgin Mary and Christ were there,
On Christmas Day in the morning.

Pray, whither sailed those ships all three,
On Christmas Day, on Christmas Day?
Pray, whither sailed those ships all three,
On Christmas Day in the morning?

O they sailed into Bethlehem,
On Christmas Day, on Christmas Day;
O they sailed into Bethlehem,
On Christmas Day in the morning.

And all the bells on earth shall ring,
On Christmas Day, on Christmas Day;
And all the bells on earth shall ring,
On Christmas Day in the morning.

Then let us all rejoice amain,
On Christmas Day, on Christmas Day;
Then let us all rejoice amain,
On Christmas Day in the morning.

It is typical of the simple faith of the Middle Ages that no one would raise objection to the image of the three ships sailing into little land-locked Bethlehem.

"In the Bleak Mid-winter"

Christina Rossetti is considered by many to be the best English female poet. This nineteenth-century poet wrote a number of hymns and carols, including "Love Came Down at Christmas." Her lovely, simple images are matched by the charming tune created by Gustav Holst, the early-twentieth-century composer who is best known for his orchestral piece *The Planets*.

In the bleak mid-winter
Frosty wind made moan,
Earth stood hard as iron,
Water like a stone;
Snow had fallen, snow on snow,
Snow on snow,
In the bleak mid-winter,
Long ago.

Our God, heav'n cannot hold him
Nor earth sustain;

197

Heav'n and earth shall flee away
When he comes to reign:
In the bleak mid-winter
A stable-place sufficed
The Lord God Almighty
Jesus Christ.

Enough for him, whom cherubim
Worship night and day,
A breastful of milk,
And a mangerful of hay;
Enough for him, whom angels
Fall down before,
The ox and ass and camel
Which adore.

Angels and archangels
May have gathered there,
Cherubim and seraphim
Thronged the air:
But only his mother
In her maiden bliss
Worshipped the Belovèd
With a kiss.

What can I give him,
Poor as I am?
If I were a shepherd
I would bring a lamb;
If I were a wise man
I would do my part;
Yet what I can I give him—
Give my heart.

"It Came upon the Midnight Clear"

This is the only widely accepted Christmas carol written by a Unitarian. The Reverend Edmund Hamilton Sears wrote it in 1849 when he was pastor of the Unitarian Church at Wayland, Massachusetts. It was published in 1850 by Uzziah C. Burnap, who adapted the music from a study by composer Richard S. Willis.

The religious background of the author is made clear in that, while the words obviously refer to the angels' song at the birth of Christ, no reference is actually made to that birth or to Christ Himself. The concern is more for the promise of peace than for the actuality of the event. The third stanza is often omitted.

It came upon the midnight clear,
That glorious song of old,
From angels bending near the earth,
To touch their harps of gold:
"Peace on the earth, good will to men,
From heaven's all-gracious King."
The world in solemn stillness lay,
To hear the angels sing.

Still through the cloven skies they come
With peaceful wings unfurled,
And still their heavenly music floats
O'er all the weary world;
Above its sad and lowly plains
They bend on hovering wing,
And ever o'er its Babel sounds
The blessed angels sing.

Yet with the woes of sin and strife
The world hath suffered long;
Beneath the angel-strain have rolled
Two thousand years of wrong;

199

And man, at war with man, hears not
The love song which they bring:
O hush the noise, ye men of strife,
And hear the angels sing.

O ye, beneath life's crushing load,
Whose forms are bending low,
Who toil along the climbing way
With painful steps and slow,
Look now! for glad and golden hours
Come swiftly on the wing;
O rest beside the weary road
And hear the angels sing!

For lo! the days are hastening on,
By prophet-bards foretold,
When with the ever-circling years
Comes round the age of gold;
When peace shall over all the earth
Its ancient splendors fling,
And the whole world give back the song
Which now the angels sing.

Eleven years after the writing of this vision of coming peace, the Civil War broke out. Humanity was not yet ready to listen to the angels' song.

"Joy to the World"

In 1692 Isaac Watts wrote his first hymn. He was eighteen at the time and wrote largely as a protest against the poor doggerel current in Anglican hymnals. When he complained of the low quality of such songs to his father, a deacon, his father suggested that he try to write better ones if he thought he could. Watts instantly produced his already-written hymn. Deacon Watts was impressed and took it to church on Sunday. The hymn was "lined out," that is, read out to the congregation one line at a time so that they could sing it to a familiar hymn tune. The congregation liked it and asked for another for the next week. The same request was repeated and complied with for 222 consecutive Sundays, by which time Watts had created a small revolution in the singing habits of the Anglican Church.

Watts later became an Anglican minister but continued to produce such still-sung hymns as "Alas and Did My Saviour Bleed," "When I Survey the Wondrous Cross," "O God, Our Help in Ages Past," and "Jesus Shall Reign, Where'er the Sun." In 1719, Watts published *The Psalms of David, Imitated.* In this work he put the psalms into modern English verse, allowing for the addition of Christian symbolism and doctrine to the Jewish originals. His reworking of the Ninety-eighth Psalm bears little resemblance to the original but provided the words for one of our most delightful carols, "Joy to the World." Curiously, the song makes no reference to any of the standard images of Christmas, yet its spirit is undeniably that of the best carols. A century later, Watts's words were set to a tune devised by Dr. Lowell Mason from a theme in Handel's *Messiah.*

Joy to the world! the Lord is come:
Let earth receive her King;
Let ev'ry heart prepare Him room,
And heav'n and nature sing.

Joy to the earth! the Saviour reigns;
Let men their songs employ;
While fields and floods, rocks, hills and plains,
Repeat the sounding joy.

No more let sins and sorrows grow,
Nor thorns infest the ground;
He comes to make His blessings flow
Far as the curse is found.

He rules the world with truth and grace;
And makes the nations prove
The glories of His righteousness,
And wonders of His Love.

"Lo, How a Rose E'er Blooming"

The inspiration for the words of this Christmas song comes from Isaiah 11:1: "And there shall come forth a rod out of the stem of Jesse, and a Branch shall grow out of his roots." The words and music of "Es ist ein' Ros' entsprungen" were first published in 1600 in Cologne, Germany, although the tune may date back to a century earlier. The great German musician Michael Praetorius in the year 1609 published the harmonization that is still used. Several different translations are current, but the best known in America is by Dr. Theodore Baker, an American musicologist.

> Lo, how a Rose e'er blooming
> From tender stem hath sprung!
> Of Jesse's lineage coming
> As men of old have sung.
> It came, a floweret bright,
> Amid the cold of winter,
> When half spent was the night.
>
> Isaiah 'twas foretold it,
> The Rose I have in mind,
> With Mary we behold it,
> The Virgin Mother kind.
> To show God's love aright,
> She bore to men a Saviour,
> When half spent was the night.

"Love Came Down at Christmas"

Christina Rossetti, the famous nineteenth-century English poetess, wrote the words of this carol, which were later set to music by the early-twentieth-century composer Reginald O. Morris. This carol is marked by the simplicity and sincerity of its sentiment.

> Love came down at Christmas,
> Love all lovely, Love divine;
> Love was born at Christmas,
> Stars and angels gave the sign.
>
> Worship we the Godhead,
> Love incarnate, Love divine;
> Worship we our Jesus:
> But wherewith for sacred sign?
>
> Love shall be our token,
> Love be yours and love be mine,
> Love to God and all men,
> Love for plea and gift and sign.

"O Come, All Ye Faithful"

The origins of this carol were shrouded in mystery for almost two hundred years after it was written. Only in this century has its original authorship been substantiated. It was written around 1742 by an Englishman named John Francis Wade who was living and working at the Roman Catholic center at Douay, France. There was an English university located there that served as a shelter for religious and political refugees from England's internal strife. While making his living as a music copyist, Wade composed the music and the Latin words, "Adeste Fideles." The carol was later brought to England by returning English Catholics. It was first sung at the Portuguese embassy, one of the few strongholds of Catholic culture in England at the time. Because of that, the assumption was made that the carol came from Portugal. The words were not translated for some time, but the tune ws used in non-Catholic churches in America with the words "How Firm a Foundation."

In 1841 an Anglican minister named Frederick Oakeley translated the words "Ye Faithful, Approach Ye." He later converted to Catholicism and in 1852 again translated the hymn. This time he produced the words we know as "O Come, All Ye Faithful," translating only the first, seventh, and eighth stanzas of Wade's eight-stanza Latin hymn.

This carol seems to break all the rules for proper hymns. Its lines are of unequal lengths and there isn't a rhyme anywhere in it. Yet that has not in any way limited its unflagging popularity.

O come, all ye faithful, joyful and triumphant,
O come ye, O come ye to Bethlehem.
Come and behold him, born the King of angels;
O come let us adore him, Christ the Lord.

Sing, choirs of angels, sing in exultation,
Sing, all ye citizens of heaven above.
Glory to God, all glory in the highest.
O come let us adore him, Christ the Lord.

Yea, Lord, we greet thee, born this happy morning,
Jesus, to thee be all glory given.
Word of the Father, now in flesh appearing;
O come let us adore him, Christ the Lord.

"O Come, O Come, Emmanuel"

This familiar carol most properly belongs to the period of Advent, since it celebrates the expectation of Christ's coming rather than His actual birth. It is based on the "Seven O's," the seven antiphons sung in medieval monasteries at the evening vespers service on the seven nights leading up to Christmas Eve. One was sung each night, and each celebrates a different attribute of the coming Lord. These twelfth-century Latin verses were translated and reduced to five by the nineteenth-century English carol writer John M. Neale, who also wrote "Good King Wenceslas." The tune sung today was adapted by Thomas Helmore from a number of twelfth-century plainsongs. It is these monastic chants which give this carol its particularly ancient flavor. To get the full effect, it is necessary to ignore the modern notations that break the melody down into even measures; originally there would have been no such measures—the plainsong would be chanted according to the natural rhythms of the words.

O come, O come, Emmanuel,
And ransom captive Israel,
That mourns in lonely exile here
Until the Son of God appear.

REFRAIN

Rejoice! Rejoice! Emmanuel
Shall come to thee, O Israel.

O come, O come, Thou Rod of Jesse, free
Thine own from Satan's tyranny;
From depths of hell Thy people save,
And give them victory o'er the grave.

REFRAIN

O come, Thou Dayspring, come and cheer
Our spirits by Thine advent here;

Disperse the gloomy clouds of night,
And death's dark shadows put to flight.

REFRAIN

O come, Thou Key of David, come,
And open wide our heav'nly home;
Make safe the way that leads on high,
And close the path to misery.

REFRAIN

O come, O come, Thou Lord of might,
Who once, from Sinai's flaming height
Didst give the trembling tribes Thy law,
In cloud, and majesty, and awe.

REFRAIN

"O Holy Night"

The nineteenth-century French composer Adolphe Charles Adam wrote more than fifty ballets and operas, yet he is known today almost entirely for two works: his ballet *Giselle* and the Christmas song we call "O Holy Night." In France it is known simply as "Cantique de Noël," "Song of Christmas," or by its first line, "Minuit, Chrétiens," which means "Midnight, Christians." The very familiar English words are by John S. Dwight, an American minister who later became a musicologist. The words are not at all a direct translation but paint a much more vivid picture than does the original French, which is more doctrinal than pictorial. Although this song has been arranged for choruses and other groups of voices, it was originally meant for a single voice and is probably the best known of all Christmas solo compositions.

O holy night! the stars are brightly shining,
It is the night of the dear Saviour's birth!

Long lay the world, in sin and error pining,
'Til He appear'd, and the soul felt its worth.
A thrill of hope the weary world rejoices,
For yonder breaks a new and glorious morn!
Fall on your knees!
O hear the angel voices!
O night divine! O night when Christ was born!
O night divine! O night, O night divine!

Led by the light of Faith serenely beaming,
With glowing hearts by His cradle we stand.
So, led by light of a star sweetly gleaming,
Here came the wise men from the Orient land.
The King of Kings lay thus in lowly manger,
In all our trials born to be our friend;
He knows our need, to our weakness no stranger;
Behold your King!
Before the Lowly bend!
Behold your King! your King! before Him bend.

Truly He taught us to love one another;
His law is love, and His gospel is peace;
Chains shall He break, for the slave is our brother,
And in His name all oppression shall cease.
Sweet hymns of joy in grateful chorus raise we,
Let all within us praise His holy name;
Christ is the Lord,
Oh, praise His name forever!
His pow'r and glory evermore proclaim!
His pow'r and glory evermore proclaim!

"O Little Town of Bethlehem"

Phillips Brooks was an Episcopal clergyman with a church in Philadelphia when he journeyed to the Holy Land in 1865. On Christmas
Eve, he rode on horseback from Jerusalem to Bethlehem. At dusk he

stood outside the village, in the Field of the Shepherds, and watched the night stealing through the silent streets. Then he attended the five-hour service at the Church of the Nativity. All of this created a vivid impression on his mind, but it was three years later before he was moved to put pen to paper as he prepared for the Christmas services in his Philadelphia church. He gave the resulting five stanzas to his church organist, the local businessman Lewis Redner. He asked him to write a tune for it and jokingly said that if the tune was good enough, he would name it "St. Lewis" after him. Redner was stumped until the night before Brooks wanted the song to be sung by the Sunday school children. Then he awoke during the night with an idea, which he jotted down. The next morning he harmonized it and heard it performed for the first time. It was December 27, 1868. Brooks was delighted with the tune and named it "St. Louis," changing the spelling to spare any embarrassment. It first appeared in the Episcopal Hymnal in 1892, the year before Brooks's death, and has gone on to become one of the favorite American carols.

O little town of Bethlehem,
How still we see thee lie!
Above thy deep and dreamless sleep
The silent stars go by;
Yet in thy dark streets shineth
The everlasting Light;
The hopes and fears of all the years
Are met in thee tonight.

For Christ is born of Mary,
And gathered all above,
While mortals sleep, the angels keep
Their watch of wondering love.
O morning stars, together
Proclaim the holy birth!
And praises sing to God the King,
And peace to men on earth.

How silently, how silently,
The wondrous gift is giv'n!
So God imparts to human hearts
The blessings of His heav'n.

No ear may hear His coming,
But in this world of sin,
Where meek souls will receive Him, still
The dear Christ enters in.

Where children pure and happy   [This verse is
Pray to the blessèd Child,   usually omitted.]
Where misery cries out to thee,
Son of the mother mild;
Where charity stands watching
And faith holds wide the door,
The dark night wakes, the glory breaks,
And Christmas comes once more.

O holy Child of Bethlehem!
Descend to us, we pray;
Cast out our sin and enter in,
Be born in us today.
We hear the Christmas angels
The great glad tidings tell;
O come to us, abide with us,
Our Lord Immanuel.

"O Tannenbaum"

This is one of Germany's very favorite carols. Its origins are completely shrouded in obscurity, having appeared sometime in the Middle Ages. It has never been as popular outside Germany, perhaps because the simplicity of the original words is difficult to translate without their becoming doggerel. The tune of this carol is also used for the Maryland state song, "Maryland, My Maryland." The following is the most familiar traditional English version.

O Christmas tree, O Christmas tree,
How lovely are your branches.

In summer sun, in winter snow,
A dress of green you always show.
O Christmas tree, O Christmas tree,
How lovely are your branches.

O Christmas tree, O Christmas tree,
With happiness we greet you.
When decked with candles once a year,
You fill our hearts with yuletide cheer.
O Christmas tree, O Christmas tree,
With happiness we greet you.

"O Thou Joyful Day"

This carol began in the sixteenth century as a series of Latin verses,
"O sanctissima." These verses were a hymn to the Virgin and had
nothing to do with Christmas. The tune to which they were sung
may be a Sicilian folk song or possibly an obscure operatic air. It was
first published with these words in the late eighteenth century. The
English version is not a real translation of the original Latin but is a
brand-new Christmas verse. This English version is anonymous, having appeared some time after the original publication.

O thou joyful day,
O thou blessed day,
Holy, peaceful Christmastide.
Earth's hopes awaken,
Christ life hath taken.
Laud Him, O laud Him on ev'ry side.

O thou joyful day,
O thou blessed day,
Holy, peaceful Christmastide.
King of glory,
We bow before thee,
Laud Him, O laud Him on ev'ry side.

"Once in Royal David's City"

Mrs. Cecil Frances Alexander wrote many hymns especially for children, to help explain the Gospel messages to them. The best of her many songs have been carried down to the present day and have served as an inspiration for adults as well as children. Her 1848 collection *Hymns for Little Children* included her two best-known works, "Once in Royal David's City" and "There Is a Green Hill Far Away." Besides writing hymns and carols, Mrs. Alexander was also the wife of the primate of Ireland. The composer Henry Gauntlett was also an organist and organ designer. Besides his tune for this lovely carol, he wrote more than ten thousand other hymns.

Once in royal David's city
Stood a lowly cattle-shed,
Where a mother laid her Baby
In a manger for His bed;
Mary was that mother mild,
Jesus Christ her little Child.

He came down to earth from heaven,
Who is God and Lord of all,
And his shelter was a stable
And His cradle was a stall;
With the poor, and mean, and lowly,
Lived on earth our Saviour holy.

And, through all His wondrous childhood,
He would honor, and obey,
Love, and watch the lowly maiden
In whose gentle arms He lay;
Christian children all must be
Mild, obedient, good as He.

For He is our childhood's pattern,
Day by day like us He grew:

He was little, weak, and helpless,
Tears and smiles like us He knew;
And He feeleth for our sadness,
And He shareth in our gladness.

And our eyes at last shall see Him,
Through His own redeeming love;
For that Child so dear and gentle
Is our Lord in heav'n above;
And He leads His children on
To the place where He is gone.

Not in that poor lowly stable,
With the oxen standing by,
We shall see Him, but in heaven,
Set at God's right hand on high;
When like stars His children crowned,
All in white shall wait around.

"Shepherd, Shake Off Your Drowsy Sleep"

This traditional carol from Besançon in the eastern part of France was first published in 1842. The tune is probably seventeenth century in origin. The harmonization usually seen today was arranged by the English composer John Stainer. The English translation of "Berger, secoue ton sommeil profond" is anonymous.

Shepherd, shake off your drowsy sleep,
Rise and leave your silly sheep;
Angels from Heav'n around are singing,
Tidings of great joy are bringing.

REFRAIN
Shepherd! the chorus come and swell!
Sing Noel, O sing Noel!

See how the flow'rs all burst anew,
Thinking snow is summer dew;
See how the stars afresh are glowing,
All their brightest beams bestowing.

REFRAIN

Shepherd, then up and quick away!
Seek the Babe ere break of day.
He is the hope of ev'ry nation,
All in Him shall find salvation!

REFRAIN

"Silent Night"

"Silent Night" is probably the most popular Christmas carol in the
world today. Yet probably no other carol was written under such unlikely circumstances and with so many ironic results. Most of us are
familiar with the rough outline of the story from various TV versions,
but there is a great deal that they leave out.

The song was composed in its entirety on Christmas Eve, 1818.
The touching words were composed by Father Josef Mohr, who was
the illegitimate son of a seamstress and an army deserter. The Salzach
River flowed near the site of the St. Nicholas' Church at Oberndorf,
eleven miles northwest of Salzburg, Austria, where Father Mohr was
the assistant priest. This closeness of the river had caused rust in the
organ so that it could not be played. (More picturesque versions of
the story insist on a mouse nibbling at the bellows as the cause of the
malfunction.) Faced with the prospect of a Christmas Eve service
with no music, Father Mohr sat down and wrote three six-line stanzas
of poetry, each beginning *"Stille Nacht! Heilige Nacht!"* He gave this
poem to his organist Franz Grüber and asked him to set it to music
that could be sung by the choir and accompanied on a guitar.
Grüber's presence was somewhat odd in that he worked as a schoolteacher in Arnsdorf, several miles away, and was also organist for a

church there. But he had a stepson play for him there so he could supplement the family income by playing for his friend Mohr in Oberndorf. This was a lucky chance, since what more appropriate place for the best-loved carol to originate than in St. Nicholas' Church? Grüber's other church was named Our Lady of the Swamps: it is hard to imagine "Silent Night" being written there.

It took Grüber only a couple of hours to set the words to music and write out the parts. That even left time for a rehearsal with the choir before the midnight service began. The arrangement was as simple as possible. Mohr sang tenor and Grüber sang bass and accompanied on the guitar. After each stanza was sung in two parts, the choir repeated the last two lines in four-part harmony. As far as Mohr and Grüber knew, they had done no more than get through an awkward situation that night. Neither knew that they had achieved immortality.

In the spring of 1819, a master organ builder came to work on the rusted organ at Oberndorf. No one knows how he came to see or hear the carol. Perhaps Grüber showed it to him along with some of his other compositions to get the response of this man who had seen so much more of the world; perhaps the organ builder just ran across it in the organ loft. Whatever the circumstances, he copied the song and took to singing it on his rounds of the Austrian villages where he worked. It was then acquired from him by two strolling families of folk singers, much like the Trapp Family Singers of *The Sound of Music*. The Rainers and the Strassers made it a part of their regular repertory, although they knew nothing about who had written it. It began to become more and more popular. In 1834 the Strassers sang the "Song from Heaven," as they called it, for the king of Prussia. He ordered that it be sung every Christmas Eve by his cathedral choir. The Rainers first brought the song to America in 1839, when it was sung at the Alexander Hamilton Monument in New York City.

By the middle of the nineteenth century the song had gained worldwide popularity, but no one knew who had written it. It was variously attributed to Joseph or Michael Haydn, Mozart, or even God Himself without the benefit of any intervening composer. In 1854 leading musical authorities received a letter from the small town of Hallein near Salzburg. The letter was from one Franz Grüber, a schoolteacher, who had the audacity to claim that he had written the tune of the holy song. Granted he did produce a manuscript that seemed authentic, but few authorities wanted to accept such an insignificant source for the world-famous song. Thus the last eight and a half years of Grüber's life were involved in controversy over whether he had written the song or not. Living in small villages as he had, he had not even been aware of the popularity of the song until over thirty years after it had spread around the world. We can only speculate on what he must have felt the first time he heard the "Song from Heaven" and recognized his own hurry-up composition from decades before.

And what of Mohr, whose words had inspired the song? Sadly, he had always had a drinking problem and was frequently in trouble with the Church authorities. He was transferred twelve times in eight years. His two-year stay at Oberndorf had been the longest time he spent anywhere. Eventually he was sent to the village of Wagrain, where he died of pneumonia in 1848. As he was penniless, his parishioners had to take up a collection to bury him. He was buried on St. Nicholas' Day. He never heard of the "Song from Heaven."

If it had not been for Mohr and the guitar to replace the organ, there would have been no "Silent Night." Ironically, one of the things he was chided for by the Church authorities was for bringing the guitar into the church service.

Around 1900 the original St. Nicholas' Church was torn down because the river that had rusted the organ was now eating at the foundations. Between 1924 and 1936 the Silent Night Chapel was built on the spot. It seats twenty-two people in pews and has a headset arrangement so that one can listen to the original setting of "Silent Night" on the site of its premiere. There is also a carved wooden nativity scene, like the one around which the carol was first sung. There is one very odd thing about this manger scene, which is not apparent. When the new St. Nicholas' Church was being built, a sculpture was designed to show Mohr and Grüber and their famous composition. However, no likeness of Mohr existed. The sculptor therefore asked that a cast be made of Mohr's skull so that he would have at least some idea of the rough contours of his head and face. Mohr was therefore disinterred at Wagrain and his skull sent to Vienna. After the cast was made, the skull was accidentally sent back to Oberndorf instead of Wagrain. The Oberndorf city fathers decided to keep it.

Wagrain protested bitterly, but to no avail. The skull was placed in the carved wooden nativity scene. So today Mohr's body lies in Wagrain while his head is in Oberndorf on the site where he penned those words which gave him an immortality he never knew of.

The translation we know today of "Silent Night" first appeared in 1863. Its author was unknown until 1959, when it was determined to have been the Reverend John Freeman Young, who would become the Episcopal bishop of Florida in 1867.

Silent night, holy night,
All is calm, all is bright
Round yon Virgin Mother and child!
Holy Infant so tender and mild,
  Sleep in heavenly peace.

Silent night, holy night,
Shepherds quake at the sight,
Glories stream from heaven afar,
Heavenly hosts sing alleluia;
  Christ, the Saviour, is born.

Silent night, holy night,
Son of God, love's pure light
Radiant beams from Thy holy face,
With the dawn of redeeming grace,
  Jesus, Lord, at Thy birth.

"Sleep, My Little Jesus"

The composer of this lovely Christmas lullaby, Adam Geibel, was re-markable in that he worked as organist, composer, and publisher in spite of being blind. Born in Baden, Germany, he made Philadelphia his home from 1862 until his death in 1933. The words were written by a Unitarian minister from Rochester, New York, William C. Gan-nett.

Sleep, my little Jesus,
On Thy bed of hay,
While the shepherds homeward
Journey on their way.
Mother is Thy shepherd
And will her vigil keep:
Did the voices wake Thee?
O sleep, my Jesus, sleep!
Softly sleep, sweetly sleep,
My Jesus, sleep!

Sleep, my little Jesus,
While Thou art my own!
Ox and ass Thy neighbors,
Shalt Thou have a throne?
Will they call me blessed?
Shall I stand and weep?
Be it far, Jehovah!
O sleep, my Jesus, sleep!
Softly sleep, sweetly sleep,
My Jesus, sleep!

Sleep, my little Jesus,
Wonder-baby mine!
Well the singing angels
Greet Thee as divine.

Through my heart, as heaven,
Low the echoes sweep
Of glory to Jehovah!
O sleep, my Jesus, sleep!
Softly sleep, sweetly sleep,
My Jesus, sleep!

"There's a Song in the Air"

Josiah Gilbert Holland gave up the practice of medicine after a short career and turned to writing and editing. He was instrumental in establishing *Scribner's Magazine* and edited it for a number of years. This American poet, novelist, journalist, and editor published his famous Christmas carol in 1872 in a volume entitled *The Marble Prophecy and Other Poems*. He died in 1881 without ever hearing the tune with which his words would henceforth be associated.

In July 1904 Professor Karl P. Harrington of Wesleyan University was vacationing in New England. He was a teacher of Latin and a musicologist. One of his tasks at that time was the editing of the 1905 edition of the Methodist Hymnal. There was a tune for Holland's poem by the English composer Alfred George Wathall, but it did not seem sufficient to Harrington. So he sat down at the old family organ and composed a new one. It was printed in the new hymnal as the second tune for the song, along with thirteen other tunes by Harrington. Today Wathall's tune is forgotten and only Harrington's is sung. The setting of these words was not easy because of the unusual arrangement of the poem: four lines of six syllables each, followed by two lines of twelve.

There's a song in the air!
There's a star in the sky!
There's a mother's deep prayer,
And a baby's low cry!
And the star rains its fire while the beautiful sing,
For the manger of Bethlehem cradles a King!

There's a tumult of joy
O'er the wonderful birth,
For the Virgin's sweet boy
Is the Lord of the earth.
Ay! the star rains its fire while the beautiful sing,
For the manger of Bethlehem cradles a King!

In the light of that star
Lie the ages impearled;
And that song from afar
Has swept over the world.
Every hearth is aflame, and the beautiful sing
In the homes of the nations that Jesus is King!

We rejoice in the light,
And we echo the song
That comes down through the night
From the heavenly throng.
Ay! we shout to the lovely evangel they bring,
And we greet in His cradle our Saviour and King!

"Thou Didst Leave Thy Throne"

This hymn was written by Emily Elizabeth Steel Elliott. She was the niece of Charlotte Elliott, the author of "Just As I Am, Without One Plea." Her father was rector of St. Mark's Church, Brighton, England. She wrote more than two hundred hymns, but only this one is still in common use today. It was first published in 1864. The tune was composed in 1876 by Timothy R. Matthews, a clergyman and amateur organist in the Church of England, who composed more than one hundred hymn tunes. He called his tune "Margaret," although subsequent publishers have sometimes called it "Elliott" after the author of the words.

Thou didst leave Thy throne
And Thy kingly crown
When Thou camest to earth for me;

But in Bethlehem's home
Was there found no room
For Thy holy nativity.
O come to my heart, Lord Jesus!
There is room in my heart for Thee.

Heaven's arches rang
When the angels sang,
Proclaiming Thy royal degree;
But of lowly birth
Didst Thou come to earth,
And in great humility.
O come to my heart, Lord Jesus!
There is room in my heart for Thee.

The foxes found rest,
And the birds their nest
In the shade of the forest tree;
But Thy couch was the sod,
O Thou Son of God,
In the deserts of Galilee.
O come to my heart, Lord Jesus!
There is room in my heart for Thee.

Thou camest, O Lord,
With the living word
That should set Thy people free;
But with mocking scorn,
And with crown of thorn,
They bore Thee to Calvary.
O come to my heart, Lord Jesus!
There is room in my heart for Thee.

When the heavens shall ring,
And the angels sing,
At Thy coming to victory,
Let Thy voice call me home,
Saying, "Yet there is room,
There is room at my side for thee."
And my heart shall rejoice, Lord Jesus,
When Thou comest and callest for me.

It is interesting to note that the last couplet, which is the same in all but the last stanza, is sometimes made uniform throughout to simplify the printing process. Thus the poem loses its final summation for the sake of space.

"The Twelve Days of Christmas"

This carol is an anonymous reminder of a form popular in the Middle Ages, the "counting song." We have similar songs today, such as "This old man he played one, he played knick-knack on my thumb. . . ." This type of song is almost a nursery rhyme, although some were more bent on teaching than mere entertainment. Some songs counted thus: one God; two Testaments; three in the Trinity; four Evangelists; five senses; six days of work in the week; seven liberal arts; eight persons saved in the Ark, or Beatitudes; nine Muses, or kinds of angels; ten Commandments; eleven faithful Apostles; and twelve Apostles altogether, or heavenly gates, or Jewish tribes, or Articles of the Creed. "The Twelve Days of Christmas" is unique among Christmas carols in being entirely about getting gifts and having nothing else to do with the season.

> On the first (second, third, etc.) day of Christmas
> My true love sent to me:
> 1. A partridge in a pear tree.
> 2. Two turtle doves and a partridge in a pear tree.
> 3. Three French hens, two turtle doves, etc.
> 4. Four colly birds, three French hens, etc.
> 5. Five gold rings! Four colly birds, etc.
> 6. Six geese a-laying, five gold rings! etc.
> 7. Seven swans a-swimming, six geese a-laying, etc.
> 8. Eight maids a-milking, seven swans a-swimming, etc.
> 9. Nine ladies dancing, eight maids a-milking, etc.
> 10. Ten lords a-leaping, nine ladies dancing, etc.
> 11. Eleven pipers piping, ten lords a-leaping, etc.
> 12. Twelve drummers drumming, eleven pipers piping, etc.

"We Three Kings of Orient Are"

This is one of the few modern carols in which both words and music are by a single author. The Reverend John Henry Hopkins, Jr., was Rector of Christ's Church, Williamsport, Pennsylvania, when he wrote it about 1857. It was first published in his very popular work *Carols, Hymns, and Songs*, in 1862. It was the only American carol to appear in *Christmas Carols New and Old*, the English collection by H. R. Bramley and John Stainer that was very influential in bringing about the revival of carol-singing. Hopkins wrote many other hymns and songs, but none ever equaled the popularity of this one. It has always appealed to children because of the dramatic device of assigning each verse to a different king and therefore, often, a different singer. This carol is based more on the legends that grew up around the Wise Men than the original account in Matthew.

THE THREE KINGS: We three kings of Orient are,
Bearing gifts we traverse afar
Field and fountain, moor and mountain,
Following yonder star.

REFRAIN

O star of wonder, star of night,
Star with royal beauty bright,
Westward leading, still proceeding,
Guide us to thy perfect light.

MELCHIOR: Born a King on Bethlehem's plain,
Gold I bring to crown Him again;
King forever, ceasing never
Over us all to reign.

REFRAIN

CASPAR:
Frankincense to offer have I,
Incense owns a Deity nigh;
Prayer and praising, all men raising,
Worship Him, God on high.

REFRAIN

BALTHAZAR:
Myrrh is mine; its bitter perfume
Breathes a life of gathering gloom;
Sorrowing, sighing, bleeding, dying,
Sealed in the stone-cold tomb.

REFRAIN

ALL:
Glorious now behold Him arise,
King, and God, and Sacrifice;
Heav'n sings Alleluia;
Alleluia the earth replies.

REFRAIN

"We Wish You a Merry Christmas"

This familiar traditional carol recalls the waits and carolers of old England as they go from door to door, singing blessings on the house and asking for some good cheer in return. Numerous versions of this exist with many other verses. In this version, "figgy pudding" is the reward sought, an unsweetened dish made with figs and often containing suet (fat), originally boiled in a bag, but now often steamed or boiled without a bag.

> We wish you a Merry Christmas,
> We wish you a Merry Christmas,
> We wish you a Merry Christmas
> And a Happy New Year!
>
> We want some figgy pudding,
> We want some figgy pudding,
> We want some figgy pudding
> And a cup of good cheer!
>
> We won't go until we get some,
> We won't go until we get some,
> We won't go until we get some,
> So bring it out here!
>
> We wish you a Merry Christmas,
> We wish you a Merry Christmas,
> We wish you a Merry Christmas
> And a Happy New Year!

Presumably, between the somewhat surly third verse and the once again good-spirited fourth verse the carolers' wishes were granted and the cup of good cheer brought out. Perhaps the caroling was of such a quality that the threat not to leave was what speeded the host's hospitality.

"What Child Is This?"

The earliest reference to the haunting folk song "Greensleeves" was in the year 1580. It was so popular and familiar that it is mentioned several times in Shakespeare's *The Merry Wives of Windsor*. The tune has been used for many purposes, including a party song for the

Cavaliers during the English Civil War and as a prison lament for Macheath in *The Beggar's Opera*. The original words are still familiar, "Alas, my love, ye do me wrong/To cast me off discourteously," but for most Americans the words most sung to this tune were written by the Victorian English hymnist and insurance company executive William Chatterton Dix.

What Child is this, Who, laid to rest,
On Mary's lap is sleeping?
Whom angels greet with anthems sweet,
While shepherds watch are keeping?

REFRAIN
This, this is Christ the King,
Whom shepherds guard and angels sing:
Haste, haste to bring Him laud,
The Babe, the Son of Mary.

Why lies He in such mean estate
Where ox and ass are feeding?
Good Christian, fear: for sinners here
The silent Word is pleading.

REFRAIN

So bring Him incense, gold, and myrrh,
Come, peasant, king, to own Him;
The King of kings salvation brings,
Let loving hearts enthrone Him.

REFRAIN

"While Shepherds Watched Their Flocks by Night"

This carol was written by Nahum Tate and first published in the supplement to his 1696 *New Version of the Psalms of David*. It was written as a singable paraphrase of Luke 2:8–14. At that time such a hymn could be sung to any number of tunes, and so none became specifically associated with it at that time. The tune we usually sing in America today was adapted from Handel's 1728 opera *Siroë, King of Persia*. Besides this carol, Tate is best known for later becoming Poet Laureate of England and writing a version of *King Lear* that had a happy ending and was more popular than Shakespeare's for 150 years.

> While shepherds watched their flocks by night,
> All seated on the ground,
> The angel of the Lord came down,
> And glory shone around.
> "Fear not," said he, for mighty dread
> Had seized their troubled mind;
> "Glad tidings of great joy I bring
> To you and all mankind.
>
> "To you, in David's town, this day,
> Is born of David's line,
> The Saviour, who is Christ the Lord;
> And this shall be the sign;
> The heavenly Babe you there shall find
> To human view displayed,
> All meanly wrapped in swathing bands,
> And in a manger laid."
>
> Thus spake the seraph, and forthwith
> Appeared a shining throng
> Of angels, praising God, who thus
> Addressed their joyful song:
> "All glory be to God on high,
> And to the earth be peace;
> Good-will henceforth from heaven to men
> Begin, and never cease."

Christmas Oratorio

Johann Sebastian Bach composed his *Christmas Oratorio* in 1734. He was at that time employed as cantor of the Thomasschule of Leipzig, a post he held until his death in 1750. His duties consisted of teaching a class in Latin, training singers and instrumentalists, playing the organ at two churches, and also organizing and directing all musical activities at these churches. As if all that were not enough, he was also responsible for composing all the special music and copying out all the parts for singers and instrumentalists. That Bach had time to compose at all is amazing; that he turned out a volume of music almost unequaled in history is astounding; that this music is not just eighteenth-century Muzak but some of the most sublime expressions of the human spirit ever created is beyond belief. During his twenty years at Leipzig, Bach composed some 250 cantatas alone, an average of one a month. Each cantata ran from twelve to forty minutes in length and usually involved chorus, orchestra, and soloists. Bach composed each work, copied all the parts, taught the performers, and conducted the performance. When asked about his life, Bach replied simply, "I worked hard."

The *Christmas Oratorio* is actually a set of six cantatas composed to be performed one at each of six services between Christmas and Epiphany in 1734–35. The texts are taken mostly from Matthew and Luke and are appropriate for each of the services. The six parts tell the story of Joseph and Mary and of Christ's birth, the appearance of the angels to the shepherds, the coming of the shepherds to the manger, the naming of Jesus, the coming of the Wise Men to Herod, and the Magi's visit to Bethlehem. The work is written for orchestra, chorus, and soprano, alto, tenor, and bass soloists. Today it is more frequently performed as a single work than as six separate cantatas.

Bach's music was the culmination of the polyphonic form, the weaving of different melodies together to form a unified whole. But by his time the polyphonic form was considered old-hat and Bach along with it. His music was never fully appreciated in his lifetime; it was too old-fashioned. After his death, the authorities at Leipzig, who had always felt that he neglected his duties as a teacher, resolved that "the school needs a choirmaster and not a music director." His music fell quickly into disuse and survived only as manuscripts in attics and basements. It was Mendelssohn who rediscovered the wonders of J. S. Bach eighty years later when he happened upon a manuscript of the *St. Matthew Passion,* one of the greatest of all choral works, at an auction of a cheese seller's goods. It was being sold as scrap paper.

Hänsel and Gretel

The best-known full-length Christmas opera has nothing to do with Christmas. *Hänsel and Gretel* is traditionally performed at Christmastime, yet Christmas is not even mentioned in the opera. However, because of its delightful fairy-tale plot, its wonderful gingerbread scenery, and its celebration of childhood it has become a beautifully appropriate addition to the Christmas season.

Engelbert Humperdinck was a disciple of Richard Wagner. Wagner's operas are known for their heavy (some would say "murky") exploration of German mythology, their elaborate orchestration, and their advanced harmonies. In the hands of Wagner, a musical genius, this blend of the mythological past and the musical future was eminently successful. Very few other composers, however, were able to carry on his tradition or extend it in any way.

Humperdinck had his greatest success through an unlikely means. His sister wrote a little play for her children to perform at home based on the familiar story by the Brothers Grimm of the two children lost in the wood. Humperdinck wrote some little songs for them to sing. It was perhaps the simplicity of this beginning that accounted for the opera's success. Expanding his simple tunes into an opera gave him a core of basic, folklike melody at the heart of the modern Wagnerian harmonic structure of his work. The opera was first performed a few days before Christmas in 1893 at Weimar, Germany. It became tremendously popular in Germany and soon throughout the world. A whole series of fairy-tale operas sprang up in imitation. Fairy tales were easier to relate to than heavy mythology, and the new emphasis on folklike melodies made the works more "hummable."

Hänsel and Gretel is still frequently performed, especially at Christmastime. The Metropolitan Opera has presented it more than one hundred times, and it was the first complete opera broadcast by radio from the stage of the Met, on Christmas Day, 1931.

An interesting note on the cast: the part of Hänsel is written for a mezzo-soprano, that is, a medium-high woman's voice. This may seem odd, since Hänsel is a little boy, but composers have frequently used women's voices to depict young men or boys, presumably to give the feeling of an adolescent sound before the voice has changed. This casting is often balanced in modern productions by the fact that the part of the witch (also written for a mezzo-soprano) is often played by a tenor, to heighten the humor and grotesqueness of the role. In operatic circles, the part of a man played by a woman is called a "trousers role"; no one has made up a polite term for a man playing a woman's role.

Messiah

On August 22, 1741, George Friedrich Handel began to act strangely. He shut himself into his room, sat at his desk, and almost did not eat or sleep for three weeks while he worked. When his servants tried to get him to eat, he would flare up at them, eyes blazing. If he ate, he continued to work with the hand that didn't hold the bread. He behaved like a madman, and perhaps he was—divinely mad.

The German-born Handel came to London in 1710 at the age of twenty-five. He immediately became the toast of the town when his opera *Rinaldo* proved to be a big success. Always a prolific composer, he turned out dozens of the popular Italian operas that the aristocratic audience clamored for. But in 1728 disaster struck—in a most unlikely form. A rowdy work called *The Beggar's Opera* was produced in London. A risqué satire on Italian opera and current politics, it contained a score made up of a host of popular tunes of the day (including one from one of Handel's operas) fitted out with new words. It was a smash hit. This was something the common people could enjoy, without having to know Italian or the conventions of the stilted operatic format of the time. Italian opera and its prime composer, Handel, began struggling for its life.

One of the steps Handel took to try to regain popularity was the composition of oratorios. The oratorio was a different format from opera in that the work was not staged, so it did not have to be specifically dramatic and it could be composed in English, which no serious opera of the time could be. He produced fifteen of these in the years leading up to 1741 with varying success. The fickleness of the public was a source of great disappointment to him, and the once-lionized composer found himself being treated as an old-timer. Financially, he was in difficult straits.

When his fit of mad composition came upon him in 1741, he did not even have a commission that he was working on. The new work he was composing might never be performed for all he knew at the time. It did not matter. It was a different, higher voice than that of the public which he was listening to as the days passed without food and rest.

A servant found him one day weeping at his desk. He rushed forward to help, but Handel looked up at him with a great light shining through the tears of his eyes. "I did think I did see all Heaven before me, and the great God Himself," he said. He had just completed the "Hallelujah Chorus."

Messiah was completed in twenty-four days, an incredibly short time for a work that takes nearly three hours to perform in its entirety. The completed manuscript was then put aside for the next seven weeks. Finally the Lord Lieutenant of Ireland asked him to visit Dublin and give some charity concerts there. He brought it with him. On April 13, 1742, the first performance of the *Messiah* was given in Dublin.

The *Messiah* was slow catching on in London. It was first performed there in 1743, with much less success than in Dublin. That first performance had been a tremendous event for the Dublin audience, which had been asked that ladies not wear hoops that evening and gentlemen leave their swords at home in order to accommodate an extra hundred people in the hall. London did not fully accept the *Messiah* until the famous performance at which King George II, moved by the inspiration of the piece, rose at the beginning of the "Hallelujah Chorus." The entire audience stood with him and established a custom that exists to this day of rising in homage to this most sublime and stirring piece of music.

Before his death, annual performances of the *Messiah* had become traditional, with Handel conducting. It was at that time usually performed at Easter. The two centuries since its composition have produced no change in the popularity of the *Messiah*, but there have been many changes made in how it is performed. Handel himself changed the work according to the musical resources he had on hand: sometimes orchestra, sometimes organ alone; sometimes a male alto, sometimes a female one. The result is considerable confusion about just what Handel wanted. The work was reorchestrated in 1789 by Mozart to suit changing tastes, and that is the version we usually hear. In the nineteenth century it became popular to have huge festival choruses, and there would sometimes be as many as five thousand voices performing the work that Handel wrote for a chorus of about twenty-four.

Today the *Messiah* is thought of as a Christmas work; at least, that is when most performances of it are presented. Actually, the work is divided into three sections, only the first of which deals with Christmas. Starting with the prophecies about Christ's birth, the first part is highlighted by the joyous chorus "For unto Us a Child Is Born" and the angels' song to the shepherds. There is very little actual narrative, being more descriptions of the emotions produced by the joyous tidings. The second part tells of Christ's Crucifixion and Resurrection, again without actually telling a story. The second part ends with the "Hallelujah Chorus" and is often referred to as the Easter section, the first part being called the Christmas section. The third part is a contemplation on the meaning of Christ's ministry and its promise of resurrection for all believers.

The text, mostly a compilation of biblical writings, was provided to Handel by his friend Charles Jennens, although there is some doubt whether he wrote it or merely took credit for what his secretary had written. Jennens did not appreciate what Handel had done. He wrote to a friend: "I shall show you a collection I gave Handel, called *Messiah*, which I value highly, and he has made a fine entertainment out of it, though not near so good as he might and ought to have done. I have with great difficulty made him correct some of the grossest faults in the composition." A more monstrous example of misplaced egotism would be difficult to find.

The *Messiah* is a living part of our Christmas tradition. Few churches let the season go by without performing at least one or two of the great choruses. In a major city, one usually has a choice of several complete performances. Radio and TV broadcast the presentations of famous orchestras as part of Christmas Eve programming.

The *Messiah* is one of the supreme achievements of human art. Its polyphonic writing, the weaving of melody against melody in the different voice and instrumental parts, has few equals in all the world of music; and the lyricism of its gentle airs is truly touching. But it goes beyond the bounds of mere ability and rises to inspiration. As Milton Cross puts it, "Never a religious man in the same sense as

Bach, Handel became the God-intoxicated man while writing *Messiah*." Sheer joy and glory fill the whole work and make it especially appropriate to the Christmas season when the joy of Christ's birth fills all our hearts.

A curious footnote: Handel is buried in Westminster Abbey. Above his grave stands a statue of him holding a score of *Messiah* while angels wheel above his head. The word "Messiah" is misspelled.

The Nutcracker

Tchaikovsky's *Nutcracker* is the best-loved and, in fact, the only major Christmas ballet in the standard repertory of today's companies. *The Nutcracker* is so popular that many ballet troupes finance all the rest of their productions by the many performances of *The Nutcracker* that they put on each Christmas. Thousands of children are brought to the Christmas holiday matinees, and yet this is a ballet for adults as much as for children. Like Christmas itself, *The Nutcracker* is a delight for all ages.

The original story, "The Nutcracker and the Mouse King," was written in 1816 by the famous writer of fantastic tales E. T. A. Hoffmann. (Hoffmann had many connections with music: he was himself a composer and took the middle name Amadeus as homage to his idol Wolfgang Amadeus Mozart; not only were his stories adapted as ballets and operas, he was himself made the leading character in Offenbach's opera *The Tales of Hoffmann*.) The story was translated from its original German into French by Alexandre Dumas (the elder), the author of *The Three Musketeers*, in 1845. In 1891 the great French choreographer Marius Petipa wrote a scenario with his assistant Lev Ivanov which was based on Dumas' translation. The commission for writing the music went to the great Russian composer Peter Ilich Tchaikovsky, with whom Petipa had previously collaborated on the *Sleeping Beauty* ballet.

In March of 1892 Tchaikovsky conducted an orchestral performance of a suite of music from the soon-to-be-produced ballet. The
music was a grand success and boded well for the premiere of the
ballet itself. This suite is still heard in its original form both on
recordings and as a standard in light classical concerts.

The ballet was first performed on December 17, 1892, at St. Peters-
burg. It was not a success! The main reason may have been the com-
plaint, still sometimes heard, that the entire first act of the ballet is
dominated by children, and that the real ballet is located almost entirely in the second act. Another problem was that audiences still
weren't ready for such symphonic ballet scores as Tchaikovsky gave
them. They were used to music that merely accompanied the dancing
without attempting too much on its own. This had caused confusion
and lack of success in Tchaikovsky's two previous ballets, *Swan Lake*
and *Sleeping Beauty*. Yet it was Tchaikovsky's contributions to the
field of ballet music that eventually raised the standard of such compositions and made it worthwhile for serious composers to venture
into the field. The ballet scores of Tchaikovsky are among the most
beautiful and familiar ever written.

The story of *The Nutcracker* takes place on Christmas Eve. Two
children, Clara and Fritz, are given a number of magical presents by a
magician named Drosselmeyer. One of them is a nutcracker shaped
like a small man. The children quarrel over him before going to bed.
Clara sneaks out of bed because she cannot sleep for thinking of her
nutcracker. She finds a full-scale battle in progress between an army of
toy soldiers, led by the nutcracker, and an army of mice led by the
seven-headed King of the Mice. In an act of great bravery, Clara hurls
her slipper at the Mouse King, stunning him and turning the tide of
battle. The nutcracker is transformed into a handsome prince. In
gratitude for her help, the nutcracker prince takes Clara on an
enchanted journey to the Kingdom of the Sweets, which is presided
over by the Sugarplum Fairy. There are dances by snowflakes and
Arabian, Chinese, and Russian dancers. The finale is provided by the
famous Waltz of the Flowers.

One of the reasons for *The Nutcracker*'s popularity is the opportunity it offers for spectacular scenic effects. Sleds fly, snowflakes dance,
hordes of mice throng the stage. For many New York children, it just
wouldn't be Christmas if they didn't go to the City Ballet and see the

giant Christmas tree that magically grows out of the stage floor until it touches the ceiling of the high stage. *The Nutcracker*, both as music and as ballet, is filled with Christmas magic. Some of the major companies that present annual Christmas productions of this perennial favorite are the American Ballet Theatre, the New York City Ballet, the San Francisco Ballet, and Ballet West in Salt Lake City. The music of *The Nutcracker* Suite also provides the accompaniment for some of the most magical dancing of all in Walt Disney's *Fantasia*.

More Serious Music for Christmas

CHRISTMAS CONCERTO
An orchestral piece by the seventeenth-century Italian composer Arcangelo Corelli, officially titled Concerto Grosso in G Minor.

CHRISTMAS EVE
Nicolai Rimsky-Korsakov wrote this Russian opera in 1895 based on a Gogol fairy tale.

THE CHRISTMAS TREE
Christmas hymns and carols were arranged into a piano solo by the virtuoso composer Franz Liszt.

L'ENFANCE DU CHRIST
A French oratorio by Hector Berlioz, this 1854 work is not directly concerned with Christ's birth but with his childhood.

FANTASIA ON CHRISTMAS CAROLS
English composer Ralph Vaughan Williams created this work for baritone, chorus, and orchestra in 1912.

ST. NICHOLAS
This Christmas cantata by the English composer Benjamin Britten tells the story of St. Nicholas' life and first appeared on CBS television in 1959.

☙ Popular ☙

"All I Want for Christmas Is My Two Front Teeth"

This was one of the first major-selling Christmas novelty records. It presents no warm Christmas sentiments, but does express an image that advertisers have found to be irresistible down through the years, the cute child with the gap in his front teeth. The song was written in 1946 by Don Gardner. The song found true fame only in 1948 when recorded by Spike Jones and his City Slickers for RCA Victor. The charm of the song was greatly enhanced by the sound of air whistling through the missing teeth of the title.

"The Chipmunk Song"

This is one of the oddest of the popular Christmas songs, as its success depended entirely on the novelty of the gimmick it employed. By speeding up the tape recording, composer Ross Bagdasarian was able to make his voice sound high and squeaky like a chipmunk's. He created a trio of "chipmunks" singing, in harmony, this song, which is also called "Christmas, Don't Be Late," and released it in 1958 under his pseudonym David Seville. The song was tremendously popular for several seasons and won a Grammy Award from the National

Academy of Recording Arts and Sciences for the best recording of 1958 in the children's category. "David Seville" later did many other novelty recordings, including "My Friend, the Witch Doctor."

"The Christmas Song"

This is one of the loveliest of all popular Christmas songs and its subtitle, "Chestnuts roasting by an open fire," has become one of the most pleasant standard images of the season, even though few of us have experienced the sensation except in this song. Written in 1946 by Mel Torme and Robert Wells, the best-known version of this song is the exceptionally warm, velvety rendition given it by Nat King Cole.

"Frosty the Snowman"

Frosty is one of the most successful additions to modern Christmas imagery. The song was written in 1950 by Steve Nelson and Jack Rollins. It was recorded by Gene Autry and was the best-selling Christmas record of 1951. Frosty had some of the elements of a fairy tale, with its snowman who comes to life with the addition of a magical silk hat. There is also some fairy-tale poignancy as Frosty begins to melt in the sun and so must hurry away, promising to return some day. A TV Christmas cartoon and record album were based on the story of the song in 1969. Frosty has also found his way into that golden realm of Christmas merchandising where he has appeared as dolls, on coloring books, as candy, and in many other manifestations that might have taxed the ingenuity of even the most magical of silk hats.

"Here Comes Santa Claus Right down Santa Claus Lane"

The simplicity of this tune made it a popular one for children to sing. It was written in 1946 by Gene Autry and Oakey Haldeman, and the popular singing cowboy also made the first successful recording of the song. It adds little to the imagery of Christmas except the dubious geographical reference to Santa Claus Lane.

"I Saw Mommy Kissing Santa Claus"

This novelty record was the most popular Christmas song of 1952. It was written by Tommie Connor and sung by Jimmy Boyd, whose lively naïveté is one of the record's chief assets. The lyrics tell quite simply of sneaking down the stairs one Christmas Eve to discover Mommy kissing Santa Claus under the mistletoe. We are to assume, it is hoped, that it was actually Daddy in a Santa Claus suit.

"I'll Be Home for Christmas"

This is one of the most masterful, nostalgic ballads ever written for Christmas. It sums up the sense of longing for reunion and for the past when all could come together in the peace of the season. This sense was especially important at the song's first release in 1943, when millions of servicemen were scattered around the world and the thought of being home for Christmas was the dearest hope they could imagine. Written by Walter Kent, Kim Cannon, and Buck Ram, it was first recorded by Bing Crosby in a memorable version on Decca Records.

"It's Beginning to Look Like Christmas"

Meredith Willson originally wrote this familiar description of Christmas decorations in 1951. It was recorded then by Bing Crosby. In 1963 Willson used it again as an important theme song in his Christmas musical on Broadway, *Here's Love*. This fairly successful Broadway show was based on the film *Miracle on 34th Street*. Willson is best known for his other Broadway musicals, *The Music Man* and *The Unsinkable Molly Brown*.

"Jingle Bell Rock"

Rock music has not shown itself to be very expressive of the gentler emotions of Christmas. This is one of the very few successful rock Christmas songs, and it is a very gentle rock, far removed from today's "hard" and "acid" varieties. The song was written by Joe Beal and Jim Boothe and recorded by Bobby Helms in 1957. Like many rock lyrics, it is very difficult to say exactly what it is about. The music is not as annoying as one might expect, but is actually rather pleasant in a mindless sort of way.

"Jingle Bells"

This is one of the most familiar of all secular carols. It was composed
in 1857 by J. Pierpont for a local Boston Sunday school ceremony. It
was originally titled "One Horse Open Sleigh," but became known
by the words of its refrain. The second verse is usually omitted, which
is understandable when you read it. This carol is unusual in that it is
only about wintertime and does not mention Christmas at all.

Dashing through the snow
In a one-horse open sleigh,
O'er the fields we go
Laughing all the way;
Bells on bobtail ring,
Making spirits bright;
O what fun it is to sing
A sleighing song tonight!

REFRAIN

Jingle Bells! Jingle Bells!
Jingle all the way!
Oh, what fun it is to ride in a one-horse open sleigh!
Jingle Bells! Jingle Bells!
Jingle all the way!
Oh, what fun it is to ride in a one-horse open sleigh!

A day or two ago
I thought I'd take a ride,
And soon Miss Fannie Bright
Was seated by my side;
The horse was lean and lank,
Misfortune seem'd his lot,
He got into a drifted bank,
And then we got upsot!

REFRAIN

"The Little Drummer Boy"

This delightful Christmas song was written in 1958 by Katherine Davis, Henry Onorati, and Harry Simeone. It has been recorded by many choral groups and soloists with choral backup. The story concerns a little boy who journeys to Bethlehem to give the Christ Child the only gift he possesses—the ability to tap out a rhythmic ditty on his snare drum. The great charm of the piece derives from the continuous drumlike sound of the lower voices of the chorus, which accelerates and grows more exciting as the little drummer comes to the stable and offers his gift.

This song has been the basis for two animated television features. Both were narrated by Greer Garson. The first was made in 1968 by NBC. The voices were provided by José Ferrer and the Vienna Boys Choir. The story contained some additional plot elements, including a sick lamb, the Magi, and a band of gypsy kidnapers. The second version was called "The Little Drummer Boy, Book Two." It appeared in 1976 on the NBC network. The story concerns the preservation of some precious bells from falling into the hands of the Roman tax collectors. Each of these TV shows was a half hour long, and they have been frequently repeated.

"Rudolph the Red-Nosed Reindeer"

Rudolph is the best-known modern Christmas character. His addition is probably the only major change made in our image of Santa Claus since Clement Moore wrote "A Visit from St. Nicholas" in 1822.

Rudolph was born in the spring of 1939, the creation of Robert L. May, an advertising copywriter for Montgomery Ward Stores and the brother-in-law of composer Johnny Marks. May dreamed up Rudolph for a Christmas pamphlet as a promotion gimmick for Ward's. Shoppers would be given the verse story of the red-nosed reindeer and how he saved Santa's trip on a foggy Christmas Eve. This was used for several years. In 1947 the chairman of Ward's made an outright gift of the copyright to its creator, May, who found a book publisher for it. One hundred thousand copies were snapped up at the book stores that year. In 1949 May's brother-in-law, Johnny Marks, put words and music to the story of Rudolph and had the song published. Finding the right singer for the song was not easy. Marks thought he had Perry Como lined up, but the Como people wanted a line in the song changed. Marks, who was not about to change even a comma in what he was sure was a hit, looked elsewhere. Gene Autry, the famed cowboy and country-and-western singer was approached, but he thought the song too childish for his image. Marks had a demonstration record made up by a country singer and sent it to Autry, who liked what he heard. With the added push of strong approval from his wife, Autry agreed to record it.

"Rudolph the Red-Nosed Reindeer" was released in September of 1949 by Columbia Records and raced to the top of the popular music ratings charts, surpassing all Columbia releases that year. At Christmas of 1949 the record was nearing the two million mark in sold copies and out-distanced all Autry's previous hits by far. It was number one for months on the television program "Your Hit Parade." Today more than ninety million copies have been sold of the more than three hundred different recordings of the song. Rudolph has appeared in his own TV shows and on all sorts of Christmas merchandise. Only one song has surpassed Rudolph's popularity, and that is "White Christmas."

"Santa Claus Is Comin' to Town"

This is the third-best-selling Christmas song of all time, yet it almost didn't get recorded. It was written in 1932 by Haven Gillespie and songwriter J. Fred Coots. They tried for two years to get someone to take a chance on the song, but even Eddie Cantor, who employed Coots as a staffwriter, wasn't interested. It was Ida Cantor, Eddie's wife, who persuaded him to give the song a chance. So he used it on his radio show one week before Thanksgiving in 1934. It was an instantaneous success. The most successful recording was made by Bing Crosby and the Andrews Sisters, although the second most successful by Perry Como has also sold millions.

"Silver Bells"

This familiar Christmas song was introduced in the 1951 Christmas film *The Lemon Drop Kid*, starring Bob Hope. The song is unusual in that it concerns itself entirely with the sights and sounds of Christmas in the city, rather than the usual country setting of most carols. The words were written by Jay Livingston and the music by Ray Evans. Although Bob Hope and Marilyn Maxwell sang it in the movie, it was Bing Crosby who made a record hit out of it.

"Sleigh Ride"

This is an unusual Christmas composition in that Leroy Anderson originally wrote it as a purely instrumental piece in 1948. It is still sometimes performed that way in concert, and its bright, hoofbeat rhythm and imitation of a horse's whinny have helped make it a popular piece for symphonic band. Words by Mitchell Parish were added in 1950 and it became a best-selling record.

"White Christmas"

In 1942 Irving Berlin composed the score for a musical motion picture called *Holiday Inn*. The plot was somewhat silly, about an inn that was opened only on holidays, but it provided the excuse for a dozen songs about different holidays of the year. And it had a wonderful cast led by Bing Crosby, Fred Astaire, and Marjorie Reynolds. It was sure to be a hit, and Berlin knew he had at least one truly great song in the score. Everyone agreed on the set, thought all the songs were good, and were sure Berlin had a real hit on his hands with that Valentine Day song, "Be Careful, It's My Heart." By the time the Oscars were given out for that year, they were beginning to realize what the real winner was: the Oscar for best song of 1942 went to "White Christmas," which had all along been Crosby's favorite.

"White Christmas" is the all-time favorite popular Christmas song. It has sold more than 100 million records. Bing Crosby's recording is the single best-selling record in history. By the time *Holiday Inn* was remade in 1954, the real star of the show was recognized and the film was named *White Christmas*.

"White Christmas" is a completely secular song. There is very little specific about the words. Rather, they seem like disjointed memories of Christmases long ago: children, sleigh bells, snow. But no one can resist the nostalgia and simplicity of the tune, and polls have indicated its Christmas popularity in America is exceeded only by "Silent Night" among all Christmas music.

"Winter Wonderland"

This pleasant Christmas song is unusual in that it doesn't actually mention Christmas at all. It is entirely about two people in love who stroll about in the snow and dream indoors in front of the fireplace. It was written by Felix Bernard and Dick Smith in 1934. The best-selling version was recorded in 1950 by the Andrews Sisters.

More Pop Songs for Christmas

This is a good test of age: see how many lyrics you can remember from these songs from the last thirty-odd years. As you will notice from this list and the preceding songs, Christmas popular music in this country would almost not exist but for the ever-welcome voice and style of the late, truly great Bing Crosby.

BLUE CHRISTMAS
Written in 1945 and originally recorded separately by Hugo Winterhalter and Ernest Tubb. Elvis Presley made this a big hit in the fifties.

245

CHRISTMAS DREAMING (A LITTLE LATE THIS YEAR)
Frank Sinatra sang this 1947 hit by Lester Lee and Irving Gordon.

CHRISTMAS IN KILLARNEY
Both Dennis Day and Bing Crosby recorded versions of this Irish reminiscence by John Redmond, James Cavanaugh, and Frank Weldon.

HAVE YOURSELF A MERRY LITTLE CHRISTMAS
Judy Garland introduced this song in the 1944 picture *Meet Me in St. Louis*. The words and music are by Hugh Martin and Ralph Blaine.

IF IT DOESN'T SNOW ON CHRISTMAS
Gene Autry sang this 1949 song by Milton Pascal and Gerald Marks.

LET IT SNOW! LET IT SNOW! LET IT SNOW!
This 1945 standard by Sammy Cahn and Jule Styne doesn't mention Christmas, but paints a lovely picture of a winter snowscape.

MELE KALIKAMAKA
The Hawaiian expression for "Merry Christmas" was incorporated into a song by R. Alex Anderson and recorded in 1950 by Bing Crosby and the Andrews Sisters.

SANTA BABY
Eartha Kitt recorded this 1953 hit by Joan Javits, Phil Springer, and Tony Springer.

THE SECRET OF CHRISTMAS
Written by Sammy Cahn and Jimmy van Heusen, this song was introduced in the 1959 film *Say One for Me* by Bing Crosby.

SING A SONG OF SANTA CLAUS
The Ames Brothers recorded this 1952 song by Mann Curtis.

SLEIGH BELL SERENADE
Paul Francis Webster and Sonny Burke wrote this 1952 hit for Bing Crosby.

THAT CHRISTMAS FEELING
Bing Crosby recorded this Jimmy van Heusen-Johnny Burke song in 1951.

WE NEED A LITTLE CHRISTMAS
This song first appeared in the Broadway musical *Mame* by Jerry Herman in 1966.

YOU'RE ALL I WANT FOR CHRISTMAS
Glen Moore and Seger Ellis wrote this song in 1948 for Bing Crosby.

CHRISTMAS on the PAGE

❧ Stories ❧

A Child's Christmas in Wales

Dylan Thomas gave the twentieth century some of its greatest poetry, filled with the songlike rhythms of his native country, Wales. This reminiscence of Christmas is in prose, but it sings like poetry and its song transcends all national boundaries. It was originally a radio script, which Thomas wrote and read over the Welsh region station of the British Broadcasting Corporation as part of a regular series of programs he had. It was later published separately and has been recorded on records and turned into a television drama.

The story is not a straightforward narrative, but rather poetic memories that blend together into a single great memory called Christmas. As Thomas puts it, "All the Christmases roll down the hill towards the Welsh-speaking sea, like a snowball growing whiter and bigger and rounder, . . . In goes my hand into that wool-white bell-tongues ball of holidays resting at the margin of the carol-singing sea, and out comes . . ." And the memories come pouring out. They are everyday and special, tinged with the glow of reminiscence. There is the fire Thomas remembers trying to put out with snowballs; he and his friends carol the haunted house, and when a thin little voice joins the harmony from inside they run for the comfort of home; there are feasts, and there are gifts. Thomas describes all the glories that lurk in and overflow his stocking of a Christmas morning, including "a celluloid duck that made, when you pressed it, a most unducklike noise, a mewing moo that an ambitious cat might make who wishes to be a cow; and a painting-book in which I could make the grass, the trees, the sea, and the animals any colour I pleased: and still the dazzling sky-blue sheep are grazing in the red field under a flight of rain-bow-beaked and pea-green birds." This wonderful story is rather like that painting-book, full of the colorful memories of childhood which were probably never like that, but are nonetheless real for never having happened.

"Christmas Phantoms"

The great Russian writer Maxim Gorki wrote a very unusual Christmas story. It was a bitter response to the sentimental tragedies that are too often decked out in Christmas garb with no attention paid to the realities of the world around us. The story begins with the author relating the Christmas story that he wrote for the annual Christmas publications. It featured a blind beggar and his wife who wandered off into the snow and froze to death. But before they died, a vision of Jesus came to the beggar and so he died happily if poignantly. But that night, in a dream, the author's bedroom was crowded with all those pathetic figures he had used so lightly in so many stories over the years and a booming voice chastised him.

"And all the others are also heroes of your Christmas stories—children, men and women whom you made to freeze to death in order to amuse the public. See how many there are and how pitiful they look, the offspring of your fancy! . . ."

I was staggered by this strange indictment. Everybody writes Christmas stories according to the same formula. You take a poor boy or a poor girl, or something of that sort, and let them freeze somewhere under a window, behind which there is usually a Christmas tree that throws its radiant splendor upon them. This has become the fashion and I was following the fashion.

"You wish to arouse noble feelings in the hearts of men by your pictures of imagined misery, when real misery and suffering are nothing to them but a daily spectacle. . . . If the reality does not move them, and if their feelings are not offended by its cruel, ruthless misery, and by the fathomless abyss of actual wretchedness, then how can you

251

hope that the fictions of your imagination will make them better? . . ."

I awoke in the morning with a violent headache and in a very bad humor. The first thing I did was to read over my story of the blind beggar and his wife once more, and then I tore the manuscript into pieces.

Surely sentiment and sometimes sadness are a valid part of our Christmas literature. But this odd little tale serves as a timely warning to us not to weep over those things in a story which we would turn our heads away from in real life. The Christmas spirit must live in our day-to-day lives if it is to have any meaning at any time.

"The Fir Tree"

Hans Christian Andersen, the great Danish writer of fairy tales, wrote a number of stories that we connect with winter, such as "The Little Match Girl." But only one takes place actually at Christmas, "The Fir Tree." For those of us who only remember reading this story long ago, a rereading comes as something of a shock, since it is not just a nice little children's story. The tale has a moral, and it pursues it relentlessly.

The fir tree begins as a very small tree surrounded by the delightful sights and sounds of the forest. But he is not satisfied. He dreams of seeing the world. He sees his larger comrades cut down and taken away at Christmas and he longs to go too, sure that they are going to a glorious new life. But then the time comes when he is big enough and he is cut down and taken away. He is set in a salon and heavy ornaments cause his limbs to droop. Candles scorch his branches. He is frightened by the children who dance and sing about him and finally swoop down on him to rob his branches of the goodies concealed there. When Christmas is over, he is thrown out in the yard. To see the sky and the trees once again is a joy to him, and he realizes he never knew when he really had it good. But then a servant comes and chops him up for firewood.

"The Gift of the Magi"

William Sydney Porter had an unusual career as a writer, and it might never have happened if he hadn't been thrown in jail. He had done some newspaper writing, but it had never led to anything, so he worked in a Texas bank as a teller. An unexplained shortage led to charges of embezzlement against him. He was probably innocent, but he fled the country to avoid trial. He might have been safe, but his wife was dying and he returned to be with her. He was arrested and sent to jail for three years. To pass the time, he began writing. After he got out, he had his first collection of stories published in 1904. He was forty-two years old. In the last seven years of his life he wrote hundreds of stories, enough to fill fourteen volumes. The pseudonym which he chose, and which has become far more familiar than his own name, was O. Henry. The greatest popular strength of his stories was also their greatest weakness: the surprise ending. Because of these often contrived plot devices, critics refused to take his work seriously although the people loved them.

One of his most successful stories was "The Gift of the Magi," first published in 1905. Here the surprise ending was not a gratuitous plot twist, but the revelation and embodiment of the theme of the story. The plot is a very familiar one. Jim and Della live in the city and have almost no money. Christmas is coming, and Della worries how she will be able to afford a present for Jim. Finally she decides to sell the thing she loves most, her beautiful long hair, to get money to buy a silver chain for Jim's watch, which is his proudest possession. When she gives it to him, he reveals that he has sold his watch to buy a beautiful set of combs for her to wear in her hair.

The style of the story is mildly chatty, with many author's asides and a light air of cynicism. But the final point is deeply felt and beautifully expressed. O. Henry closes by saying, "The magi, as you know, were wise men—wonderfully wise men—who brought gifts to the

Babe in the manger. They invented the art of giving Christmas presents. Being wise, their gifts were no doubt wise ones, possibly bearing the privilege of exchange in case of duplication. And here I have lamely related to you the uneventful chronicle of two foolish children in a flat who most unwisely sacrificed for each other the greatest treasures of their house. But in a last word to the wise of these days let it be said that of all who give gifts these two were the wisest. Of all who give and receive gifts, such as they are wisest. Everywhere they are wisest. They are the magi."

Since its publication as a story, "The Gift of the Magi" has appeared in many forms. It has been done as a musical both off-Broadway and on television with Gordon MacRae and Sally Ann Howes. The American Ballet Theatre turned it into a ballet. And it appeared on film in 1952 starring Farley Granger and Jeanne Crain as one of five stories in O. Henry's Full House.

"The Other Wise Man"

American clergyman, author, and educator Henry van Dyke is chiefly known today for his two Christmas stories, "The First Christmas Tree" and "The Other Wise Man." "The First Christmas Tree" was merely a retelling of the legend of St. Boniface and how he replaced the sacred German tree with the fir tree of Christmas. His other story was written in 1896 and is a more original parable of Christmas.

In far-off Persia, Artaban, a Wise Man, observes a new star in the heavens, a star he has been waiting for. He believes the star signifies the coming of the newborn King and Savior. Selling all his possessions, he buys three precious jewels: a sapphire, a ruby, and a pearl. He will give these to the newborn King. He hears of the other Wise Men and sets out to join them. On the first leg of his journey, he comes upon a sick traveler and cares for the man. Because of this, he arrives at the place where he expected to meet the other Magi too late. Going on to Bethlehem alone, he sees neither the other Wise

Men nor the Christ Child. Grieved, Artaban begins a lifelong search for the King of Kings. His gifts—the sapphire, the ruby, and the pearl —are one by one used to help the poor and the sick. Artaban is an old man when he comes to Jerusalem on the fateful day of Christ's crucifixion. An earthquake strikes the city as Jesus dies, and Artaban is seriously injured. As his life slips away, a gentle voice comes to his ears: "Inasmuch as you have done it unto one of the least of these my brethren, you have done it unto me." He knows that he has met his Lord.

The Second Shepherds' Play

All of our modern theater, strange as it may seem, grew out of the liturgical church service of the Middle Ages. The question-and-answer format between priest and congregation was almost a form of drama itself, and at some point actual dialogue was added to bring the biblical stories more to life. The first instance of this was at Easter. It told how the women who came to find Jesus in the tomb were met instead by an angel who asked whom they sought and told them He was not there, but was risen. This simple three-line exchange was the beginning of modern drama.

This acting out of biblical stories became very popular. It got more and more elaborate until whole plays were being performed, first at the altar and then at the porch of the church. As the subject matter broadened and the natural rough humor of the times began to creep in, the plays were moved out of the church entirely, into the streets. There were great festival days on which whole cycles of plays were given, sometimes as many as forty-eight or more. These plays told everything from the creation of the world and the flood down to the more modern miracles of favorite saints. The plays were performed by the different guilds of tradesmen in the town. Each guild had its own play; for instance, the shipbuilders' guild might do the story of Noah's Ark. Every year the same guild would do the same play. The plays were mounted on wagons so that they could be taken through the streets of the town. Thus, by sitting in one place, one could behold the whole history of the world in a single day.

Most of these plays are lost to us now, but several complete or near-complete cycles have survived, and one of them seems to be the work of a master. This is the Wakefield Cycle, from Yorkshire, England. It contains the Christmas masterpiece *The Second Shepherds' Play*. This work was written around 1385, which means that the language is extremely archaic. There are, however, many good modern versions and the work is well worth reading and performing. The blending of honest good humor and devotion is extraordinary. (It is the "Second" Shepherds' Play because there was another play about shepherds in the cycle.)

Three shepherds are tending their herds on a bitter cold night. They grumble and complain amusingly. Along comes Mak, a shepherd with a bad reputation. He complains that he has been given a bad deal, that no one ever trusts him. They trust him, but make him lie down between them as they go to sleep, just in case. Mak uses a spell to keep them asleep and steals a sheep, which he takes home to his wife, Gill. When the three shepherds come looking, they bundle up the sheep to look like a newborn baby. Gill groans as if she has just finished labor, and Mak sings a lullaby. The shepherds can't find their sheep anywhere about the hut, although they comment they never met with a more foul-smelling infant. Mak takes an oath that he doesn't have the sheep, saying, "If I have your sheep, may I eat my newborn son!" The shepherds are about to go away when they realize that they have been unneighborly in not offering any presents for the child. They go back and ask to see him. Mak tries to stop them, but they are insistent. The size of the baby's nose makes them suspicious. Mak claims the nose was broken, that's all. The shepherds give Mak a good bouncing in a blanket and go off. Suddenly an angel rises up and announces the birth of Christ. The three shepherds hurry to Bethlehem and give presents of cherries, a bird, and a ball to the newborn Babe. They go off singing happily in the cold night.

In a more sophisticated age, this juxtaposition of Mak's "son" with the Son of God would have been a blasphemous parody. But to the people of the Middle Ages it was perfectly natural for religion to spill over into everyday life. No one questioned how far it was to Bethlehem and no one saw anything wrong with laughing riotously at Mak's antics and a moment later standing in awe at the side of the cradle. Jesus was a part of their lives, and He could join in their pleasures. Simple happiness and simple devotion blend beautifully in this little masterwork from the Middle Ages.

Dickens

After the period of prohibition imposed by the Puritans, Christmas returned to England with the Restoration. But it was not Christmas as it had once been. The splendor was gone out of it. The elaborate feastings and pageantry passed out of favor and more and more Christmas became a quiet celebration in individual homes. This was a good thing in that it helped eliminate the abuses of Christmas, but with them also many fine old traditions began to disappear.

The Industrial Revolution further hastened what looked like the imminent death of the old-style Christmas with its innocent feasting and games, plum pudding and mince pie, evergreens and mistletoe. The motto of the time was "Work!" and the poor were too oppressed to celebrate, while those who were well off did not want to waste the time and money. Christmas became a workday.

A number of writers still wrote in praise of Christmas, but their writing had a flavor of nostalgia over the all-but-gone past. They spoke of what Christmas had once been, not what it now was or what it could become. This attitude has endured to the present day and is part of the bittersweet pleasure of all Christmas celebrations: no matter how delightful the present day, it can never hold a candle to those brisk Christmas mornings of memory.

One writer believed that Christmas could still be alive and well— and almost single-handedly made it so. Charles Dickens felt what Christmas could do for himself, and he set about doing the same for the rest of the world.

His first blow struck for the cause was a short sketch called "A Christmas Dinner," which described the conviviality of a family as it

257

gathers around the Christmas table. The past is forgiven and forgotten as all join in the spirit of the season.

Dickens' next story on the subject will sound more familiar. It tells of an unpleasant, cranky type who is annoyed by other people's cheerfulness on Christmas Eve. He is taken by supernatural beings to view scenes of family happiness and goodness, which convince him of the error of his ways and cause him to reform when he awakens the next day. Sound familiar? You may be surprised to learn that this story was not Dickens' best-known work but was a short story called "The Goblins Who Stole a Sexton," contained in *The Pickwick Papers*. The story is an entertaining one, but it does not capture the imagination because the Christmas setting is almost incidental to the tale. It is merely a ghost story told around the fire at an old-time Christmas festivity. The description of the other Christmas games and frivolities is much more delightful and points more to what was to come in his later writings. Dickens wrote rhapsodically of the time of year which was so important to him:

> Christmas was close at hand, in all his bluff and hearty honesty; it was the season of hospitality, merriment, and open-heartedness; the old year was preparing, like an ancient philosopher, to call his friends around him and amidst the sound of feasting and revelry to pass gently and calmly away. . . .
>
> And numerous indeed are the hearts to which Christmas brings a brief season of happiness and enjoyment. How many families whose members have been dispersed and scattered far and wide, in the restless struggles of life, are then reunited, and meet once again in that happy state of companionship and mutual goodwill which is a source of such pure and unalloyed delight, and one so incompatible with the cares and sorrows of the world that the religious belief of the most civilized nations and the rude traditions of the roughest savages alike number it among the first joys of a future condition of existence provided for the blest and happy! How many old recollections and how many dormant sympathies does Christmas time awaken!
>
> We write these words now, many miles distant from the spot at which, year after year, we met on that day, a merry and joyous circle. Many of the hearts that throbbed so gaily then have ceased to beat; many of the looks that shone so brightly then have ceased to glow; the hands we grasped have grown cold; the eyes we sought have hid

their lustre in the grave; and yet the old house, the room, the merry voices and smiling faces, the jest, the laugh, the most minute and trivial circumstances connected with those happy meetings, crowd upon our mind at each recurrence of the season, as if the last assemblage had been but yesterday! Happy, happy Christmas, that can win us back to the delusions of our childish days, that can recall to the old man the pleasures of his youth, that can transport the sailor and the traveller, thousands of miles away, back to his own fireside and his quiet home!

Seven years passed before Dickens found his fullest expression of the Christmas spirit. The year 1843 was not a good one for him. He had an unparalleled popular success with his previous works, *Pickwick Papers*, *Nicholas Nickleby*, *Oliver Twist*, *The Old Curiosity Shop*, and *Barnaby Rudge*. But in 1843 he was in the midst of writing and publishing serially his new novel *Martin Chuzzlewit*. It was not well received, yet he had to keep turning out the monthly installments and trying desperately to regain the public's favor before his financial situation became impossible. He was also in a mental turmoil over the terrible plight of the poor. During October 1843 he went to Manchester to make several speeches appealing for aid to the working class. While he walked the streets with these images in his mind an idea came to him. He modeled it roughly on the "The Goblins Who Stole a Sexton" and decked it out with details from his own life, and he worked on it feverishly while still writing *Martin Chuzzlewit*. He finished it and took it to his publisher by the second week in November. Because he wanted it to be of the first quality, he worked on the design of the book himself, selecting the illustrator, the bindings, and the paper, having the illustrations hand-tinted, and keeping the price as low as possible so that his work could be afforded by the people he aimed it at. A few days before Christmas the new little book appeared.

Financially it was not a success. Dickens had succeeded too well in keeping down the price of the book. Although it sold well, he made very little from it in its initial sales. He also had to suffer the indignity of seeing many cheaply made pirated versions of his work appear on both sides of the Atlantic. The copyright laws were not very strict then, and almost anyone could steal a writer's work. Dickens brought suit against one such pirate. This unethical publishing firm defended its version of Dickens' story by saying that it had made "very considerable improvements." Dickens won the suit, but the firm's bankruptcy left him with no settlement and court costs to pay.

It took Dickens a good while to realize just how completely he had succeeded even though he had not made much money. He wrote other Christmas books, one each year. In 1844 he wrote *The Chimes*, of which he said, "I believe I have written a tremendous book, and knocked the Carol out of the field." He was wrong. Nothing he or any other writer would ever conceive would knock the *Carol* out of the field. A *Christmas Carol* remains to this day, next to the Nativity itself, the best-known and best-loved Christmas story of all. Scrooge has passed into the language as a synonym for "miser," and the Ghosts of Christmas Past, Present, and Future have haunted us all. Christmas has bloomed again as a time to think of one's fellow man and to strive to deserve the ultimate compliment that is paid to the reformed Scrooge:

> . . . and it was always said of him, that he knew how to keep Christmas well, if any man alive possessed the knowledge. May that be truly said of us, and all of us! And so, as Tiny Tim observed, God Bless Us, Every One!

A *Christmas Carol* was the ultimate embodiment of what Dickens called "the Carol philosophy," that Christmas was "a good time: a kind, forgiving, charitable, pleasant time: the only time I know of, in the long calendar of the year, when men and women seem by one consent to open their shut-up hearts freely, and to think of other people below them as if they really were fellow-passengers to the grave, and not another race of creatures bound on other journeys."

There is a famous story, which may not be true but which should be, about a poor costermonger's girl in Drury Lane who was told of Dickens' funeral. "Dickens dead?" she asked tearfully. "Then will Father Christmas die too?"

MARLEY

The first spirit to visit Scrooge is Marley's ghost, Marley having been his partner in business until his death. Dickens selected the name of this ghostly and far-from-silent partner in an amusing fashion. At a St. Patrick's Day party in the year in which he wrote and published *A Christmas Carol*, Dickens met a doctor who practiced medicine in Piccadilly. Knowing that Dickens peopled his stories with unusual names, this doctor suggested that his own family name was quite unusual: Marley. According to the story, Dickens merely replied, "Your name will be a household word before the year is out." Thus the spirit of the forgotten Dr. Miles Marley is aroused every year by the clanking chains of his namesake, the late Jacob Marley.

TINY TIM

In came little Bob, the father, with at least three feet of comforter exclusive of the fringe, hanging down before him; and his thread-bare clothes darned up and brushed, to look seasonable; and Tiny Tim upon his shoulder. Alas for Tiny Tim, he bore a little crutch, and had his limbs supported by an iron frame! . . .

"And how did little Tim behave?" asked Mrs. Cratchit. . . .

"As good as gold," said Bob, "and better. Somehow he gets thoughtful sitting by himself so much, and thinks the strangest things you ever heard. He told me, coming home, that he hoped the people saw him in church, because he was a cripple, and it might be pleasant to them to remember upon Christmas Day, who made lame beggars walk and blind men see."

The Spirit of Christmas Yet to Come shows Scrooge that same happy Cratchit household as it will be in the future. But there is one difference, "a vacant seat in the poor chimney corner, and a crutch without an owner, carefully preserved."

"But however and whenever we part from one another, I am sure we shall none of us forget poor Tiny Tim—shall we—or this first parting that there was among us?"

"Never, father!" cried they all.

"And I know," said Bob, "I know, my dears, that when we recollect how patient and how mild he was; although he was a little, little child; we shall not quarrel easily among ourselves, and forget poor Tiny Tim in doing it."

"No, never, father!" they all cried again.

"I am very happy," said little Bob, "I am very happy!"

Mrs. Cratchit kissed him, his daughters kissed him, the two young Cratchits kissed him, and Peter and himself shook hands. Spirit of Tiny Tim, thy childish essence was from God!

We all know that Tiny Tim did not die, that the converted Scrooge helped to save him. Tiny Tim is one of the most familiar names in popular English literature, and it is difficult to imagine a Christmas season without Tiny Tim in one of his many movie or TV incarnations waving his tiny crutch and crying "God bless us, every one!" Yet the original manuscripts of *A Christmas Carol* show that Tiny Tim was to be called Little Fred. Most of us would agree that the name change was a wise one. It is difficult to hold back the tears at the thought of Tiny Tim; it is hard to imagine being anything but annoyed at someone named Little Fred.

The inspiration for the character of Tiny Tim probably came from a visit to Dickens' sister Fanny and her invalid son Harry Burnett in 1843, the year that the book was published. Unlike Tiny Tim, Harry Burnett did not find a second father and live happily ever after; he died while still a child.

THE WIT AND WISDOM OF SCROOGE

"A merry Christmas, uncle! God save you!" cried a cheerful voice. It was the voice of Scrooge's nephew, who came upon him so quickly that this was the first intimation he had of his approach.

"Bah!" said Scrooge, "Humbug!"

He had so heated himself with rapid walking in the fog and frost, this nephew of Scrooge's, that he was all in a glow; his face was ruddy and handsome; his eyes sparkled, and his breath smoked again.

"Christmas a humbug, uncle!" said Scrooge's nephew. "You don't mean that, I am sure."

"I do," said Scrooge. "Merry Christmas! what right have you to be merry? what reason have you to be merry? You're poor enough."

"Come, then," returned the nephew gaily. "What right have you to be dismal? what reason have you to be morose? You're rich enough."

Scrooge having no better answer ready on the spur of the moment, said, "Bah!" again; and followed it up with "Humbug."

"Don't be cross, uncle," said the nephew.

"What else can I be," returned the uncle, "when I live in such a world of fools as this? Merry Christmas! Out upon merry Christmas! What's Christmas time to you but a time for paying bills without money; a time for finding yourself a year older, and not an hour richer; a time for balancing your books and having every item in 'em through a round dozen of months presented dead against you? If I could work my will," said Scrooge, indignantly, "every idiot who goes about with 'Merry Christmas,' on his lips, should be boiled with his own pudding, and buried with a stake of holly through his heart. He should!"

"At this festive season of the year, Mr. Scrooge," said the gentleman, taking up a pen, "it is more than usually desirable that we should make some slight provision for the poor and destitute, who suffer greatly at the present time. Many thousands are in want of common necessaries; hundreds of thousands are in want of common comforts, sir."

"Are there no prisons?" asked Scrooge.

"Plenty of prisons," said the gentleman, laying down the pen again.

"And the Union workhouses?" demanded Scrooge. "Are they still in operation?"

"They are. Still," returned the gentleman, "I wish I could say they were not."

"The Treadmill and the Poor Law are in full vigour, then?" said Scrooge.

"Both very busy, sir."

"Oh! I was afraid, from what you said at first, that something had occurred to stop them in their useful course," said Scrooge. "I'm very glad to hear it."

"Under the impression that they scarcely furnish Christian cheer of mind or body to the multitude," returned the gentleman, "a few of us are endeavouring to raise a fund to buy the Poor some meat and drink, and means of warmth. We choose this time, because it is a time, of all others, when Want is keenly felt, and Abundance rejoices. What shall I put you down for?"

"Nothing!" Scrooge replied.

"You wish to be anonymous?"

"I wish to be left alone," said Scrooge. "Since you ask me what I wish, gentlemen, that is my answer. I don't make merry myself at Christmas, and I can't afford to make idle people merry. I help to support the establishments I have mentioned: they cost enough: and those who are badly off must go there."

"Many can't go there; and many would rather die."

"If they would rather die," said Scrooge, "they had better do it, and decrease the surplus population."

"A Merry Christmas to us all, my dears. God bless us!"

Which all the family re-echoed.

"God bless us every one!" said Tiny Tim, the last of all.

He sat very close to his father's side, upon his little stool. Bob held his withered little hand in his, as if he loved the child, and wished to keep him by his side, and dreaded that he might be taken from him.

"Spirit," said Scrooge, with an interest he had never felt before, "tell me if Tiny Tim will live."

"I see a vacant seat," replied the Ghost, "in the poor chimney corner, and a crutch without an owner, carefully preserved. If these shadows remain unaltered by the Future, the child will die."

"No, no," said Scrooge. "Oh no, kind Spirit! say he will be spared."

"If these shadows remain unaltered by the Future, none other of my race," returned the Ghost, "will find him here. What then? If he be like to die, he had better do it, and decrease the surplus population."

Scrooge hung his head to hear his own words quoted by the Spirit, and was overcome with penitence and grief.

But he was early at the office next morning. Oh he was early there. If he could only be there first, and catch Bob Cratchit coming late! That was the thing he had set his heart upon.

And he did it; yes he did! The clock struck nine. No Bob. A quarter past. No Bob. He was full eighteen minutes and a half behind his time. Scrooge sat with his door wide open, that he might see him come into the Tank.

His hat was off, before he opened the door; his comforter too. He was on his stool in a jiffy; driving away with his pen, as if he were trying to overtake nine o'clock.

"Hallo!" growled Scrooge, in his accustomed voice as near as he could feign it. "What do you mean by coming here at this time of day?"

"I'm very sorry, sir," said Bob. "I *am* behind my time."

"You are?" repeated Scrooge. "Yes. I think you are. Step this way, if you please."

"It's only once a year, sir," pleaded Bob, appearing from the Tank. "It shall not be repeated. I was making rather merry yesterday, sir."

"Now, I'll tell you what my friend," said Scrooge, "I am not going to stand this sort of thing any longer. And therefore," he continued, leaping from his stool, and giving Bob such a dig in the waistcoat that he staggered back into the Tank again: "and therefore I am about to raise your salary!"

Bob trembled, and got a little nearer to the ruler. He had a momentary idea of knocking Scrooge down with it; holding him; and calling to the people in the court for help and a strait-waistcoat.

"A merry Christmas, Bob!" said Scrooge, with an earnestness that could not be mistaken, as he clapped him on the back. "A merrier Christmas, Bob, my good fellow, than I have given you, for many a year! I'll raise your salary, and endeavour to assist your struggling family, and we will discuss your affairs this very afternoon, over a Christmas bowl of smoking bishop, Bob! Make up the fires, and buy another coal-scuttle before you dot another i, Bob Cratchit!"

Scrooge was better than his word. He did it all, and infinitely more; and to Tiny Tim, who did NOT die, he was a second father. He became as good a friend, as good a master, and as good a man, as the good old city knew, or any other good old city, town or borough, in the good old world.

DICKENS ON *A CHRISTMAS CAROL*

Charles Dickens, speaking about himself in the third person, described the composition and subsequent reception of *A Christmas Carol* in a letter to a friend:

"Over which *Christmas Carol* Charles Dickens wept and laughed and wept again, and excited himself in a most extraordinary manner in the composition; and thinking whereof he walked about the black streets of London, fifteen and twenty miles many a night when all the sober folks had gone to bed. Its success is most prodigious. And by every post all manner of strangers write all manner of letters to him about their homes and hearths, and how this same *Carol* is read aloud there, and kept on a little shelf by itself. Indeed, it is the greatest success, as I am told, that this ruffian and rascal has ever achieved.

A REVIEW OF *A CHRISTMAS CAROL*

The great English novelist William Makepeace Thackeray reviewed *A Christmas Carol* in February 1844, just a few months after its initial publication. He was so inspired and influenced by Dickens' work that he would later publish his own series of Christmas books. His comments stand as an enduring tribute to Dickens and an unusual example of graciousness from one writer to another:

> Who can listen to objections regarding such a book as this? It seems to me a national benefit, and to every man or woman who reads it a personal kindness. The last two people I heard speak of it were women; neither knew the other, or the author, and both said, by way of criticism, "God bless him!" A Scotch philosopher, who nationally does not keep Christmas, on reading the book, sent out for a turkey, and asked two friends to dine—this is a fact! Many men were known to sit down after perusing it, and write off letters to their friends, not about business, but out of their fulness of heart, and to wish old acquaintances a happy Christmas. Had the book appeared a fortnight earlier, all the prize cattle would have been gobbled up in pure love and friendship, Epping denuded of sausages, and not a turkey left in Norfolk. . . .
>
> As for Tiny Tim, there is a certain passage in the book regarding that young gentleman, about which a man should hardly venture to speak in print or in public (any more than he would of any other affections of his private heart). There is not a reader in England but that little creature will be a bond of union between the author and him; and he will say of Charles Dickens, as the woman just now, "God bless him!" What a feeling is this for a writer to be able to inspire, and what a reward to reap.

A *CHRISTMAS CAROL* IN OTHER MEDIA

A *Christmas Carol* was published just before Christmas, 1843; in less than two months, there were, not one, but two different stage adaptations being presented in London theaters. (Copyright laws being what they were, Dickens received nothing for any of the adaptations of his work, except his own reading version, which he performed widely on his lecture tours.) Since that time, *A Christmas Carol* has been adapted into every form imaginable: movies, TV, radio, records, cartoons, musical comedies, and marionettes. It must stand as one of the most frequently adapted works in the history of literature.

The number of play versions of the story is impossible to estimate. It has probably been performed by every church group and amateur little theater in the English-speaking world. The local library will yield up dozens of current adaptations for such groups. No single stage version has ever gained such widespread acceptance as to become the definitive version, but all follow the story more or less accurately.

The movies picked up Dickens' story early in their career. The first version was produced in 1908, and there were at least four more silent films based on *A Christmas Carol* before the introduction of sound in 1929. The year 1935 saw the first sound version, and 1938 produced the movie starring Reginald Owen, the earliest version still current on TV screens. This adaptation rather emphasizes the sentimentality of the story and plays down Dickens' emphasis on the horrors of poverty. Scrooge himself is nicer than he might be.

The best-known and probably best film version is the 1951 production starring Alastair Sim. This movie follows Dickens' book very closely and gives full weight to the more grotesque scenes, such as the ragpickers arguing over the belongings of the dead Scrooge in the vision of Christmas yet to come. The performance by Sim is a joy to behold. He captures both the dried-up bitterness of old Scrooge and the irrepressible, manic joy of Scrooge reborn.

In 1970 Albert Finney starred as the miser in *Scrooge*, an elaborate color musical version. The only major rewards in viewing this film are

Finney's performance and the appearance of Sir Alec Guinness and Dame Edith Evans as two of the ghostly visitors.

During the depression, Lionel Barrymore was famous for his interpretation of Scrooge on a yearly radio broadcast, which was also released on records. He might have done a truly memorable film performance were it not for the crippling illness that left him in a wheelchair for the rest of his life. Radio versions have also featured Alec Guinness and Franklin Delano Roosevelt. On records, Scrooge has been interpreted by Laurence Olivier, Ralph Richardson, Basil Rathbone, and Ronald Colman. Television has had numerous adaptations, including one for marionettes in 1948. A 1955 musical version on CBS-TV featured a libretto by Pulitzer Prize-winning playwright Maxwell Anderson, Fredric March as Scrooge, and Basil Rathbone as Marley. A 1956 production was narrated by Vincent Price. In the realm of cartoons, Walt Disney produced a version featuring mice in the leading roles, and *Mr. Magoo's Christmas Carol* has become a seasonal staple on TV.

There was even an operatic version of *A Christmas Carol*. It was composed for the British Broadcasting Corporation in 1963.

Of all the film versions of *A Christmas Carol*, only one ever won an Oscar. Can you guess which one? If you guess a film that features mere flesh and blood, you aren't in the spirit of the thing. A 1970 cartoon version with the voices of Alastair Sim and Michael Redgrave won the Oscar for best animated feature. Richard Williams produced this very imaginative film by animating the original drawings which John Leech had provided for the first publication of Dickens' immortal, often-imitated classic.

Washington Irving

When Charles Dickens wrote his Christmas pieces, there was another author whose writing on Christmas he probably had in mind. Two years before the composition of *A Christmas Carol*, Dickens wrote to this author: "There is no living writer, and there are very few among the dead, whose approbation I should feel so proud to earn. And with everything you have written, upon my shelves, and in my thoughts, and in my heart of hearts, I may honestly and truly say so. . . . I should like to travel with you, astride the last of the coaches, down to Bracebridge Hall." The author he addressed was the American Washington Irving, and he was referring to that writer's famous story of the Christmas celebration at the mythical home of an English squire, Bracebridge Hall. This sketch was published in 1819 in *The Sketch Book of Geoffrey Crayon*, which also contained Irving's most famous story, that of the Headless Horseman in "The Legend of Sleepy Hollow." The story of Bracebridge Hall, with its celebration of all the antique customs, was a first reminder to the British people of the glorious traditions they were in great danger of allowing to fall into total ruin. It kept smoldering the coals that would be blown into glorious life a few years later by the literary bellows that was Charles Dickens. Let us go down by coach with Irving and Dickens to see how Old Christmas may be truly kept.

The dinner was served up in the great hall, where the squire always held his Christmas banquet. A blazing crackling fire of logs had been heaped on to warm the spacious apartment, and the flame went sparkling and wreathing up the wide-mouthed chimney. . . .
We were ushered into this banquetting scene with the sound of minstrelsy; the old harper being seated on a stool beside the fireplace, and twanging the roast beef of old England, with a vast deal more power than melody. Never did Christmas board display a more goodly and gracious assemblage of countenances; those who were not handsome were, at least, happy; and happiness is a rare improver of your hard-favoured visage. The parson said grace, which was not a short familiar one, such as is commonly addressed to the deity, in these unceremonious days; but a long, courtly, well-worded one, of the ancient school. There was now a pause, as if something was expected, when suddenly the Butler entered the hall, with some degree of bustle; he was attended by a servant on each side with a large wax light, and bore a silver dish, on which was an enormous pig's head, decorated with rosemary, with a lemon in its mouth, which was placed with great formality at the head of the table. The moment this pageant made its appearance, the harper struck up a flourish; at the conclusion of which

the young Oxonian, on receiving a hint from the squire, gave, with an air of the most comic gravity, an old carol, the first verse of which was as follows:

> *Caput apri defero*
> *Reddens Laudes Domino.*
> The boar's head in hand bring I,
> With garlands gay and rosemary.
> I pray you all synge merily,
> *Qui estis in convivio. . . .*

When the cloth was removed, the butler brought in a huge silver vessel of rare and curious workmanship, which he placed before the squire. . . . The old gentleman's whole countenance beamed with a serene look of in-dwelling delight, as he stirred this mighty bowl. Having raised it to his lips, with a hearty wish of a merry Christmas to all present, he sent it brimming round the board, for every one to follow his example according to the primitive custom; pronouncing it "the ancient fountain of good fellowship, where all hearts met together." . . .

After the dinner table was removed, the hall was given up to the younger members of the family, who, prompted to all kind of noisy mirth by the Oxonian and Master Simon, made its old walls ring with their merriment as they played at romping games. I delight in witnessing the gambols of children, and particularly at this happy holiday-season, and could not help stealing out of the drawing room on hearing one of their peals of laughter. . . .

The door suddenly flew open, and a whimsical train came trooping into the room, that might almost have been mistaken for the breaking up of the court of Fairy. That indefatigable spirit, Master Simon, in the faithful discharge of his duties as lord of misrule, had conceived the idea of a Christmas mummery, or masqueing; and having called in to his assistance the Oxonian and the young officer, who were equally ripe for any thing that should occasion romping and merriment, they had carried it into instant effect. The old housekeeper had been consulted; the antique clothes presses and wardrobes rummaged and made to yield up the reliques of finery that had not seen the light for several generations; the younger part of the company had been privately convened from the parlour and hall, and the whole had been bedizzened out, into a burlesque imitation of an antique masque.

Master Simon led the van as "ancient Christmas," quaintly apparel'd in short cloak and ruff, and a hat that might have served for a village steeple, from under which, his nose curved boldly forth, with a frost bitten bloom that seemed the very trophy of a December blast. He was accompanied by the blue-eyed romp, dished up as "Dame mince pie," in the venerable magnificence of faded brocade, long stomacher, peaked hat, and high heeled shoes. The young officer figured in genuine Kendal Green as Robin Hood; the fair Julia in a pretty rustic dress as Maid Marian. The rest of the train had been metamorphosed in various ways; the girls trussed up in the finery of their great grandmothers, and the striplings bewhiskered with burnt cork, and fantastically arrayed to support the characters of Roast Beef, Plum Porridge, and other worthies celebrated in ancient masqueings. The whole was under the control of the Oxonian, in the appropriate character of Misrule. . . .

It was inspiring to see wild-eyed frolick among the chills and glooms of winter, and old age throwing off its apathy, and catching once more the freshness of youthful enjoyment. I felt an interest in the scene, also, from the consideration that these fleeting customs were posting fast into oblivion; and that this was, perhaps, the only family in England in which the whole of them were still punctiliously observed. There was a quaintness, too, mingled with all this revelry, that gave it a peculiar zest; it was suited to the time and place; and as the old manor house almost reeled with mirth and wassail, it seemed echoing back the joviality of long-departed years.

Poetry

Christmas has inspired some of our greatest poets. John Milton, T. S. Eliot, Robert Browning, and Sir Walter Scott all penned works in honor of the joyous season; so did Ogden Nash, for that matter. Christmas is one of those subjects that almost everyone has to write about eventually. This makes the realm of Christmas poetry a rather large one. Entire books have been devoted to the subject. Therefore, we will not attempt to cover the whole field, but will rather offer some samples of the delights to be found in this particularly evergreen branch of literature.

Christmas

Leigh Hunt, 1836

Christmas comes! He comes, he comes,
Ushered with a rain of plums;
Hollies in the window greet him;
Schools come driving post to meet him;
Gifts precede him, bells proclaim him,
Every mouth delights to name him; . . .
And he has a million eyes
Of fire, and eats a million pies,
And is very merry and wise;
Very wise and very merry,
And loves a kiss beneath the berry. . . .

O plethora of beef and bliss!
Monkish feaster, sly of kiss!
Southern soul in body Dutch!
Glorious time of great Too-Much!

Too much heat, and too much noise,
Too much babblement of boys;
Too much eating, too much drinking,
Too much ev'rything but thinking;
Solely bent to laugh and stuff,
And trample upon base Enough;
Oh, right is thy instinctive praise
Of the wealth of Nature's ways.
Right thy most unthrifty glee,
And pious thy mince-piety! . . .

Shakespeare and Christmas

Some say that ever 'gainst that season comes
Wherein our Saviour's birth is celebrated,
The bird of dawning singeth all night long:
And then, they say, no spirit dare stir abroad;
The nights are wholesome; then no planets strike,
No fairy takes, nor witch hath power to charm,
So hallow'd and so gracious is the time.

Shakespeare

It is a curious fact that this passage from *Hamlet* is the only one devoted to the topic of Christmas in all of the writings of Shakespeare. The great poet who dealt so completely with all the emotions of humanity for some reason was uninterested in that most joyous season of the year. He uses the word "Christmas" only three times in all the mass of his works, each time to describe a time of year only, not to talk about the day itself.

The humorous writer Max Beerbohm offered an amusing reason for this omission. He asserted that Anne Hathaway, Shakespeare's wife, was born on Christmas Day. It is known that the marriage was not the happiest, as was evidenced by the famous bequest in Shakespeare's will leaving Anne Hathaway the "second-best bed." Did the

273

Bard have his own painfully personal reason for not wanting to think about a time of year that gave him little cause for rejoicing? Behind every great man is a woman; perhaps that's why Shakespeare wrote so many tragedies.

A Christmas Carol

Christina Rossetti

Before the paling of the stars,
Before the winter morn,
Before the earliest cock-crow
Jesus Christ was born:
Born in a stable,
Cradled in a manger,
In the world His hands had made
Born a stranger.

Priest and king lay fast asleep
In Jerusalem,
Young and old lay fast asleep
In crowded Bethlehem:
Saint and angel, ox and ass,
Kept a watch together,
Before the Christmas daybreak
In the winter weather.

Jesus on His mother's breast
In the stable cold,
Spotless Lamb of God was He,
Shepherd of the fold:
Let us kneel with Mary maid,
With Joseph bent and hoary,
With saint and angel, ox and ass,
To hail the King of Glory.

A Christmas Carroll

In this seventeenth-century poem George Wither happily describes the
boisterous joy of Christmas in that long-gone era.

So, now is come our joyfulst FEAST;
Let ever man be jolly.
Each Roome, with Ivie leave is drest;
And every Post, with Holly.
Though some Churles at our mirth repine,
Round your foreheads Garlands twine,
Drowne sorrow in a Cup of Wine.
And let us all be merry.

Now, all our Neighbours Chimneys smoke,
And CHRISTMAS blocks are burning;
Their Ovens, they with bakt-meats choke,
And all their spits are turning.
Without the doore, let sorrow lie:
And, if for cold, it hap to die,
We'll bury't in a CHRISTMAS Pie.
And evermore be merry.

Now, every LAD is wondrous trim,
And no man minds his Labour.
Our Lasses have provided them,
A Bag-pipe, and a Tabor.
Young men, and Mayds, and Girles & Boyes.
Give life, to one anothers Joyes:
And, you anon shall by their noyse,
Percieve that they are merry.

The Client now his suit forbeares,
The Prisoners heart is eased,
The Debtor drinks away his cares,
And, for the time is pleased.

Though others purses be more fat,
Why should we pine or grieve at that?
HANG SORROW, CARE WILL KILL A CAT.
And therefore let's be merry.

The Bells

In the first section of his poems *The Bells*, Edgar Allan Poe describes the sound of the sleigh or sledge bells that are such an important part of our nostalgic Christmas sounds.

Hear the sledges with the bells,
Silver bells!
What a world of merriment their melody foretells!
How they tinkle, tinkle, tinkle,
In the icy air of night!
While the stars that oversprinkle
All the heavens seem to twinkle
With a crystalline delight;
Keeping time, time, time,
In a sort of Runic rhyme,
To the tintinnabulation that so musically wells
From the bells, bells, bells, bells,
Bells, bells, bells—
From the jingling and the tinkling of the bells.

Besides A *Christmas Carol in Prose*, as Dickens' work is more completely known, Charles Dickens actually wrote one Christmas carol. It was published in the famous Christmas chapter of *The Pickwick Papers*, and later set to the tune of "Old King Carol" and published in a songbook.

A CHRISTMAS CAROL

I care not for Spring; on his fickle wing
Let the blossoms and buds be borne;
He woos them amain with his treacherous rain,
And he scatters them ere the morn.
An inconstant elf, he knows not himself,
Nor his own changing mind an hour,
He'll smile in your face, and, with wry grimace,
He'll wither your youngest flower.

Let the Summer sun to his bright home run,
He shall never be sought by me;
When he's dimmed by a cloud I can laugh aloud,
And care not how sulky he be!
For his darling child is the madness wild
That sports in fierce fever's train;
And when love is too strong, it don't last long,
As many have found to their pain.

A mild harvest night, by the tranquil light
Of the modest and gentle moon,
Has a far sweeter sheen, for me, I ween,
Than the broad and unblushing noon.
But every leaf awakens my grief,
As it lieth beneath the tree;
So let Autumn air be never so fair,
It by no means agrees with me.

But my song I troll out, for CHRISTMAS stout,
The hearty, the true, and the bold;
A bumper I drain, and with might and main
Give three cheers for this Christmas old!
We'll usher him in with a merry din
That shall gladden his joyous heart,
And we'll keep him up, while there's bite or sup,
And in fellowship good, we'll part.

In his fine honest pride, he scorns to hide
One jot of his hard-weather scars;

They're no disgrace, for there's much the same trace
On the cheeks of our bravest tars.
Then again I sing till the roof doth ring,
And it echoes from wall to wall—
To the stout old wight, fair welcome to-night,
As the King of the Seasons all!

As in most of his Christmas writings, Dickens is not concerned with the specifically religious nature of the holiday but with the cheerfulness and good feeling between people. Also, Christmas to him is not just a day but an entire season, just like spring, summer, and autumn in the other stanzas. His overflow of fellow-feeling could not be confined to a mere day.

Christmas Night of '62

William G. McCabe
In the Army of Northern Virginia, 1862

The wintry blast goes wailing by,
The snow is falling overhead;
I hear the lonely sentry's tread,
And distant watch-fires light the sky.

Dim forms go flitting through the gloom;
The soldiers cluster round the blaze
To talk of other Christmas days,
And softly speak of home and home.

My sabre swinging overhead,
Gleams in the watch-fire's fitful glow,
While fiercely drives the blinding snow,
And memory leads me to the dead.

My thoughts go wandering to and fro,
Vibrating 'twixt the Now and Then;
I see the low-browed home agen,
The old hall wreathed with mistletoe.

And sweetly from the far-off years
Comes borne the laughter faint and low,
The voices of the Long Ago!
My eyes are wet with tender tears.

I feel agen the mother kiss,
I see agen the glad surprise
That lighted up the tranquil eyes
And brimmed them o'er with tears of bliss,

As, rushing from the old hall-door,
She fondly clasped her wayward boy—
Her face all radiant with the joy
She felt to see him home once more.

My sabre swinging on the bough
Gleams in the watch-fire's fitful glow,
While fiercely drives the blinding snow
Aslant upon my saddened brow.

Those cherished faces are all gone!
Asleep within the quiet graves
Where lies the snow in drifting waves,—
And I am sitting here alone.

There's not a comrade here to-night
But knows that loved ones far away
On bended knees this night will pray:
"God bring our darling from the fight."

But there are none to wish me back,
For me no yearning prayers arise.
The lips are mute and closed the eyes—
My home is in the bivouac.

A Visit from St. Nicholas

The most famous Christmas poem of all was not meant for publication, and if it had been up to its author, none of us would ever have heard of it. On the evening of December 23, 1822, the distinguished scholar Clement Clarke Moore recited for his children a little nothing he had composed. Some guests were permitted to listen to this charming but not-quite-dignified recitation. One of them copied the poem for her own pleasure. The following Christmas she sent the poem anonymously to the Troy *Sentinel* in New York, which published it on December 23, the anniversary of its composition. The editor included a note: "We know not to whom we are indebted for the description of that unwearied patron of children, but from whomever it may have come, we give thanks for it." All the world soon felt the same, but Moore felt it beneath the dignity of an author of classical verse and a publisher of sermons. It was not until 1844 that he allowed the poem to appear in his collected works, finally acknowledging his authorship.

Moore drew upon a number of sources for his description of the jolly gift-giver. The antecedents of his reindeer names may be seen in Gnasher and Cracker, the two goats who pulled the cart of Thor, the thunder god. More directly, Washington Irving had included St. Nicholas in his *Knickerbocker History*. But the children may have recognized someone more familiar around the house: the caretaker of the Moore home was a Dutchman named Jan Duyckinck. He was fat, jolly, and bewhiskered and was known for the old pipe whose stump he kept clenched in his teeth. As is so often the case, the world owes great thanks to this almost forgotten man, for without him there might never have been *A Visit from Saint Nicholas*.

'Twas the night before Christmas, when all through the house
Not a creature was stirring, not even a mouse;
The stockings were hung by the chimney with care,
In hopes that St. Nicholas soon would be there;

The children were nestled all snug in their beds,
While visions of sugar-plums danced in their heads;
And mamma in her kerchief and I in my cap
Had just settled our brains for a long winter's nap,
When out on the lawn there arose such a clatter,
I sprang from my bed to see what was the matter.
Away to the window I flew like a flash,
Tore open the shutters, and threw up the sash;
The moon, on the breast of the new-fallen snow,
Gave a lustre of midday to objects below;
When what to my wondering eyes should appear
But a miniature sleigh and eight tiny reindeer,
With a little old driver, so lively and quick,
I knew in a moment, it must be St. Nick.
More rapid than eagles his coursers they came,
And he whistled and shouted and called them by name:
"Now Dasher! now Dancer! now Prancer! now Vixen!
On, Comet! on, Cupid! on, Donder and Blitzen!
To the top of the porch! To the top of the wall!
Now, dash away, dash away, dash away, all!"
As dry leaves that before the wild hurricane fly,
When they meet with an obstacle, mount to the sky,
So up to the housetop the coursers they flew,
With the sleigh full of toys and St. Nicholas too.
And then, in a twinkling, I heard on the roof
The prancing and pawing of each little hoof.
As I drew in my head and was turning around,
Down the chimney St. Nicholas came with a bound.
He was dressed all in fur, from his head to his foot,
And his clothes were all tarnished with ashes and soot;
A bundle of toys he had flung on his back,
And he looked like a peddler just opening his pack.
His eyes: how they twinkled! his dimples: how merry!
His cheeks were like roses, his nose like a cherry;
His droll little mouth was drawn up like a bow,
And the beard on his chin was as white as the snow.
The stump of a pipe he held tight in his teeth,
And the smoke, it encircled his head like a wreath:
He had a broad face, and a little round belly,
That shook, when he laughed, like a bowl full of jelly;
He was chubby and plump, a right jolly old elf;

And I laughed, when I saw him, in spite of myself,
A wink of his eye and a twist of his head
Soon gave me to know I had nothing to dread.
He spoke not a word, but went straight to his work,
And filled all the stockings; then turned with a jerk,
And laying his finger aside of his nose,
And giving a nod, up the chimney he rose.
He sprang to his sleigh, to his team gave a whistle,
And away they all flew like the down of a thistle;
But I heard him exclaim, ere he drove out of sight,
"Happy Christmas to all, and to all a good-night!"

Did you read that? Did you find yourself saying the lines before you got to them on the page? Most of us are surprised to find that, out of all the great literature we are exposed to and even forced to memorize at some time or other in school, it is a silly little Christmas poem which has so imprinted its good cheer and fun upon our minds that it is the only work we can quote almost word for word.

Quickly, A QUIZ!

1. What were mamma and I wearing?

2. How fast were the reindeer?

3. How many reindeer have names starting with the letter *D*?

4. What were St. Nick's clothes made of?

5. How big was St. Nick?

6. How does he let the narrator know he was nothing to dread?

7. How does he get up chimneys?

8. How many times does he whistle in the whole poem?

9. Is he ever referred to as Santa Claus?

No peeking, we hope. If you can't have the honor system at Christmas, when can you have it?

ANSWERS:

1. *Mamma was in her kerchief and I was in my cap. Presumably they were both also in nightgowns, as it sounds much too chilly to be running around in nothing but a hat.*

2. *"More rapid than eagles."*

3. *Three: Dasher, Dancer, and Donder.*

4. *All of fur, "from his head to his foot."*

5. *Moore never specifically states how big St. Nick is, but his descriptions indicate that he is much smaller than the full size person we usually picture. His "miniature sleigh" is drawn by "tiny reindeer"; he is the "little old driver" with a "little round belly" and he is referred to as an "elf," which is usually pictured as smaller than a man.*

6. *By "a wink of his eye and a twist of his head." We don't quite see how this complicated maneuver is meant to be reassuring, but we suppose you had to be there.*

7. *By "laying his finger aside of his nose, and giving a nod." There is some principle at work here not yet known to science.*

8. *Twice.*

9. *No.*

How did you do on the test? How did you do on the earlier test, the one about the nativity stories in the Gospels? Does it make you feel strange to know that you are more familiar with *A Visit from St. Nicholas* than with the nativity story?

'Twas the night after Christmas, and all through the house
We were paying each one for our Yuletide carouse.
I felt in my tummy a burden like lead
And visions of tumors careered through my head.
Martha tumbled and tossed, at last breathed with a sob,
"I've got 'pendicitis—I'm sure of it, Bob." . . .
I swore about sunrise, "It's not worth the price.
Believe me, *next* Christmas we dine on boiled rice!"

> from *The Aftermath—December Twenty-sixth*
> by Julia Boynton Green

In 1929 humorist Ring Lardner sent out these Christmas greetings
to his friends.

> How utterly ridiculous you'd feel,
> How damned unpleasant,
> If you sent just a card to us
> And *we* sent *you* a present.
>
> In order that no such thing
> Can happen to you, comma,
> This card is all you'll get from Ring,
> His kiddies or their momma.

To Jesus on His Birthday

Edna St. Vincent Millay

For this your mother sweated in the cold,
For this you bled upon the bitter tree:
A yard of tinsel bought and sold;
A paper wreath; a day at home for me.
The merry bells ring out, the people kneel;
Up goes the man of God before the crowd;
With voice of honey and with eyes of steel
He drones your humble gospel to the proud.
Nobody listens. Less than the wind that blows
Are all your words to us you died to save.
Oh Prince of Peace! Oh Sharon's dewey rose!
How mute you lie within your vaulted grave.
 The stone the angel rolled away with tears
 Is back upon your mouth these thousand years.

They all were looking for a king
To slay their foes and lift them high;
Thou cam'st, a little baby thing
That made a woman cry.
    George Macdonald, *That Holy Thing*
    from *Paul Faber, Surgeon*

CHRISTMAS
on
FILM

The history of Christmas in the movies is somewhat difficult to trace because it is hard to determine exactly what is a Christmas movie. The simplest way to define it would be as a movie about the Nativity. If you define it that way, then there are almost no Christmas movies. The basic reason is that the story of Christ's birth is too short and doesn't have the necessary elements of plot and conflict. There were a few silent films as early as 1909 which dealt exclusively with the Nativity, but this was possible because movies were so much shorter then and did not have to have all the elements of good drama.

Other films set in Christ's time have included the nativity scene briefly as part of the story. Often this appears almost as a frozen picture with voice-over narration telling the story. Thus, movies such as King of Kings, The Greatest Story Ever Told, and Ben Hur deal briefly with the Nativity, but can hardly be considered Christmas movies.

Many other movies that are not really about Christmas use Christmas as a setting or background. This is an old writer's device. If you want to write a story in which something sad happens, the best way to do it is to set it at the happiest time you can think of. The contrast between the sad occurrence and the cheerful background make it all the more poignant. Thus the viewer must be prepared in dramatic movies when everyone sits down to a happy Christmas dinner. It probably means that news of a death is about to arrive, romance is about to sour, or the boat is about to sink.

One is sorely tempted to say that Christmas movies are the ones they show on TV at Christmastime.

Perhaps the best and only definition possible of a Christmas movie is that it takes as its theme some aspect of the Christmas spirit, be it Santa Claus, gift-giving, or the joy of family reunion. Let's look at the movies themselves before someone asks for a definition of Christmas spirit.

All Mine to Give

This 1958 film stars Glynis Johns and Cameron Mitchell as the pioneer parents of six children in early Wisconsin. Much of the film traces their hardships in carving out a place for themselves. With the untimely death of the parents, the oldest boy is faced with the impossibility of caring for the younger children. On Christmas morning he sets out to find homes for them among the neighboring families. The Christmas setting heightens the poignancy of this touching story.

Beyond Tomorrow

This 1940 fantasy tells the story of three rich, lonely men played by Charles Winninger, Harry Carey, and C. Aubrey Smith. They hit on the idea of dropping their wallets in the street and sharing Christmas with whoever is honest enough to return them. Only two are returned, by Richard Carlson and Jean Parker. The three men play Cupid, and all seems to be on the right track until a plane crash kills all three. Trouble sets in for the young couple, as the man has become a successful singer and is being wooed away by the traditional gorgeous vamp. The three men return as ghosts to try to finish up what they started before they receive their final call to the "Great Beyond."

The Bishop's Wife

This 1947 comedy featured Cary Grant as an angel named Dudley. He is sent to earth to aid David Niven, the bishop, who is having troubles with his wife, Loretta Young, as well as financial troubles in raising money for a new cathedral. Dudley performs a number of delightful Christmas miracles to set all to rights. Also on hand is an excellent supporting cast, including Monty Woolley, James Gleason, Elsa Lanchester, and Gladys Cooper.

Christmas Eve

In this 1947 comedy-drama, Ann Harding plays an eccentric and wealthy widow who faces a dilemma on Christmas Eve. Her unscrupulous nephew is going to have her committed to an asylum in order to gain control of her financial affairs. She depends on her three adopted sons to show up and save her, even though they are scattered around the world. The three wards are played by George Raft, George Brent, and Randolph Scott. With that threesome on your side, could there be any doubt that good triumphs?

Christmas in Connecticut

This pleasant film is a welcome and frequent part of TV's holiday fare. Released in 1945, it stars Barbara Stanwyck as an unmarried writer who has sold a number of articles describing the joys of married life on a Connecticut farm from a first-person viewpoint. Her publisher, Sydney Greenstreet, decides it would be good for her to have a war hero, Dennis Morgan, as her family's Christmas guest. The fun concerns her attempts to produce a reasonable facsimile of a farm and a husband so she won't lose her job.

Christmas in July

This excellent 1940 movie has little to do with Christmas except its infectious spirit of the delight of gift-giving. Preston Sturges, the master of the screwball comedy, directed this often-hilarious film. Dick Powell plays a man who thinks he has won a slogan contest. He immediately begins playing Santa Claus to everyone in the neighborhood—all on credit. Christmas overspenders will appreciate his plight when he finds that he didn't win the contest.

Holiday Affair

This pleasant 1949 comedy-drama stars Janet Leigh as a young war widow with a child. She is working as a comparison shopper when she meets Robert Mitchum, a toy salesman, at Christmastime. They are great opposites—she needing someone who can accept responsibility and he just wanting to run away and build boats—but of course they fall in love. Wendell Corey is on hand as the stuffy lawyer she finally throws over to go with her heart.

Holiday Inn

The story of this popular movie concerns a song-and-dance man who creates an inn that opens only on holidays. This gives the excuse for a dozen holiday songs by Irving Berlin. Love interest is provided by Bing Crosby and Fred Astaire good-naturedly competing for the heart of Marjorie Reynolds. This film would have no more to do with Christmas than any other month of the year if it weren't for Bing's crooning of "White Christmas," which won the Oscar for Best Song of 1942 and turned into the biggest-selling record of all time.

The Holly and the Ivy

This excellent English film from 1954 takes a family Christmas reunion as its setting. A strong-willed vicar comes to realize that he has failed his children in the ways they most needed him. All is gradually set right against the background of the English Christmas scene. This somewhat slow story is kept strongly alive by the cast, headed by Ralph Richardson and featuring Celia Johnson, Margaret Leighton, and Denholm Elliott.

I'll Be Seeing You

This sentimental 1945 drama stars Ginger Rogers as a convict who is allowed to go home for Christmas. On the train she meets Joseph Cotten, a soldier returning home from World War II with severe emotional problems as he must adjust to civilian life. Their love affair helps to restore both of them to the joys of life. The supporting cast includes Shirley Temple, Spring Byington, and Chill Wills.

It's a Wonderful Life

And this is a wonderful movie. It's great that they show it every Christmas, but about four times a year would not be too often for this lovely, loving film.

Jimmy Stewart plays a small-town banker whose biggest dream has always been to leave this small town and see the world where he can amount to something. But he is always thwarted in his efforts to leave because he keeps sacrificing himself for the other people of the town. When it looks as though his company must fail and a lot of people lose their savings, it is his world travel money that goes to save them; when the unscrupulous millionaire Lionel Barrymore tries to take the company over after the death of Stewart's father, it is Jimmy who cancels his travel plans to stay and preserve the company; when his uncle (Thomas Mitchell) foolishly loses a great sum of money, it is Jimmy who takes the blame and faces jail. This is the situation on Christmas Eve. He has given his all to his family and his town, and now he faces ruin and disgrace. He stands at the edge of the bridge and looks down into the ice-clogged, swirling waters below him. He climbs the rail. But before he can jump, there is another splash. Without thinking, with the great humanity that has always trapped him in this small town, he leaps to rescue the other person from the dark waters. But as he slowly comes to realize, it is not just a person he has saved but his own rather inept guardian angel, Clarence, played by Henry Travers. In a self-pitying moment, Jimmy wishes that he had never been born. Clarence, who is hoping to earn his wings on this case, grants his wish and takes him on a tour of his hometown to see what it would be like if he had never lived. It is a hopelessly different world. The corrupt millionaire runs the town as a vice jungle; a misguided girl he helped at a crucial moment is a dance hall girl; the pharmacist he saved from a fatal error when he was just a delivery boy is an ex-convict and a drunk. The whole town reeks of the cynicism and the self-disgust that he had always stood against without even knowing it. He begs for his life to be restored, willing to face personal shame and ruin if these people he has known and loved can be restored, too. His wish is granted and he waits happily to be taken to jail. But it is not to be. There are earthly miracles, too, and the townspeople pour out their love and their money to save him in a joyous affirmation that one man's life can make a big difference in the world, even if he never leaves home.

And Clarence wins his wings.

Even if this film were set on the Fourth of July, it would be a Christmas film, perhaps the best of all. It is filled with unsickly sentiment and with principles that are unashamedly part of the American and the Christmas spirit. Frank Capra directed and co-authored this 1946 film. Donna Reed plays Jimmy Stewart's wife and equals him in some of the most amusing, touching, and honest love scenes imaginable. What do you call a tearjerker that inspires only tears of joy?

The Lemon Drop Kid

This Damon Runyan story has twice been made into a movie, the first time in 1934 with Lee Tracy and Helen Mack. The much better known and still-shown version was made in 1951 with Bob Hope and Marilyn Maxwell. The story concerns a typical Runyan character, played by Hope, who gets into trouble when he gives a big gangster's moll a wrong tip at a dog track. To atone, he has to come up with ten grand by Christmas morning. From that point, the plot becomes typically confused, but it basically concerns Hope dressing up as Santa in a wild scheme to get the necessary cash. Hope and Maxwell introduce the well-known song "Silver Bells" in this film, which is chockful of typically amusing gags and antics by Hope and a supporting cast that includes Lloyd Nolan and William Frawley.

Meet John Doe

This 1941 film is sometimes warm and amusing, sometimes hard-bitten and cynical. A bored newspaper reporter (Barbara Stanwyck) fills a slow news day by making up a letter from "John Doe," an average citizen so upset by modern conditions that he is going to jump from the roof of City Hall on Christmas Eve. Tremendous publicity results and she has to produce a real John Doe. She hires an out-of-work baseball player (Gary Cooper) to play the part. Easy-going and simple, he sees nothing wrong with the scheme. A national cult springs up of organizations devoted to helping all the "John Does" in the land and learning to be friends and good neighbors. It all looks wonderful, but then Cooper finds that he is being used to realize the political ambitions of an unscrupulous millionaire (Edward Arnold). When he tries to tell the people the truth, Arnold reveals him as a fake and all the John Doe clubs are disbanded in a fit of disillusionment. Cooper disappears for months. Then on Christmas Eve, he goes to the roof of City Hall. He is going to jump, not to prove a point, but because he has become the real John Doe and he owes it to all the people who believed in him. Arnold's men try to stop him from becoming a martyr, but it is Stanwyck who saves him. The tough reporter has seen the truth, that people can be good, that a bunch of average men can stand up to anyone if they'll just believe. She reminds him of the "first John Doe," whose birthday is celebrated on Christmas. He comes down with her to begin the fight again.

Miracle on 34th Street

This is probably the best-known and one of the best of all Christmas movies. It has had two interesting side effects: probably more people know on what street Macy's Department Store is located than the address of any other store in the world; and this film solidified for all time the idea that Kris Kringle is just another name for Santa Claus. (It is actually a corruption of *Christkind*, the "Christ Child" who brings gifts to much of northern Europe at Christmastime.)

Edmund Gwenn plays Kris Kringle, a harmless old eccentric who lists eight reindeer as his next of kin and claims that he really is Santa, although he lives in an old folks' home on Long Island. He is hired by Macy's to play Santa Claus, but doubts as to his sanity lead to a courtroom trial. The final proof of his identity is provided by the Post Office, which decides to dump all the Santa Claus mail they have on him as an easy way of getting rid of it. He is therefore proclaimed authentic by an agency of the United States Government.

The story is also about the romance of John Payne, who sort of believes, and Maureen O'Hara, who has taught her daughter Natalie Wood that it is wrong to believe in fairy tales and Santa Claus. Without ever really finding definite proof, all come by the end to realize the importance of believing in things that can't be proved.

Twentieth Century-Fox didn't realize what it had on its hands when it released this film in 1947. It came out in the spring, of all times. It was a tremendous hit and won three Academy Awards, including Best Supporting Actor for Edmund Gwenn. The film was made into a book, appeared three times in TV adaptations, and was the basis for Meredith Willson's Broadway musical *Here's Love*. According to National Telefilm Associates, this film appears on TV more often than any other.

Remember the Night

This touching film features Fred MacMurray as an assistant D.A. preparing to go home for the Christmas holidays. A shoplifter is to be held until after the recess for her day in court, but MacMurray is concerned about her having to spend Christmas in jail. When he finds she has no place to go, he invites her to his home in Indiana. Played by Barbara Stanwyck, the worldly-wise shoplifter goes to take advantage of him, but learns from the influence of a simple down-home Christmas and ends up loving him. When the case is brought up in court, he tries to lose it, but she pleads guilty to save him from jeopardizing his position. They promise to wed after she has paid her debt to society. Mitchell Leisen directed this 1940 script by Preston Sturges, well known as the writer and director of some of the greatest "screwball comedies."

Tenth Avenue Angel

This overly sentimental movie came out in 1947 (a good Christmas year for the streets of New York; besides this and *Miracle on 34th Street*, Christmas was also the setting for a film called *It Happened on Fifth Avenue*). The story is of a little dreamer growing up in New York's tenements. Margaret O'Brien is the little girl who has trouble distinguishing between reality and make-believe as she plays matchmaker for her aunt, Angela Lansbury, and an ex-convict, George Murphy. The climax comes when she sees a calf kneel in the deserted stockyards at midnight on Christmas Eve, proving her mother right in her assertion that the animals kneel at the moment of Christ's birth.

Three Godfathers

This Western shows allegorically how the birth of Christ touches even the most hardened souls. The movie was made twice: once in 1936 with Chester Morris, Lewis Stone, and Walter Brennan; and again in 1948 with John Wayne, Pedro Armendariz and Harry Carey, Jr., with John Ford directing. The story tells of three bandits escaping from the law across the Arizona desert. They come upon a dying woman who is about to give birth. Their hearts are melted and they aid her in delivering her child. When she dies, they are left with the self-imposed and rather joyful responsibility of caring for the infant. This symbolic Christ Child causes them to reform, even in the face of approaching death.

White Christmas

"If at first you do succeed, try it again bigger" often seems to be Hollywood's motto. Occasionally it works out well, as in this 1954 remake of *Holiday Inn.* This version is more lavish and was the first film shot in VistaVision, a process for improving the quality of the print. Wisely, Bing Crosby was back to sing the title song and also introduced the song "Count Your Blessings" as part of the revised score. He was most ably assisted by Danny Kaye, Rosemary Clooney, and Vera-Ellen.

Actors Playing Santa

Edmund Gwenn won the Oscar for playing Santa Claus in *Miracle on 34th Street*, and a lot of us can't picture anyone else in the role. But a lot of rather unlikely actors have donned the red suit and whiskers for a few minutes in the course of a movie, usually with comic effect.

ACTOR	MOVIE AND YEAR
Frank Morgan	*Dangerous Nan McGrew* (1930)
Robert Livingston	*Three Godfathers* (1936)
Tex Ritter	*Down the Wyoming Trail* (1939)
Cary Grant	*My Favorite Wife* (1940)
Edward G. Robinson	*Larceny, Inc.* (1942)
Monty Woolley	*Life Begins at 8:30* (1942)
Robert Cummings	*The Bride Wore Boots* (1946)
Errol Flynn	*Never Say Goodbye* (1946)
Bob Hope	*The Lemon Drop Kid* (1951)

Christmas Film Music Quiz

A greal deal of Christmas music appears in films as musical numbers or as background. This quiz is just for fun. Number one is a gift.

1. In which two films does Bing Crosby sing "White Christmas"?

2. Doris Day sang a song called "Christmas Story" in which film?

3. What song did Bing Crosby teach his young choristers in *Going My Way?* Deanna Durbin also sang it in *Lady on a Train.*

4. Bob Hope didn't introduce it, but what popular Christmas song first appeared in his movie *The Lemon Drop Kid?*

5. Ray Bolger and June Haver performed a musical version of "A Visit from St. Nicholas" in which movie?

6. In what very un-Christmas-sounding movie did Judy Garland sing a song called "Merry Christmas"?

7. Just one more Bing Crosby question: in which film did he sing "The Secret of Christmas"?

8. The song "Have Yourself a Merry Little Christmas" was sung by whom to whom in which movie?

9. When Franchot Tone catches up with and takes care of the murderer of Robert Young in *Three Comrades,* it is in front of a cathedral. The choir inside is singing what appropriate anthem?

10. All right, this is really, *positively* the last Bing Crosby question: he and his cohorts sang "It Came upon the Midnight Clear" in which film?

11. Joan Hackett tried to teach broken-down cowboy Charlton Heston some Christmas songs in which movie? (P.S. His singing was no threat to Bing Crosby.)

1. Holiday Inn (1942) *and* White Christmas (1954).
2. On Moonlight Bay (1951).
3. *"Silent Night"*—Going My Way (1944); Lady on a Train (1945).
4. *"Silver Bells"* (1951).
5. Look for the Silver Lining (1949).
6. In the Good Old Summertime (1949).
7. Say One for Me (1959).
8. *Judy Garland to Margaret O'Brien in* Meet Me in St. Louis (1944).
9. *"Hallelujah Chorus" from Handel's* Messiah—Three Comrades (1938).
10. High Time (1960).
11. Will Penny (1968).

Other Films

These are some of the other films that may crop up on TV around Christmastime and relate more or less to the season.

BUSH CHRISTMAS
This mild-mannered Australian Western is about some kids who outwit horse thieves at Christmastime (1947).

CHRISTMAS HOLIDAY
This was Deanna Durbin's first stab at an adult dramatic role. A night-club hostess reminisces with a young soldier on Christmas Eve about the no-good she married and tried to reform. Gene Kelly, of all people, plays the heavy (1944).

THE CHRISTMAS MARTIAN

This Canadian film tells of a Martian who crashes in the North Woods at Christmastime and is rescued by youngsters (1971).

THE CHRISTMAS THAT ALMOST WASN'T

An Italian film, marking the directorial debut of actor Rossano Brazzi. The owner of the North Pole attempts to evict Santa Claus (1966).

THE CHRISTMAS TREE

This tearjerker stars William Holden and Virna Lisi. A little boy is exposed to radiation and develops leukemia. The film tells of his last few months and his death on Christmas Eve (1969).

COME TO THE STABLE

Loretta Young and Celeste Holm both won Oscar nominations for their roles as two French nuns who come to America and, starting with nothing, use devotion, charm, and persistence to build a children's hospital (1949).

THE LADY IN THE LAKE

A Philip Marlowe detective story set at Christmastime. It is chiefly notable for director-star Robert Montgomery's technique of using the camera only to show what the hero sees, so you see him only in such ways as reflected in mirrors (1946).

LARCENY, INC.

Based on the Broadway play *The Night Before Christmas*, this comedy describes the farcical mix-ups when an ex-con tries to go straight. The cast includes Edward G. Robinson, Jane Wyman, Broderick Crawford, Jack Carson, and Anthony Quinn (1942).

SANTA CLAUS

This Mexican film is based on a play by e. e. cummings. The story is a morality fable that pits Santa against Satan in the setting of Santa's workshop (1959).

SANTA CLAUS CONQUERS THE MARTIANS

Martians kidnap Santa from the North Pole in this children's fantasy (1964).

SANTA'S CHRISTMAS CIRCUS

A little girl and her friends are taken to the North Pole by a good-hearted clown (1966).

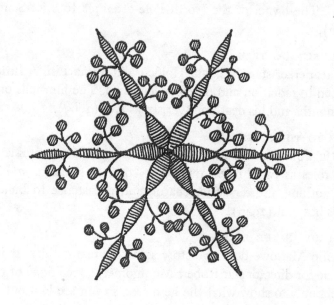

CHRISTMAS
on the
SMALL SCREEN

For television, Christmas is a "special" time of year. Regular programming is pre-empted to bring us dozens of specials. We are taken around the world to see how the season is celebrated by our favorite entertainers, religious leaders, or just plain folks. By simply flipping the channels we may spend Christmas Eve with Billy Graham, the Pope, or the King Family, according to our personal preference. Every version of A Christmas Carol is on, along with animated versions of popular Christmas songs. While Penn State plays Arizona on one channel, the Boston Symphony plays Handel on another.

In the midst of all this scrambling for attention, there are certain shows that stand out from the hundreds of others. Some are one-time events, religious services from the great cathedrals or special performances of music. Others are stories of Christmas which we never tire of no matter how many years they are repeated. It is this select group of enduring TV classics that we will consider here.

Amahl and the Night Visitors

This heart-warming Christmas opera may be the world's best-known English-language opera, thanks to its repeated exposure on television. It was originally commissioned by the NBC television network and was the first opera to be written specifically for TV. It was first presented on December 24, 1951. For many years it was shown every Christmas with several different casts, but in recent years it was not repeated until the completely new production of 1978, featuring Metropolitan Opera star Teresa Stratas. It has also become a Christmas regular in music schools and churches and local productions. The unusual success of this opera can be attributed to the great sense of theater that composer-librettist Gian-Carlo Menotti brings to the work. The music is of a high quality, yet it never interferes with the ongoing story, and the easy, natural setting of the words makes the story both intelligible and delightful for a modern audience. Menotti has composed many other works for the stage, but none has achieved the widespread popularity of this little Christmas legend.

The story concerns a small crippled boy, named Amahl, who lives with his mother, a poor shepherdess, in the Italian mountains. One day Amahl tells his mother that three Kings have come to their house; the child's mother does not believe such a fantastic tale—she is too trapped in the harsh realities of their life even to dream of such wonders. However, it is no child's fantasy, for the Magi have indeed come to Amahl's house and are invited to rest. When they tell of the gifts they are bringing to the newborn King who will reign with peace and love, Amahl longs to add his own poor present. But all he has is the tiny crutch he has carved himself. In a moment of unthinking love and devotion he steps forward to place his crutch with the other, more splendid gifts. Miraculously, he can walk. He sets out with the Kings to offer his thanks at that manger which all wise men have sought through the centuries.

"A Charlie Brown Christmas"

This "Peanuts" Christmas special was first produced in 1965 and has been shown every year since on the CBS television network. Charles M. Schulz, who created the "Peanuts" comic strip, wrote the script for this half-hour animated cartoon. The story features Charlie Brown, Lucy, Linus, Snoopy, and all the other "Peanuts" regulars. Everyone is too concerned about what they are receiving for Christmas, which causes Charlie Brown to try to find the real meaning of the season. Both the humor and the sentiment are effectively underplayed, just as in the comic strip, so the children are never cutely precocious. Vince Guaraldi provides the pleasant and unobtrusive jazz piano background for the action. This is a Christmas treat that can be appreciated as much, if not more, by adults as by children.

"A Christmas Memory"

Truman Capote wrote this lovely short story in 1956. In 1966 it was filmed for TV and has been shown several times since. The film was written by Eleanor Perry and directed by Frank Perry and starred Donnie Nelvin and Geraldine Page. It is one of the loveliest Christmas specials ever done for television.

The story is a reminiscence of growing up in a large family of indifferent and unimaginative relatives. The one exception is an elderly cousin who is referred to by Buddy, the narrator, simply as "my friend." She is treated as a child by the other adults, and so the two lonely people find solace in each other. When winter begins to chill the air in November, she happily announces, "It's fruitcake weather!"

That means they must get together their savings and begin to prepare the dozens of fruitcakes they make each year. The struggle to get enough money to beg or bargain for the necessary ingredients is half the fun. And when the cakes are made, they don't just go to relatives, they are given in a true Christmas spirit to those who have touched the two friends' lives in some way, even strangers, missionaries, and traveling salesmen. The joy is in the giving. She expresses a thought that is a profound one for our commercial lives: "It's bad enough in life to do without something *you* want; but confound it, what gets my goat is not being able to give somebody something you want *them* to have."

She has a great sense of the specialness and uniqueness of every moment, every thing, every person. She and Buddy go out into the woods to fell their own Christmas tree. Bringing it back, they are offered money for it by a man who points out that they can always get another one. They can certainly use the money, but she refuses because "there's never two of anything."

The story is amusing, involving, and ultimately deeply touching. Buddy grows up and goes away, to see his friend only on rare occasions. Inevitably there comes the day when he finds he will never see her again. He is filled with that most painful joy, of happiness remembered and unrecoverable, as he looks toward the sky "as if I expected to see, rather like hearts, a lost pair of kites hurrying toward heaven."

"The Homecoming"

This story by Earl Hamner, Jr., is best known for the television version made of it in 1971 and the series "The Waltons" which grew out of that special. The original is often repeated at Christmastime. It starred Patricia Neal (a performance for which she won the Golden Globe Award), Richard Thomas, and Cleavon Little.

The story concerns the Walton family's preparations for Christmas in 1933, the height of the depression. They are upset because the father is late in returning home from a trip. He is feared caught in a severe storm, but does eventually return in time—along with the miracle of freshly cut flowers in the middle of winter.

"How the Grinch Stole Christmas"

This is one of the most delightful modern additions to the realm of children's literature as well as television. The little book is by Theodore Geisel, who writes under the pen name Dr. Seuss. The tale is told with humorous verse and the inimitable drawings for which Dr. Seuss is famous.

The TV cartoon version first appeared in 1966. Narrated by Boris Karloff, it used the style of Dr. Seuss's drawings and added songs for an extra treat. This show is happily repeated every Christmas. The story tells how the evil Grinch (a wonderful name! almost as good as Scrooge) attempted to steal all the Christmas presents and therefore all the Christmas joy from the town of Who-ville. When he learns that Christmas joy is not dependent on getting presents, he repents and discovers the meaning of Christmas for himself.

"The Legend of Silent Night"

This television film was first presented by the ABC network on Christmas Day, 1968, and has been repeated often since. As the title suggests, it is not a documentary approach but rather a dramatic retelling of the story of the writing of the world's best-loved Christmas carol. The original story upon which the film was based is by Paul

Gallico, best known as author of *The Poseidon Adventure*. Kirk Douglas narrates and James Mason stars as Franz Grüber. The Vienna Boys Choir and the United Nations Choir provide the Christmas music in this inspiring TV movie.

Other TV Specials

Try to recall some of these Christmas specials from yesteryear. If you can remember most of them, you'd better give your eyes a rest.

THE BEAR WHO SLEPT THROUGH CHRISTMAS
This 1974 animated NBC show about a bear who tries to avoid hibernating so he can enjoy Christmas featured the voices of Tom Smothers, Arte Johnson, and Barbara Feldon.

CHRIST IS BORN
John Huston narrated this 1966 ABC story of Christ's birth told against historic scenes of the Holy Land.

CHRISTMAS IN APPALACHIA
Charles Kuralt narrated this 1965 CBS news documentary.

CHRISTMAS IN THE HOLY LAND
Art Linkletter conducted this 1959 CBS tour of the scenes of Christ's homeland.

CHRISTMAS 'TIL CLOSING
A 1955 NBC drama starring Hume Cronyn, Jessica Tandy, and Eileen Heckart in a story of parents and children trying to solve their problems at Christmas.

THE COMING OF CHRIST
Great Renaissance paintings illustrated Christ's nativity and life while Alexander Scourby narrated biblical passages in this 1960 NBC program.

THE CRICKET ON THE HEARTH
A 1967 NBC special based on Dickens' Christmas book about a mysterious stranger who affects the lives of a small village featured Danny and Marlo Thomas, Ed Ames, Hans Conried, and Roddy McDowall.

A CRY OF ANGELS
This 1963 NBC show told the story of the writing of Handel's *Messiah*.

THE DANGEROUS CHRISTMAS OF RED RIDING HOOD
or OH WOLF, POOR WOLF
Bob Merrill and Jule Styne wrote the music and lyrics for this 1965 ABC story of Little Red Riding Hood's adventures on the way to her grandmother's Christmas party, with Cyril Ritchard, Vic Damone, Liza Minnelli, and the sixties rock group the Animals.

A DREAM FOR CHRISTMAS
An all-black cast featuring Hari Rhodes and Beah Richards played this 1973 ABC story of a minister working to save his church from demolition, which was based on a story by Earl Hamner, Jr., who also wrote "The Homecoming," the basis for the TV series "The Waltons."

THE ENCHANTED NUTCRACKER
Based on the same story as the ballet, this 1961 ABC special starred Carol Lawrence and Robert Goulet.

THE FOURTH KING
An animated 1977 NBC special.

FROSTY THE SNOWMAN
Jimmy Durante, Jackie Vernon, and Billy de Wolfe provided the voices for this 1969 CBS animated version of the familiar song.

FROSTY'S WINTER WONDERLAND
Further animated adventures of Frosty in this 1976 ABC show, with the voices of Andy Griffith, Shelley Winters, and Dennis Day.

THE GATHERING
Edward Asner and Maureen Stapleton starred in this 1977 ABC drama.

THE GIFT OF THE MAGI
A musical version of the familiar O. Henry story produced in 1958 by CBS, with Gordon MacRae, Sally Ann Howes, and Tammy Grimes, and with music by Richard Adler.

THE GREAT SANTA CLAUS SWITCH
An evil magician kidnaps Santa so he can make his rounds and rob everyone in this 1970 CBS program, with Art Carney and the Muppets.

IT HAPPENED ONE CHRISTMAS
Based on the movie *It's a Wonderful Life*, this 1977 ABC special starred Marlo Thomas, Orson Welles, Wayne Rogers, and Cloris Leachman.

THE LITTLE DRUMMER BOY
Animated puppets act out a story based on the song in this 1968 NBC show, featuring the voices of Greer Garson, Jose Ferrer, and the Vienna Boys Choir.

THE LITTLE DRUMMER BOY, BOOK TWO
Further adventures of the little drummer boy from NBC in 1976, with the voices of Greer Garson and Zero Mostel.

THE LITTLEST ANGEL
Based on the children's book of the same name, this 1969 NBC musical starred Fred Gwynne, E. G. Marshall, Cab Calloway, Tony Randall, John McIver, Connie Stevens, and James Coco in the story of the child angel who has trouble adjusting to heaven until his humble gift is chosen most worthy for the Christ Child.

MIRACLE ON 34TH STREET
There have been three TV versions based on the familiar movie: (1) 1955, CBS, with Thomas Mitchell, Teresa Wright, Macdonald Carey, and Hans Conried; (2) 1959, NBC, with Ed Wynn, Peter Lind Hayes, Mary Healy, and Orson Bean; (3) 1973, CBS, with Sebastian Cabot, Tom Bosley, and Jane Alexander.

MR. MAGOO'S CHRISTMAS CAROL
A musical, animated version of Dickens' story, with Jim Backus, Jack Cassidy, and Morey Amsterdam providing voices for the music of Bob Merrill and Jule Styne.

NESTOR, THE LONG-EARED DONKEY
A 1977 ABC animated special, with the voices of Roger Miller and Brenda Vaccaro.

THE NIGHT THE ANIMALS TALKED
Sammy Cahn and Jule Styne provided lyrics and music for this 1970 ABC animated version of Christ's birth as seen through the eyes of the animals.

THE NUTCRACKER
NBC presented two versions of the great ballet in 1977: (1) American Ballet Theatre, choreographed by Mikhail Baryshnikov; (2) the Bolshoi Ballet from Russia, introduced by former First Lady Betty Ford.

ONCE UPON A CHRISTMAS TIME
In 1959 NBC presented this musical version of a Paul Gallico story about New England villagers who struggle with the head of an orphanage to allow them to bring the orphans into their homes for Christmas, featuring Claude Rains, Patty Duke, Margaret Hamilton, Charles Ruggles, and Kate Smith.

ONE RED ROSE FOR CHRISTMAS
A 1958 CBS drama, with Helen Hayes and Patty Duke, about an abandoned child who creates problems for the mother superior when brought to an orphanage at Christmastime.

RUDOLPH THE RED-NOSED REINDEER
Burl Ives sang and narrated for this 1964 NBC animated musical.

RUDOLPH'S SHINY NEW YEAR
More adventures of Rudolph in this 1976 animated ABC special, with Red Skelton, Frank Gorshin, and Morey Amsterdam.

SANTA CLAUS IS COMIN' TO TOWN
A 1970 animated story for ABC, with the voices of Fred Astaire, Mickey Rooney, and Keenan Wynn.

SILENT NIGHT! LONELY NIGHT!
Originally a Broadway play by Robert Anderson with Henry Fonda, Barbara Bel Geddes, and Lois Nettleton, this 1969 NBC version of two middle-aged New Englanders drawn together by their common

problems on Christmas Eve featured Lloyd Bridges, Shirley Jones, Cloris Leachman, Carrie Snodgress, and Jeff Bridges.

THE SILVER WHISTLE

This 1959 CBS show, with Eddie Albert, about an old vagabond who livens things up at an old folks' home was based on a Broadway play starring Jose Ferrer.

THE STINGIEST MAN IN TOWN

A 1956 NBC musical version of A Christmas Carol, with Basil Rathbone, Vic Damone, Johnny Desmond, Patrice Munsel, and the Four Lads; an animated version of this musical appeared on NBC in 1978 with the voices of Walter Matthau, Tom Bosley, Theodore Bikel, Robert Morse, and Dennis Day.

THE STORY OF THE FIRST CHRISTMAS SNOW

A 1975 animated NBC special about a French shepherd boy, blinded by lightning, who still longs for the first snowfall, featuring the voices of Angela Lansbury and Cyril Ritchard.

THE TINY TREE

Johnny Marks, who wrote "Rudolph, the Red-Nosed Reindeer," provided music and lyrics for this 1975 NBC animated musical of a tiny pine tree that becomes a beautiful Christmas tree, with the voices of Buddy Ebsen, Paul Winchell, and Roberta Flack.

'TWAS THE NIGHT BEFORE CHRISTMAS

This 1974 CBS cartoon features the voices of Tammy Grimes, Joel Grey, John McIver, and George Gobel in a story of a small-town newspaper that denounces Santa as a fraud.

A VERY MERRY CRICKET

A 1974 ABC cartoon musical that won an Emmy Award with its story of a cricket who spreads the Christmas spirit throughout New York.

THE YEAR WITHOUT A SANTA CLAUS

A 1974 ABC show about a cold that prevents Santa from making his rounds, featuring Shirley Booth, Mickey Rooney, and Dick Shawn.

YES, VIRGINIA, THERE IS A SANTA CLAUS!

Jim Backus narrated this 1974 ABC cartoon, which won an Emmy with the story of the famous newspaper editorial of the same title.

CHRISTMAS
on the
TABLE

The food of Christmas has always been one of its glories. The Christmas meal is festive and decorative, and what it may lack in subtlety, it more than makes up for in substance. The following recipes do not cover the full range of international Christmas foods. Entire books have been written on the subject without exhausting the possibilities. These recipes represent some of the wonderful diversity available to us at this joyous time of year. The recipes, unless otherwise noted, are taken from that wonderful kitchen aid *The Doubleday Cookbook*, by Jean Anderson and Elaine Hanna, and most of the introductory material is theirs also. The recipes are arranged thus: Entrées, Breads, Desserts, and Drinks.

Goose

Before the European advent of the turkey, the goose was one of the favorite Christmas meals. Goose is still a prime contender in some countries such as Denmark, where it is traditionally stuffed with apples and prunes.

Preheat oven to 325° F. Prepare bird for roasting in the same way as the turkey. Also rub inside well with half a lemon before stuffing. Prick skin well all over with a sharp fork so fat underneath will drain off during cooking. Rub skin well with salt (this helps to crispen skin). Place bird breast side up on a rack in a shallow roasting pan and roast uncovered, draining off drippings as they accumulate and pricking as needed. (*Note*: for a particularly crisp skin, raise oven temperature to 450° F. during last ½ hour of roasting. Also drain all drippings from pan and spoon ¼–½ cup ice water over bird.)

Roasting times with oven temperature of 325° F.:

4–6 pounds	2¾–3 hours
6–8 pounds	3–3½ hours
8–12 pounds	3½–4½ hours
12–14 pounds	4½–5 hours

An apple and prune stuffing can be prepared with 8 ounces each of prunes and bread crumbs and 1 pound of cooking apples. Wash the prunes and soak them overnight in cold water. Use the same water the next day to simmer them until moderately soft. Drain and pit the prunes. Chop them finely and mix with the bread crumbs. Add the cored, peeled, chopped apples and a little of the prune juice if necessary to bind the mixture.

As goose is very rich, plain side dishes will suit it best.

Pheasant

Two birds that were very popular at medieval England feasts were the swan and the peacock. Assuming that they won't be available at the neighborhood supermarket, there is another medieval favorite that is slightly more accessible, although it, too, will take some hunting.

Preheat over to 350° F. Prepare the pheasant in the same way as the turkey. Brush well with melted butter or margarine. Place breast side up on a rack in a shallow roasting pan and roast uncovered, basting often with drippings or brushing with additional melted butter. A farm-raised pheasant should weigh 2–4 pounds. At 350° F., it will take approximately 1½–2½ hours to roast.

Suckling Pig

If you'd like to try the modern-day version of a boar's head, roast suckling pig is for you. Suckling pigs are 6 to 8 weeks old and weigh from 10 to 20 pounds. There is little meat on them, but what there is approaches pâté in richness. Some people like to munch the richly browned skin, but for most tastes it is too leathery. Suckling pigs must always be especially ordered, sometimes as much as a week or two ahead. The best size is in the 14- to 18-pound range—large enough to contain some meat, small enough to fit in most home ovens. To figure number of servings, allow about 1¼ pounds pig per person (most of the weight is bone).

TIP: To keep the pig cool until roasting time (you can't get a suckling pig in the refrigerator unless you clear virtually everything else out), place in an extra-large roasting pan and set on a porch or just outside the door (suckling pig is cold weather food, so the outdoor temperature should be just about right unless it's below freezing; in that case, you'll have to make accommodations inside). Turn a large washtub upside down over the pig and weight down with bricks or large rocks to remove temptation from neighborhood dogs. When inviting guests, tell them what you plan to serve—some people are squeamish about seeing a whole pig on a platter. Makes 10–12 servings.

1 *(15-pound) suckling pig, dressed*
1 *tablespoon salt*
1 *teaspoon pepper*
1 *recipe Chestnut Mushroom Stuffing* (see below)
¼ *pound butter, softened to room temperature*

GARNISHES

1 *small red apple or 1 lemon*
1 *pint fresh cranberries*
12 *laurel or English ivy leaves*

Preheat oven to 350° F. Wipe pig inside and out with a damp cloth and dry with paper toweling. Rub inside well with salt and pepper. Lay pig on its side and stuff loosely; wrap remaining stuffing in foil and refrigerate. Close cavity with skewers and lace together to close. Place a large, sturdy rack in an extra-large shallow roasting pan; lay a triple thickness of foil diagonally on top, allowing plenty of overhang. Lift pig onto foil so it, too, is diagonal to the pan, bend hind legs forward and front legs backward into a "praying" position so pig crouches. Turn up foil edges, forming a "pan" to catch drips. Rub pig with butter; cover ears and tail with bits of foil and force a foil ball about the size of an apple into the mouth. Roast uncovered, brushing occasionally with butter, 18 minutes per pound. Meanwhile, string cranberries and leaves into 2 garlands. Save 2 cranberries for pig's eyes. About 1 hour before serving, place foil package of stuffing in oven to heat. When pig is done, lift carefully to an extra-large platter; remove skewers, lacing, and foil. Place an apple or lemon in pig's mouth, 1 cranberry in each eye (secure with toothpicks) and lay garlands around neck. Place extra stuffing in a separate dish and skimmed drippings in a gravy boat.

CHESTNUT MUSHROOM STUFFING

   4 medium-size yellow onions, peeled and coarsely chopped
   2 cloves garlic, peeled and crushed
   4 large stalks celery, coarsely chopped (do not include tops)
   ¼ cup butter or margarine
   1 pound fresh mushrooms, wiped clean and sliced thin
   ¼ cup minced parsley
   ½ teaspoon sage
   ½ teaspoon thyme
   1 tablespoon salt
   ¼ teaspoon pepper
   ¾ cup melted butter or margarine
   8 cups soft bread crumbs, or 2 (8-ounce) packages poultry stuffing mix
   1 pound chestnuts, shelled, peeled, and quartered
   ¼ cup dry sherry (optional)

Stir-fry onions, garlic, and celery in butter in a large, heavy skillet over moderate heat 8–10 minutes until golden; add mushrooms, parsley, sage, thyme, salt, and pepper and heat, stirring occasionally, 8–10 minutes. Mix with all remaining ingredients (use a 6-quart kettle) and use to stuff pig. About 465 calories per cup.

HOW TO CARVE SUCKLING PIG: Set platter on table so pig's head is to left of carver. First, remove the hams or hind legs, then divide pig into chops by cutting along the backbone, then down along each rib. See that each person receives both chops and ham or leg meat. About 1135 calories for each of 10 servings with Chestnut Mushroom Stuffing.

Turkey

Turkey is the main course in more Christmas dinners than any other type of meat or fowl. The high proportion of meat to unusable bone and fat makes it an ideal bird for a feast. Turkeys were domesticated in Mexico long before Spanish explorers found them and introduced them into their homeland. From there they spread throughout Europe and gradually replaced most of the native Christmas feast foods.

BASIC PREPARATION FOR COOKING: Remove paper of giblets from body (save giblets for gravy or use in stuffing). Also remove any loose fat from body cavity. Wipe bird with a damp cloth but do not wash (most birds coming to market today are beautifully cleaned and dressed; washing them merely destroys some of their flavor). Singe off any hairs and remove pinfeathers. Sprinkle neck and body cavities with salt.

SAGE AND ONION DRESSING: There are many possible stuffings for turkey. This is a good basic one. Makes about 2 quarts, enough to stuff a 10–12-pound bird.

> 4 medium-size yellow onions, peeled and minced
> 1 cup water
> 6 cups soft white bread cubes
> 2 teaspoons sage
> ½ cup melted butter or margarine
> 2 teaspoons salt
> ¼ teaspoon pepper

Simmer onions and water, covered, 20 minutes. Off heat, mix in remaining ingredients. About 215 calories per cup. Spoon stuffing *loosely* into both body and neck cavities. If you pack stuffing into a bird, it will become tough and rubbery in cooking. If you have more stuffing than the bird will hold, simply wrap the leftover in foil and bake alongside the bird in the pan. (*Note:* Do not stuff a bird until *just* before roasting; and *do not* let a stuffed bird stand at room temperature because of the danger of food poisoning.)

TO TRUSS A BIRD: After stuffing bird, skewer or sew openings shut, then truss by folding the wings back and underneath body and tying drumsticks close to body so bird will have a more compact shape and roast more evenly.

BREAST-UP METHOD FOR A WHOLE BIRD: This is the preferred way today; it produces an exquisitely brown bird. Preheat oven to 325° F.

Prepare turkey as above and place breast side up on a rack in a shallow roasting pan. Insert meat thermometer in thigh or stuffing, not touching bone, and roast uncovered, according to times given below. Baste, if you like, with melted butter or margarine every ½–¾ hour. If bird browns too fast, tent breast loosely with foil.

Roasting times with oven temperature of 325° F.:

4–8 pounds	2½–3½ hours
8–12 pounds	3½–4½ hours
12–16 pounds	4½–5½ hours
16–20 pounds	5½–6½ hours
20–24 pounds	6½–7 hours

Internal temperature when done will be 180–85° F.

BREAST-DOWN METHOD FOR A WHOLE BIRD: Though this method produces juicier breast meat, it has disadvantages: The breast skin is apt to stick to the rack and tear as the turkey is being turned and the act of turning a hot, hefty turkey is both difficult and dangerous. Preheat oven to 325° F. Prepare turkey for roasting as directed and place breast side down in a V rack in a shallow roasting pan. Roast, uncovered, until half done according to the above roasting chart, turn breast side up, insert thermometer in thickest part of inside thigh, not touching bone, and continue roasting, uncovered, until done. Baste, if you like, during cooking with drippings or melted butter.

FAST FOIL METHOD FOR A WHOLE BIRD: This is the method to use for birds, especially big ones, that must be cooked in a "hurry." Turkeys cooked this way will have more of a steamed than roasted flavor. Preheat oven to 450° F. Prepare turkey for roasting as directed and place in the center of large sheet of heavy foil; brush well with softened butter, margarine, or shortening. Bring foil up on both sides of breast and make a simple overlapping fold at the top, smooth down around turkey, then crumple ends of foil up to hold in juices. Place turkey breast side up in a shallow roasting pan and roast as follows:

Ready-to-Cook Weight	Total Roasting Time
6–8 pounds	1½–2 hours
8–12 pounds	2–2½ hours
12–16 pounds	2½–3 hours

| 16–20 pounds | 3–3½ hours |
| 20–24 pounds | 3½–4 hours |

About 30–40 minutes before turkey is done, open tent of foil and fold back and away from bird so it will brown nicely. (*Note*: When roasting turkey by any of the three preceding methods, it's a good idea to cut string holding drumsticks to tail about 1 hour before bird is done so that inner legs and thighs will brown.)

Panettone

(Italian Christmas Bread)

Makes a tall 9″ loaf.

1 *recipe Basic Sweet Dough* (see below—reduce amount of scalded milk to ¾ cup)
¼ *cup butter or margarine*
3 *egg yolks, lightly beaten*
1 *cup sultana raisins*
1 *cup minced candied citron or mixed candied fruits*
½ *cup piñon nuts (optional)*
2 *tablespoons melted butter or margarine*
Confectioners' sugar

Prepare basic recipe as directed, adding the ¼ cup butter above to the scalded milk along with the butter, sugar, and salt called for in basic recipe; cool to lukewarm and stir into yeast mixture along with all but last ingredient above. Proceed as basic recipe directs. While dough is rising, prepare pan: Tear off a 30″ piece of heavy duty foil and fold over and over again until you have a strip 30″ long and 4″ wide. Grease 1 side of strip and stand greased side around the inside edge of a greased 9″ layer cake pan; secure with a paper clip to form a collar. Punch dough down, knead lightly 1–2 minutes, and shape into smooth round loaf about 9″ across. Place in pan, cover, and let rise in warm, draft-free place until doubled in bulk, about 1 hour. Toward end of rising, preheat oven to 400° F. Bake 10 minutes, reduce oven to 350° F., and bake 40–50 minutes longer until golden brown and hollow sounding when tapped. Turn out on a wire rack, dust with confectioners' sugar and cool. To serve, cut in thin wedges. About 330 calories for each of 16 wedges.

BASIC SWEET DOUGH: Makes enough for 2 10″ rings or 2 9″×5″×3″ loaves or 4 dozen rolls.

> 1 cup scalded milk
> ¼ cup butter or margarine
> ½ cup sugar
> 1 teaspoon salt
> ¼ cup warm water (105–15° F.)
> 2 packages active dry yeast
> 2 eggs, lightly beaten
> 5 cups sifted flour

Mix milk, butter, sugar, and salt and cool to lukewarm. Pour warm water into a warm large bowl, sprinkle in yeast, and stir to dissolve. Add cooled mixture, eggs, and 3 cups flour and beat well. Mix in remaining flour and knead lightly on a lightly floured board until elastic. Shape into a ball, turn in a greased bowl to grease all over, cover with cloth, and let rise in a warm, draft-free place until doubled in bulk, about 1 hour. Dough is now ready to shape and use.

Stollen

(German Christmas Bread)

1 recipe Basic Sweet Dough (see Panettone above)
½ cup sultana raisins
½ cup seedless raisins

1 cup minced blanched almonds
¾ cup minced candied fruits or a ½ and ½ mixture of citron and
candied cherries
1 teaspoon cinnamon
½ teaspoon nutmeg
1 tablespoon finely grated lemon rind
3 tablespoons melted butter or margarine
1 recipe Easy White Icing (see below)

Prepare dough as directed, adding raisins, almonds, candied fruit, cinnamon, nutmeg, and lemon rind to yeast along with lukewarm mixture. Add remaining flour, knead, and let rise as directed. Divide dough in half and shape into 2 round loaves and place in greased 9″ piepans. Or, if you prefer, make 2 braids. Brush with melted butter. Cover loaves and let rise in a warm, draft-free place until doubled in bulk, about ¾ hour. Toward end of rising, preheat oven to 375° F. Bake 35–40 minutes until golden brown. Lift to wire racks set over wax paper and, while still warm, drizzle with icing. For a festive touch, decorate with "flowers" made with blanched almond halves, candied cherries, and slivered angelica. For a shiny crust, brush dough before baking with 1 egg lightly beaten with 1 tablespoon cold water; omit icing. About 140 calories for each of 20 slices.

EASY WHITE ICING: A quick and easy topping for any hot sweet breads.

1 cup sifted confectioners' sugar
1 tablespoon cold milk
¼ teaspoon vanilla extract

Sprinkle confectioners' sugar slowly into milk and blend smooth. Mix in vanilla extract, spread on bread, and let stand until glaze hardens. Add about 25 calories to each of 20 servings.

Baked Rice Pudding

Put a lucky almond into your pudding for someone to find and you can start your Christmas feast the way the Scandinavians do. Short grain rice, *not* converted, makes the best pudding. Makes 4–6 servings.

> ⅓ *cup uncooked short grain rice*
> 1 *quart milk*
> ½ *cup sugar*
> ⅛ *teaspoon nutmeg or 1 teaspoon vanilla*
> 2–3 *tablespoons butter or margarine*

Preheat oven to 300° F. Sprinkle rice evenly over the bottom of a buttered 1½-quart casserole. Mix milk and sugar, pour over rice, sprinkle with nutmeg, and dot with butter. Bake, uncovered, 2½ hours, stirring every 15 minutes for the first 1½ hours, until lightly browned. Serve warm, topped, if you like, with cream. About 375 calories for each of 4 servings (without cream), 250 calories for each of 6 servings.

Bûche de Noël

(Christmas Log)

A rich chocolate log traditionally served on Christmas Eve in France. Makes 1 roll.

> ½ *cup sifted cake flour*
> ¾ *teaspoon baking powder*

¼ teaspoon salt
4 eggs, at room temperature
¾ cup sugar
1 teaspoon vanilla
3 (1-ounce) squares unsweetened chocolate, melted, or 3 (1-ounce)
    envelopes no-melt unsweetened chocolate
2 tablespoons very strong warm black coffee
Sifted cocoa
2 recipes Mocha or Chocolate Butter Cream Frosting (see below)

Preheat oven to 400° F. Line the bottom of a 15½"×10½"×1" jelly-roll pan with wax paper. Sift flour with baking powder and salt and set aside. With electric or rotary beater, beat eggs at high speed until foamy; slowly add sugar, a little at a time, and beat until very thick and cream colored. Mix in vanilla, blend chocolate with coffee and mix into batter. Fold in dry ingredients just until blended. Spoon into pan, spreading batter evenly. Bake 12–14 minutes until springy to the touch. Loosen edges of cake and invert on a clean dish towel heavily sprinkled with sifted cocoa. Peel off paper and cut off crisp edges with a sharp knife. Beginning at the short side, roll cake and towel up; cool completely on a wire rack. Unroll, remove towel, spread about 1 cup mocha frosting to within ½" of edges and carefully reroll. Wrap loosely in foil and chill 1 hour. With a sharp knife, cut a small piece from each end on the diagonal and reserve to make "branches." Place roll seam side down on serving plate and tuck a strip of wax paper under each side. Spread with remaining frosting, then draw fork tines in a wavy pattern the length of log to resemble bark or use a serrated ribbon tip and a pastry bag to force frosting out in a ridged bark effect. Lay trimmed-off ends on roll cut side down at an angle, off center. Press into frosting lightly, then frost edges. If you wish, sprinkle log with minced pistachio nuts and write, "Noel" in white decorative icing. About 680 calories for each of 12 servings.

MOCHA OR CHOCOLATE BUTTER CREAM FROSTING: The following is a single recipe. Two recipes are needed for the Bûche de Noël.

⅓ cup butter or margarine, softened to room temperature
2 teaspoons instant coffee powder and 2 (1-ounce) squares melted
    unsweetened chocolate (this will make mocha frosting)

or 3 (1-ounce) squares melted unsweetened chocolate or ½ cup
sifted cocoa (either of these will make chocolate frosting)
1 (1-pound) box confectioners' sugar, sifted
5–6 tablespoons light cream
2 teaspoons vanilla
¼ teaspoon salt

Cream butter until fluffy; beat in coffee powder and chocolate, or
chocolate or cocoa; beat in sugar, a little at a time, adding alternately
with cream. Mix in vanilla and salt and beat until satiny and of good
spreading consistency. If mixture seems too stiff, thin with a little additional cream.

Gingerbread Boys

Let the children help make and decorate these. Makes 2 dozen.

2½ cups sifted flour
½ teaspoon salt
2 teaspoons ginger
½ cup butter or margarine
½ cup sugar
½ cup molasses
½ teaspoon baking soda
¼ cup hot water

DECORATIONS:

Cinnamon candies ("red-hots")
Seedless raisins

EASY ICING:

1 cup sifted confectioners' sugar
¼ teaspoon salt

½ teaspoon vanilla
1 tablespoon heavy cream (about)

Sift flour with salt and ginger and set aside. Melt butter in a large saucepan over low heat, remove from heat and mix in sugar, then molasses. Dissolve soda in hot water. Add dry ingredients to molasses mixture alternately with soda-water, beginning and ending with dry ingredients. Chill dough 2–3 hours. Preheat oven to 350° F. Roll out dough, a small portion at a time, ⅛″ thick. Cut with gingerbread boy cutter, handling dough carefully, and transfer cookies to ungreased baking sheets (they should be spaced about 2″ apart). Press on cinnamon candies for buttons and raisins for eyes and bake 10–12 minutes until lightly browned. Cool 2–3 minutes on sheets, then lift to wire racks. While cookies cool, prepare icing: Mix sugar, salt, and vanilla; add cream, a few drops at a time, mixing well after each addition until icing is smooth and will hold a shape. Using a decorating tube, pipe outlines for collars, boots, cuffs, and belts. If you like, make a little extra icing, tint yellow, and use to pipe in hair. When frosting has hardened, store airtight. (Note: Gingerbread boys can be made several days ahead and piped with icing shortly before serving. If they soften in storage, warm 3–5 minutes at 350° F. to crispen, then cool on racks.) About 130 calories each.

Glorious Golden Fruitcake

The recipe for this traditional seasonal favorite comes from *Christmas with a Country Flavor.*

4 cups sifted flour
1½ teaspoons baking powder
½ teaspoon salt
2 cups butter or regular margarine
2½ cups sugar
6 eggs

¼ *cup milk*
 4 *cups chopped walnuts*
 ½ *cup chopped candied pineapple*
 1 *cup golden raisins*
 ½ *cup chopped red candied cherries*
 ½ *cup chopped green candied cherries*
 1 *tablespoon grated lemon rind*
 Pineapple Glaze (recipe follows)
 Pecan halves

Sift together flour, baking powder and salt. Reserve ¼ cup; set aside.

Cream together butter and sugar until light and fluffy. Add eggs, one at a time, beating well after addition. Add sifted dry ingredients alternately with milk, beating well after each addition.

Combine walnuts, pineapple, raisins, candied cherries, lemon rind and reserved ¼ cup flour; toss gently to coat. Stir into batter. Spread batter in greased and waxed paper-lined 10″ tube pan.

Bake in 275° oven for 2 hours 45 minutes or until cake tests done. Cool in pan on rack 30 minutes. Remove from pan; cool on rack.

Wrap fruitcake tightly in foil. Store in refrigerator up to 4 weeks. (Fruitcake keeps better if stored unfrosted.)

TO SERVE: Prepare Pineapple Glaze. Frost top of cake, letting glaze drip down sides. Decorate cake with pecan halves. Makes 1 (5 lb.) fruitcake.

PINEAPPLE GLAZE: Combine 1 cup sifted confectioners' sugar and 2 tablespoons pineapple juice; mix until smooth.

Lebkuchen

A spicy German cookie studded with candied fruits. Makes about 4½ dozen.

 3 *cups sifted flour*
 ½ *teaspoon baking soda*

1 teaspoon cinnamon
½ teaspoon nutmeg
½ teaspoon cloves
1 cup firmly packed dark brown sugar
1 cup honey, at room temperature
1 egg
1 teaspoon finely grated lemon rind
1 tablespoon lemon juice
½ cup finely chopped blanched almonds
½ cup finely chopped mixed candied orange peel and citron

FROSTING:

1 cup sifted confectioners' sugar
4–5 teaspoons milk

DECORATION:

Blanched halved almonds
Slivered or halved candied cherries

Sift flour with baking soda and spices. Beat sugar, honey and egg until well blended; add lemon rind and juice. Slowly mix in dry ingredients just until blended; stir in almonds and fruit peel. Wrap and chill 12 hours. Preheat oven to 400° F. Roll out ⅓ of dough at a time ¼" thick and cut with a 2" round cookie cutter *or* cut in rectangles 2½"×1½". Arrange 2" apart on lightly greased baking sheets and bake 8 minutes until edges are lightly browned and tops spring back when touched. Cool on wire racks. For the frosting: Mix sugar and milk until smooth; spread a little on top of each cookie *or* dip cookie tops in frosting. Decorate with almonds and cherries. Let frosting harden before storing cookies. About 80 calories per cookie.

FOR DROP COOKIES: Reduce flour to 2½ cups; drop by rounded teaspoonfuls and bake as directed. About 75 calories per cookie.

Marzipan

Delicately shaped and tinted marzipan fruits, flowers, vegetables, and animals are ancient Christmas confections. Special molds, used for the shaping, are sold in housewares departments of many large stores, also by candy supply houses. Pure almond paste can be bought at gourmet shops. Makes about ½ pound.

> ½ pound pure almond paste
> 1 egg white, lightly beaten
> 1½ cups sifted confectioners' sugar

Break up almond paste in a bowl, add egg white and about ½ cup confectioners' sugar, and mix well. Knead in remaining sugar until mixture is smooth and malleable. Marzipan is now ready to color and shape or use in other recipes. About 80 calories per 1″ ball.

TO MAKE FRUITS AND VEGETABLES: Knead in appropriate food color, drop by drop, until marzipan is the right color. Pinch off small pieces and shape as desired. To tint or shade, dilute coloring with water and paint on with an artist's brush. Pipe on stems and leaves of green Basic Butter Cream Frosting (see below). To give texture to citrus fruits and strawberries, dust a thimble with confectioners' sugar, then press over surface of candy. (Note: Beginners may find it helpful to work from real life fruit.) Stored airtight in refrigerator, candy keeps well several weeks.

BASIC BUTTER CREAM FROSTING: This recipe is enough to frost a 2-layer cake, so cut it down according to your specific needs.

> ⅓ cup butter or margarine, softened to room temperature
> 1 (1-pound) box confectioners' sugar, sifted
> 5–6 tablespoons light cream
> 2 teaspoons vanilla
> ¼ teaspoon salt

Cream butter until fluffy; beat in sugar, a little at a time, adding alternately with cream. Mix in vanilla and salt and beat until satiny and of good spreading consistency. If mixture seems too stiff, thin with a little additional cream.

VARIATIONS:

Cocoa Marzipan: Prepare marzipan, then knead in 2 tablespoons cocoa. Use to make "mushrooms" or "potatoes" (roll in cocoa after shaping and make "eyes" with a toothpick or skewer). If you prefer, roll into small (about 1") balls and dip in melted semisweet chocolate. About 85 calories per piece (undipped).

Chocolate-Dipped Marzipan: Prepare marzipan, then knead in ½ teaspoon vanilla, rum or brandy flavoring, and 1 tablespoon instant coffee powder. Sprinkle hands and board with confectioners' sugar, then roll marzipan, a little at a time, into ropes 1" in diameter. Cut in ½" lengths, flatten into ovals, and dip in melted semisweet chocolate. Before chocolate hardens, top with almond halves. Store airtight. About 125 calories per piece.

Moravian Christmas Cookies

These dark ginger-molasses cookies store beautifully, so you can make them well ahead of the Christmas rush. The Moravian women of Old Salem, North Carolina, roll them paper thin and cut in fancy shapes. Makes 4½ dozen.

> 4 cups sifted flour
> 1 teaspoon ginger
> 1 teaspoon cinnamon
> 1 teaspoon mace
> ½ teaspoon cloves
> ¼ cup butter or margarine

¼ *cup lard*
　　½ *cup firmly packed dark brown sugar*
　　　1 *cup molasses*
　1½ *teaspoons baking soda*
　　　1 *tablespoon very hot water*

Sift flour with spices. Cream butter, lard, and sugar until light and fluffy; add molasses and beat well. Dissolve soda in water. Mix ¼ of dry ingredients into creamed mixture, then stir in soda-water. Work in remaining dry ingredients, ⅓ at a time. Wrap dough and chill 4–6 hours. Preheat oven to 350° F. Roll dough, a little at a time, as thin as possible ⅛″ is maximum thickness, ¹⁄₁₆″ far better). Cut with Christmas cutters, space cookies 1½″ apart on lightly greased baking sheets, and bake about 8 minutes until lightly browned. Cool 1–2 minutes on sheets, then transfer to wire racks. When completely cool, store airtight. About 70 calories per cookie.

TO DECORATE: Make an icing by mixing 1 cup sifted confectioners' sugar with 2–3 teaspoons heavy cream. Trace outlines of cookies with icing by putting through a pastry tube fitted with a fine tip. About 80 calories per cookie.

Pepparkakor

(*Christmas Ginger Snaps*)

These gingery brown cookies are Sweden's favorite at Christmastime. They are rolled very thin, cut into stars, bells, angels, and Santa Clauses, and hung upon either the Christmas tree or the small wooden *pepparkakor* tree. Makes about 5 dozen.

　　3½ *cups sifted flour*
　　　1 *teaspoon baking soda*
　　½ *teaspoon salt*

1½ teaspoons ginger
1½ teaspoons cinnamon
1½ teaspoons cloves
1 cup butter or margarine
1 cup firmly packed dark brown sugar
2 egg whites

ICING:

4 cups sifted confectioners' sugar
2 egg whites

Sift flour with soda, salt, and spices. Cream butter and sugar until very fluffy; beat in egg whites. Slowly work in dry ingredients. Wrap and chill 12 hours. Preheat oven to 350° F. Roll out dough, a small portion at a time, ⅛" thick on a lightly floured board and cut in decorative shapes; space cookies about 1" apart on ungreased baking sheets and bake 10–12 minutes until lightly browned around the edges. Transfer to wire racks to cool. While cookies cool, prepare icing: Slowly blend confectioners' sugar into egg whites and beat until smooth. Fit pastry bag with a fine, plain tip and pipe icing onto cookies, tracing outlines, filling in details, or adding any decorative touches you wish. About 100 calories per cookie.

Pfeffernüsse

(German Peppernuts)

The secret of good "peppernuts" is to ripen the dough 2–3 days before baking and to store the cookies 1–2 weeks with a piece of apple before eating. Makes 3½ dozen.

3 cups sifted flour
1 teaspoon cinnamon

⅛ teaspoon cloves
¼ teaspoon white pepper
3 eggs
1 cup sugar
⅓ cup very finely chopped blanched almonds
⅓ cup very finely chopped mixed candied orange peel and citron
Vanilla sugar or confectioners' sugar (optional)

Sift flour with spices and set aside. Beat eggs until frothy, slowly add sugar, and continue beating until thick and lemon colored. Slowly mix in flour, then almonds and fruit peel. Wrap in foil and refrigerate 2–3 days. When ready to bake, preheat oven to 350° F. Roll, about ⅓ of dough at a time, ¼"–½" thick and cut with a 1¾" round cutter. Space cookies 1" apart on greased baking sheets and bake 15–18 minutes until light brown. Cool on wire racks and store with ½ an apple in a covered container 1–2 weeks before eating. If you like, dredge in vanilla sugar or dust with confectioners' sugar before serving. About 70 calories per cookie if not dredged in sugar, 80 calories if dredged in sugar.

Plum Pudding

The English plum pudding served at Christmas doesn't contain plums; it resembles steamed fruitcake, is made weeks ahead and mellowed in a cool, dry place. If you have no cool spot (about 50° F.), freeze the pudding or make only 1 week ahead and refrigerate. The English hide silver charms or coins in the pudding batter—and lucky the child who finds one. Makes 12 servings.

1½ cups seedless raisins
½ cup dried currants
½ cup finely chopped mixed candied fruit
1 tart apple, peeled, cored, and grated fine
Finely grated rind of 1 lemon

Finely grated rind of 1 orange
¾ cup ale or orange juice
1 cup sifted flour
1 teaspoon baking powder
½ teaspoon salt
1 teaspoon cinnamon
½ teaspoon allspice
¼ teaspoon nutmeg
1 cup fine dry bread crumbs
1 cup firmly packed dark brown sugar
⅓ cup molasses
1 cup finely ground suet
3 eggs, lightly beaten
½ cup minced, toasted, blanched almonds

Mix fruits, rinds, and ale and let stand ½ hour. Sift flour with baking powder, salt and spices, stir in remaining ingredients, add fruit mixture, and mix well. Spoon into 2 well-buttered 1-quart molds or metal bowls, cover with double thicknesses of foil, and tie firmly in place. Set on a rack in a large kettle, add boiling water to come halfway up puddings, cover, and steam 4 hours; keep water simmering slowly and add more boiling water as needed to maintain level. Cool puddings on racks with foil still intact, then store in a cool place, freeze, or refrigerate. To reheat, steam 1 hour exactly the same way you cooked them. Unmold puddings on a hot platter and decorate with holly. If you like, pour ¼ cup warm brandy over each pudding and blaze. Cut in wedges and serve with Hard Sauce. About 440 calories per serving (without sauce).

HARD SAUCE: Makes about 1 cup.

½ cup butter (*no substitute*), softened to room temperature
2 cups sifted confectioners' sugar
⅛ teaspoon salt
1 tablespoon hot water
1 teaspoon vanilla

Beat butter until creamy; gradually beat in sugar, a little at a time. Beat in remaining ingredients and continue to beat until fluffy. Serve chilled or at room temperature. About 115 calories per tablespoon.

Springerle

The original 3-D cookies, springerle date to pagan Germany when the poor, having no animals to sacrifice at the Winter Festival, made effigies of them out of cookie dough. Today, springerle are square or rectangular cookies with pressed-in designs, made either by rolling dough on a springerle board or with a springerle rolling pin (available in gourmet shops). Sometimes used, too, are individual wooden cookie blocks called *Spekulatius* blocks. Makes about 5 dozen.

> 4 cups sifted flour
> 1 teaspoon baking powder
> ½ teaspoon salt
> 4 eggs
> 2 cups sugar
> 2 teaspoons finely grated lemon rind (optional)
> Anise seeds

Sift flour with baking powder and salt. Beat eggs until lemon colored, slowly add sugar, ½ cup at a time, beating well after each addition; continue beating until very thick and pale, about 10 minutes with a mixer. Slowly mix in lemon rind and dry ingredients, beating just to blend. Wrap and chill dough 3–4 hours. Roll, ⅓ at a time, slightly less than ½" thick, keeping shape as nearly rectangular as possible and about the width of the rolling pin. Roll a lightly floured springerle rolling pin over dough 1 time, pressing firmly so dough is about ¼" thick and evenly so imprint is clear. If using springerle board, roll dough ¼" thick on lightly floured board, using regular rolling pin, then invert on lightly floured surface. If using *Spekulatius* block, roll dough ¼" thick, then press firmly and evenly, using block like a stamp. (*Note:* In warm weather, chill springerle pin or board along with dough to make rolling easier.) Cut on imprint lines to separate individual cookies, transfer to a lightly floured surface, and let stand uncovered overnight. Preheat oven to 325° F. Sprinkle greased baking sheets generously with anise seeds, lift cookies to sheets, and bake 15 minutes until golden but not brown. Cool 1 minute on sheets before transferring to racks to cool. (*Note:* Some people like to mellow springerle about a week in an airtight canister before serving.) About 110 calories per cookie.

Sugarplums

Roll fondant (see below) around small pieces of fruit—candied cherries, small pitted dates, cubes of preserved ginger, pieces of dried apricots. About 60 calories each.

FONDANT: Fondant is more a base for other confections than a candy to be eaten by itself. Makes about 1 pound.

> 2 *cups sugar*
> 1½ *cups hot water*
> ⅛ *teaspoon cream of tartar or* ¼ *teaspoon lemon juice*

Heat and stir all ingredients in a large, heavy saucepan over moderate heat until sugar dissolves; cover and boil 3 minutes. Uncover, insert candy thermometer that has been heated under hot tap, and cook *without stirring* to 238° F. or until a drop of fondant forms a soft ball in cold water. (*Note:* Wipe crystals from sides of pan with a damp pastry brush as they collect—fondant will be less apt to turn grainy.) Remove fondant from heat and let stand 1–2 minutes until bubbles subside; pour—*without scraping pan*—onto a marble slab or large, heavy platter rubbed lightly with a damp cloth; cool undisturbed until barely warm. (*Note:* If you have an extra candy thermometer, insert as soon as fondant is poured.) When fondant has cooled to 110° F., scrape from edges with a broad spatula in toward center again and again until it thickens and whitens; pick up and knead until velvety. Wrap fondant in cloth wrung out in cold water and "season" ½ hour before using. (*Note*: Covered with damp cloth and stored in an airtight jar, fondant will keep 3–4 days.) About 25 calories per 1" ball.

TO FLAVOR FONDANT: Knead in about ½ teaspoon extract (vanilla, almond, rum, spearmint, rose or orange water) or a few drops oil of peppermint or wintergreen. Add these *by the drop*, tasting as you go so you don't *overflavor*.

TO COLOR FONDANT: Dip a toothpick in desired food color, then pierce fondant in several places. Knead to distribute color; if too pale, repeat—but keep colors pastel.

Sugar Pretzels

Christmas favorites in Germany and Scandinavia. Makes 2½ dozen.

> 1 *cup butter* (*no substitute*)
> ⅔ *cup sugar*
> 2 *egg yolks, lightly beaten*
> 1 *teaspoon vanilla*
> 2 *cups plus 2 tablespoons sifted flour*

DECORATION:

> 1 *egg white, lightly beaten*
> ¼ *cup green, red, or plain sugar*

Preheat oven to 375° F. Cream butter until white, slowly add sugar, and continue beating until light and fluffy. Add egg yolks and vanilla and beat well. By hand mix in flour just until blended. Spoon mixture into a pastry bag fitted with a rosette tube and pipe pretzel-shaped cookies on greased and floured baking sheets. Make the cookies about 2½" in diameter and space them 2" apart. Brush lightly with egg white and sprinkle with colored or plain sugar. Bake 10–12 minutes until just firm but not brown. Cool 1–2 minutes, then lift to racks with a spatula. When cool, store airtight. About 110 calories per cookie.

Berliner Kränze (Wreaths): Pipe dough into 1½″–2″ wreaths, brush with egg white, and decorate with green sugar and slivers of candied red cherries. Bake as directed. About 110 calories per cookie.

Nut Rings: Pipe dough into 1″–1½″ rings, brush with egg white, and sprinkle with ground pecans, walnuts, filberts, or flaked coconut instead of colored sugar. Bake as directed. About 110 calories per cookie.

Eggnog

This nonalcoholic version of a traditional favorite makes 6 servings.

> 4 eggs, separated
> ½ cup sugar
> 2 cups cold milk
> 1 cup cold light cream
> 1½ teaspoons vanilla
> ⅛ teaspoon salt
> ¼ teaspoon nutmeg

Beat egg yolks and ¼ cup sugar until thick and cream colored; gradually add milk, cream, vanilla, salt, and ⅛ teaspoon nutmeg and beat until frothy. Beat egg whites with remaining sugar until soft peaks form and fold in. Cover and chill until serving time. Mix well, pour into punch bowl, and sprinkle with remaining nutmeg. About 250 calories per serving.

CHRISTMAS AROUND the HOUSE

That older Christmas was one we seemed to hold in our hands. After all, our hands seemed to create so much more of it then than now.

Paul Engle, "A Handmade Christmas"

Have we really lost the sense of homemade Christmas? Is it a chore each year to break out the artificial tree and the boxes of store-bought ornaments, all alike except when we've had to replace broken ones? Sure, it's pretty, but we wouldn't let a stranger cook our Christmas dinner; why do we put up decorations that are strange to us, that have nothing of ourselves in them except that we bought them?

There are a wealth of possibilities for personal decorations. String popcorn balls and wrap nuts in foil to hang on the tree. Taking down decorations isn't such a chore if you can eat them, too. Hang walnut shells that you've cracked open and put a note into, like a fortune cookie. Decorate your tablecloths for Christmas dinner by sewing on bells or other appropriate symbols. Make a crepe-paper "stained-glass window" for the lights to shine through. Cut out a silhouette and stick it to your windows to share Christmas with passersby. Even better, make a three-dimensional window display by mounting several silhouettes on cardboard several inches apart with lights between: for instance, the Magi close, then a string of lights, then the shepherds, a string of lights, then the hillsides of Bethlehem. Rig a star to shine over it all and you have a diorama to be proud of.

Ingenuity is the keyword in homemade Christmas decorations. The simplest objects that you find lying around can be combined with a touch of imagination into delightful ensembles. Natural ob-

jects that you find in your yard or in the woods are lovely additions to our Christmas festivities.

The following ideas are just to get you thinking. Some of them come from a delightful book by Margaret Perry called Holiday Magic.

Christmas Advent Calendar

An Advent calendar to mark the days from the first of December to Christmas Eve is easy to make if you have a supply of old Christmas cards at hand. The golds and silvers, the designs and trimmings on cards finish the shutters of the calendar's windows and trim the edges of the house.

Start with a sheet of dark-blue construction paper 9" by 12". Draw a line through the center, lengthwise, on the wrong side of the paper to serve as a guide.

Measure down on each side 4" and draw a line from that point to the center of the top. This will form the roof. Draw in the chimney about midway down one side of the peak—the chimney is 1¼" wide —and cut out the house. It will be 9" wide and 12" tall at the center of the roof's peak.

On the right side of the paper, mark off the windows, starting 3" down from the top of the roof. All windows are ¾" wide and ¾" tall, except the three in the third row. These are 1" tall and ¾" wide, just for variation. The top row of windows has three windows; the second, five; the third, three; the fourth, five; the fifth, three; and the sixth has two windows on either side of the door.

Leave ½" between all windows, and about ¼" between the rows, and center your rows on the house, leaving the same amount of space on each side.

The door is 1½" wide and 1½" tall.

With an X-Acto knife and a ruler edge, cut across the top and bottom of all windows and the door, and then down through the center of each. Bend back the shutters. *Don't* cut down each side of your windows, or you will lose your shutters.

Paste on strips of gold or colored designs from old Christmas cards, trimming each row of shutters with the same color. Use stick glue—it will not mar the paper.

Trim the edges of the roof and the walls of the house with strips of gold, and top the chimney with gold.

Cover the door with gold pieces; give the door and the windows on each side of it a triangular lintel of gold, and paste two golden steps below the door.

On the back of the calendar paste a lining of red shelf paper, placing it so the red side of the paper will show through the little windows. Use stick glue and fasten the red paper securely.

In each little window paste a tiny picture cut from a Christmas card—a toy, an animal, a candle, or whatever you can find. Paste the cutout onto the red shelf paper. In the doorway paste a Christmas tree.

Starting on December 1, one window should be opened each day, until on the twenty-fourth the door is opened, and there is the Christmas tree.

When all the windows are open, stand the calendar in front of a lamp. The light will shine through the red paper, giving the little house a Christmas glow.

Natural Decorations

The great outdoors offers many materials for use in making decorations. Most of them can be found lying around on the ground, often in your own back yard. The editors of *Farm Journal* offer these suggestions in *Christmas with a Country Flavor*.

Wreaths and festoons can be made on wire or rope, or around a bent coat hanger. Della Robbia wreaths, inspired by the terra-cotta wreaths made by the Della Robbia family in fifteenth-century Italy, can be constructed to hang on doors—with the greens, fruits, and cones wired together. Or use Della-Robbia-like circles as centerpieces, on a sideboard, or surrounding a punch bowl, hurricane lamp, or candles. For centerpieces the fruit can be scattered rather than wired.

Kissing balls—a favorite Christmas decoration hung from doorways or hallway light fixtures—can be made with cones, pods, all of the greens available in your area, and dried berries. Using a large Styrofoam ball as the base, attach florist's wire to the materials and then insert the ends of the wire into the Styrofoam until the ball is completely covered. Accents of gingham or plaid ribbons can add an old-fashioned touch of color.

Boxwood and other greens can be beautiful if sprayed gold, silver, or flat white. Try an arrangement of leaves and cones sprayed dull white, with a few carnations for brilliance. Apples and other fruits lend themselves well to gilding (golden apples were a traditional decoration in the early days of our country). And large leaves can be painted for a totally different look. For instance: Roll rhododendron leaves into cornucopias, wrap with facial tissue, secure with wire twist. Insert cornucopias made from 4 thicknesses of newspaper into each rhododendron leaf, stuff with paper to hold outside surface smooth. Place in 100° oven to dry; it takes about four days. Remove facial tissue, spray outside with coat of white, then 2 coats of red (let dry between coats). Remove stuffing, spray insides the same way. Circle the edge with glitter and attach a hanger and you have beautiful red cornucopias to brighten your tree.

Pine cones can be cut crosswise to form flower-like hangings or fashioned into owl shapes.

Nuts can be painted, or, in a tradition that goes back a very long time, they can be wrapped in gold or silver foil or in colored paper to be used as Christmas tree ornaments. Nuts can be wired into grape-like clusters or made into small trees. (To use nuts, pierce them with a drill or a red-hot pin and insert wire.)

Make your own nativity figures out of self-hardening clay and use natural materials for their setting. A knobby gourd becomes a tree ornament when you saw off the front to make a window and put tiny figures inside. Dried fungus, rocks, gnarled wood, all can form lovely natural settings for the lowly stable bed.

Cookie Ornaments

From *The Doubleday Cookbook* comes this idea for a delightful and delicious kind of homemade decoration, Christmas tree ornaments made of cookies.

Most Suitable Cookies: Large decorated rolled cookies, particularly fancy cutouts.

To Attach Hangers to Unbaked Cookies: "Stick" large loops of thin ribbon or thread to backs of unbaked cookies with tiny dabs of dough. Bake as directed, then decorate.

To Attach Hangers to Baked Cookies (good only for those that are not shattery-crisp): While cookies are still warm and pliable, quickly draw lengths of coarse thread through top, using a sturdy needle. Don't insert too close to edge or cookies may break. Allow 6"–8" thread for each cookie so it can easily be hung. Decorate as desired.

Medieval Christmas Castle

This is what the English would call a "proper castle." It has turrets and towers and ramparts, and a courtyard where knights in armor ride on their panoplied horses.

Place the castle under the Christmas tree or on a mantel. Or use it for other times of the year, too, when you want a "story" centerpiece.

For the towers, save soup cans, coffee cans, and all kinds of cans of various sizes. Cover them with construction paper (use stick glue), and in contrasting colors paste on small pieces for windows and doors. Top the towers with cone-shaped roofs made of about a third of a circle of construction paper. Experiment in newspaper until you find the right size to fit your tower.

For the tallest tower tape 2 soup cans together with masking tape, and then cover them with paper.

Small boxes, also covered with paper, make up part of the castle wall. For each end of the box paste on peaked pieces to form the gables that hold up the roof. Cut them to fit the side of the box and extend the paper 1" or so for the peak.

The roof is an oblong piece of paper folded in half and fitted over the end gables, secured with stick glue. Paste on snips of paper for doors and windows.

To make the bridges which connect the towers, cut a rectangle out of cardboard. Fold it twice close to the center (the space between the two folds is the walkway on top of the bridge). Cut an arch through the two sides of the resulting structure to form the bridge. Cover with construction paper that extends up beyond the bridge itself, and snip it to simulate a crenelated wall.

The ramparts are made in the same way, but without the opening that forms the bridge.

Arrange the various towers, houses, and ramparts on a large base—a large piece of dark construction paper will do—in a sort of circle, to make the courtyard.

You can add as many towers and ramparts as you like, and you can add to it year by year. The various sections are easily packed away, to be used again and again.

Toothpick Stars and Edible Ornaments

These easy and delightful suggestions are from *The LIFE Book of Christmas*. These can be especially fun for children.

TOOTHPICK STARS

All you need is a Styrofoam ball, 1″ in diameter, and a box of plastic toothpicks.

Stick all the toothpicks in the ball, forming rays. To hang, tie a thread to one of the toothpicks (make sure it is driven in securely), or to a straight pin stuck in the ball.

FRUIT FIGURES

Materials:
Variety of fresh fruit as indicated below:
Little marshmallows
Gumdrops
Small candies or raisins
Candy-coated chocolate drops
Ribbon, gold paper trim
Cotton
Holly or evergreen
Small matchboxes
Thread
Paper cup
Small Styrofoam balls
8 pipe cleaners
Yarn (or raffia)
Feathers
Toothpicks, wooden skewers and glue

352

Reindeer: For each antler, twist 2 green pipe cleaners together. Separate other ends and twist in jagged pattern. Insert each antler into lime head. Stick lime on green banana (yellow banana is too soft) with toothpick. Legs are skewers. They should be pointed at one end. Glue on small candies as eyes and nose. Ears are gumdrops attached with toothpicks. Tie ribbon around neck.

Three Wise Men: Make head of peach or small apple or orange and attach with toothpick to apple body. Glue circlets of gold trim around heads and bodies as crowns and belts. Arms are skewers with hands of Styrofoam balls. Glue on bits of cotton for mustaches and beards. Add eyes and noses of colored pins or raisins. Wrap matchboxes for gifts. Stick sprig of holly or piece of evergreen in one hand, suspend a package on thread from other hand.

Santa: Grapefruit body, peach or orange head. Hat is paper cup covered with red paper. Use cotton for mustache and beard, and for trim on hat and body.

Lady and Man: Pear body, peach or lemon head, pipe cleaner arms akimbo. Make lady's muff of two marshmallows, man's hands of Styrofoam balls. Man's hat is marshmallow decorated with paper fringe. Glue small cookie to lady's head [for hat], glue decorations on top. She has white yarn hair. Use velvet ribbons for scarves.

Girl with Pigtails: Grapefruit body, orange head. Hair is braided raffia or yarn, glued on. Devise neckpiece of feathery pastel powder puff.

Pomanders

Pomanders make delightful Christmas gifts or fragrant tree decorations and can freshen closets and drawers for years to come. This technique for making them comes from Adelma Grenier Simmons' *A Merry Christmas Herbal.* Any kind of fruit may be used, but apples and oranges are the easiest to start with.

For 6 to 8 apples or oranges you will need:

> ½ *pound whole long-stemmed cloves*
> 1 *cup (about) ground spices, including*
> > ¼ *cup ground cinnamon*
> > ¼ *cup ground cloves*
> > ¼ *cup ground nutmeg and allspice*
> > ¼ *teaspoon ground ginger*
> > ¼ *cup powdered orris root*

Select only sound fruits. Hold firmly, but do not squeeze; insert the whole cloves in close rows, but avoid placing too many in one spot as this may cause skin to break. Cloves need not touch if you roll the balls in a spice bath afterwards. Don't make holes for the cloves with a needle or other tool, for the cloves will fall out later if you do, and it doubles the time of making them.

After cloves are placed, roll your pomander in the spice mixture given above, coating it completely to keep out air. It is important to finish each pomander within twenty-four hours; it should only take you thirty to sixty minutes for each one. Keep it in the open; do not cover.

Let pomanders remain in the spice mixture in an open bowl in a warm dry place for about a week. We place ours for a centerpiece in a large copper vessel on the dining table, and the spicy aroma of curing pomanders penetrates the entire house. At the end of a week, the pomanders should be sufficiently hardened to tie up for gifts. However, they are still too fresh to store in airtight containers.

You may want to add an essence for lasting fragrance. For each orange or apple, allow about four drops of *one* of these oils: rose, patchouli, vetiver, clove, jasmine, sandalwood, bergamot, or orange blossom; for lemon pomanders, use oil of lemon verbena. These essences or oils are not to be confused with perfumes, which are diluted with alcohol. All oils smell very strong for the first few days; some, like patchouli, sandalwood, and vetiver, are even rank, but they soon mellow and blend with the other scents.

Spice and fruit pomanders without oils will be fragrant for several years. When you find their aroma fading, wash your pomanders in warm water, roll them in a fresh spice bath, and add a drop or two of clove or cinnamon oil. Let them remain in the spices for a few days, then tie with fresh ribbons.

Stained "Glass" Windows

It will be interesting to transform one or more of your windows at Christmastime and create the illusion of having a beautiful, costly, stained glass window. These effects are easily attained by anyone with a little patience. If you have a window which is already distinctive, such as a semi-circular one over your door, this is the best type to choose for decorating, as decorating only one window in the livingroom will leave an unfinished appearance.

The most beautiful effect can be attained by the use of crepe paper and black cardboard. The cardboard simulates the lead and the crepe paper the glass, so that the design is traced upon the cardboard, which is then cut to make a stencil of ½-inch width outlining the design. When the stencil has been completed, trace each section on the various colors of crepe paper. The crepe paper is then cut a trifle larger to allow space for pasting.

It is well to place the paste on the cardboard rather than on the crepe paper. You may produce gradations in the tints of the crepe paper by stretching the paper before you put it on. Sometimes we may use several thicknesses of crepe paper to modify the color, such as yellow over green to produce yellow-green.

from 1001 *Christmas Facts and Fancies*
by Alfred Carl Hottes

Some Tree Trimmings

The following bright and easy suggestions for homemade tree ornaments are from *A New Look at Christmas Decorations*, by Sister M. Gratia Listaite and N. Hildebrand.

FOIL FLAKES

Cut a strip of metallic paper 22 inches long and 2½ inches wide. Fold the paper into ½-inch pleats. Cut angular designs along both sides of the folded foil. This will form the cutout pattern of the snowflake when unfolded. Start with just a few cuts and add more as you see how they look. Run a threaded needle through each fold ½ inch from the bottom. Tie the ends of the thread together loosely. Open the snowflake like a fan until the ends come together. Join them with glue or staples and your snowflake is ready to hang on the tree.

CELLOPHANE BALLS

Make twelve circles 3 inches in diameter in clear or colored cellophane. Fold each circle in half without creasing it, then fold it again in quarters. Run a threaded needle through the pointed tip of the resultant cone-shaped figure. String all 12 figures together and form them into a ball.

CHEERY CHAIN

On the top sheet of several layers of tissue paper, trace as many circles, 2 inches in diameter, as possible. Cutting through all layers of paper, cut out the circles so that you end up with as many 2-inch circles as possible. Starting at the edge of each circle, make ½-inch cuts toward the center all around the diameter, so that the circles are surrounded by a sort of fringe. Cut drinking straws into 1¼-inch segments. Put the circles together two at a time and curl the edges. Collect a number of beads of glass, plastic, or any other bright material which can be strung. Then string all your materials in this order:

1. Two circles
2. Bead

3. Drinking straw
4. Bead
5. Repeat.

The resulting cheerful garlands will look delightful on trees or in other festive trimming.

Kissing Hoop and Goody Tree

These two easy decorations are from *Christmas Lighting and Decorating* by Theodore A. Saros.

KISSING HOOP

An old-fashioned "kissing hoop" can be made quickly and hung on a ceiling fixture, or on the tree. Simply wrap two embroidery hoops in red satin ribbon, fix one inside the other at a right angle, and tie a cluster of mistletoe in the center. A red ribbon tied at the top completes the decoration.

GOODY TREE

For the small fry, with eager fingers during Christmas time, place a "goody tree" on a table. The tree is made from heavy silver paper fashioned into a large cone. A long ½-inch dowel, which serves as the stem of the tree, is nailed to the center of a coffee can that has been covered with bright red paper. The cone-shaped "tree" is then fastened to the stick with transparent cellophane tape. Interesting designs can be created by securing candies of various shapes, sizes, and colors to the tree with both transparent and colored cellophane tape.

When the parents take down the Christmas decorations, every child will be delighted to "put away" this tree's decorations.

Ceppo

If you'd like to try the Italian version of the Christmas tree in addition to your own, this one is pretty simple to make with four wooden triangles and three pieces of doweling. It then offers as many possibilities for decorating as does a Christmas tree. A ceppo is a set of triangular shelves, each one smaller than the one below it, which form a pyramid shape rather like a Christmas tree.

This one is 48 inches high and the sides of the bottom triangle shelf measure 20 inches. The next shelf measures 17 inches, the one above it 12 inches, and the top one 8 inches. Drill holes [near each corner of] the shelves and run 1½-inch dowels through the holes. [Drill additional holes as close to the corners as possible to serve as candleholders.] Following the tradition of the ceppo, place a [pine] cone or puppet on the top shelf, and fruit and candy on the upper shelves. The lowest shelf is usually reserved for the Christmas crèche.

from A *Treasury of Christmas Decorations*,
Zelda Wyatt Schulke

Some Christmas Suggestions

Christmas is the greatest blending of the secular and the religious in all the year. It is best to realize that it is both and not try to exclude one or the other. Anything indulged in to excess is bad for us, but the pleasures of Christmas can be joyous and even worshipful when entered into in the right spirit.

Everyone knows that Christmas is a special time for children; why can't it be that special for adults? Are we so afraid of being childish that we cannot let ourselves be childlike? Try to see everything afresh, taste everything for the first time. Read the Bible story as if you never heard it before; notice the smell of pine and admire the brightness of the lights. Really hope for snow this year.

There is very little pleasure in giving gifts to the person who has everything and wants nothing. Do everyone a favor and really want something this year. Drop hints. Get excited. Try to decipher everyone else's hints. Care if you got the right thing. Try to find out the right size without asking outright. Be secretive. Hide everyone's presents. Try to find where they hid yours. No matter how unsuitable your gifts turn out to be, wear them once. That ugly pink and orange tie will remind you of Christmas no matter when you wear it.

Don't trim the tree with whatever the dime store has on special. Do your ornaments have memories for you? How can they if they're all the same? Have a tree-trimming party and invite everyone to come for a donation of one ornament. You'll have a tree filled with variety and the memories of good friends.

Don't let the store gift-wrap anything. Do it yourself, even if it's lumpy and uneven—especially if it's lumpy and uneven. Try Julklapping. Wrap it as outlandishly as possible. If the gift is the size of a postage stamp, put it in an old carton and fill the carton with three rolls of tissue paper. Write a verse on the card. Make it rhyme as badly as possible.

Christmas is not a time for dignity, it is a time for top-heavy joy. Humanity's hope has been reborn in the bleakness of midwinter. Bells are ringing, people are singing out loud in the street. There is no such thing as a quiet Christmas. The whole world trembles with the thrill of Christ's coming.

Join in the song.

CHRISTMAS
on
MY MIND

Christmas Superstitions

Midwinter has always been a time when spirits and monsters were on the prowl. It is also a time that looks forward to the coming of spring, hence a good time for fortunetelling and weather forecasting. The following is a collection of only some of the superstitions of the Christmas season. Some are associated with specific countries, some are too general to be identified with any one country.

At midnight on Christmas Eve, all water turns to wine; cattle kneel facing toward the East; horses kneel and blow as if to warm the manger; animals can speak, though it's bad luck to hear them; bees hum the Hundredth Psalm.

In Ireland, it is believed that the gates of heaven open at midnight on Christmas Eve. Those who die at that time go straight through without having to wait in purgatory.

A child born on Christmas Day or Christmas Eve is considered very lucky in some countries, but in Greece he is feared to be a Kallikantzaroi; in Poland he may turn out to be a werewolf.

The weather on each of the twelve days of Christmas signifies what the weather will be on the appropriate month of the coming year.

In Germany, a blindfolded goose will touch first the girl in the circle who will wed first.

The branch of a cherry tree placed in water at the beginning of Advent will bring luck if it flowers by Christmas.

In Devonshire, England, a girl raps at the hen house door on Christmas Eve. If a rooster crows, she will marry within the year.

You burn your old shoes during the Christmas season in Greece to prevent misfortunes in the coming year.

It's bad luck to let any fire go out in your house during the Christmas season.

It's bad luck to let your evergreen decorations fall or to throw them away. You should burn them or feed them to your cow.

If the husband brings the Christmas holly into the house first, he will rule the household for the coming year; if the wife is first, she will hold sway.

If you eat a raw egg before eating anything else on Christmas morning, you will be able to carry heavy weights.

In Hertfordshire, England, a plum cake is stuck on a cow's horn on Christmas Eve. Cider is then thrown into her face. If the cake falls forward, it will be a good harvest.

From cockcrow to daybreak of Christmas morning, the trolls roam the Swedish countryside. Stay indoors.

During the recitation of Christ's genealogy at Christmas Eve Midnight Mass, buried treasure reveals itself.

If you don't eat any plum pudding, you will lose a friend before next Christmas.

If you refuse mince pie at Christmas dinner, you will have bad luck for a year.

A loaf of bread left on the table after Christmas Eve dinner will ensure no lack of bread for the next year.

Eating an apple at midnight on Christmas Eve gives good health for a year.

You will have as many happy months in the coming year as the number of houses you eat minced pie in during Christmas.

There is some truth behind some of these superstitions. For instance, if you eat everything during Christmas that you're supposed to eat for good luck, the rest of the year has got to be an improvement once you get over your stomach ache.

Some Famous People Born on Christmas

1642 Isaac Newton—English mathematician and physicist who discovered the law of gravitation, considered by some the greatest scientist of all time.

1818 Clara Barton—organizer of the American Red Cross.

1883 Maurice Utrillo—French painter of atmosphere-filled Parisian street scenes.

1892 Rebecca West—well-known English novelist and critic.

1899 Humphrey Bogart—great American screen actor, star of *Casablanca*, *The Maltese Falcon*, and *The Caine Mutiny*, Oscar-winner for *The African Queen*.

1907 Cab Calloway—jazz band leader, famous for his "scat" singing.

1918 Anwar Sadat—President of Egypt since Nasser's death in 1970.

1924 Rod Serling—noted writer and television personality, creator of the eerie show "The Twilight Zone."

Strangely enough, the one birth we might have expected to take place on Christmas but which didn't was that of Jesus Christ.

The Twelve Days' Accounting

If you add up all the presents in the old carol "The Twelve Days of Christmas," you find that the twelfth day's shipment brings the menagerie to the following total:

12 drummers drumming
22 pipers piping
30 lords aleaping
36 ladies dancing
40 maids amilking [presumably they brought cows with them]
42 swans aswimming
42 geese alaying
40 gold rings
36 colly birds
30 French hens

22 turtle doves

12 partridges in a dozen pear trees

There have been some feeble attempts to figure the net worth of this Christmas package, but it all breaks down when you try to fix a price scale for such unusual gifts as leaping lords. Fortunately, this medieval sender didn't have to face today's postal rates.

The Christmas Season

We may think we know what we mean by the Christmas season, but every country has a slightly different idea of it. The Catholic Church's reckoning of the whole season stretches from Advent, four Sundays before Christmas, to Candlemas on February 2.

Most countries start festivities or preparations from two to three weeks before Christmas (often St. Nicholas' Day) and end on Epiphany, January 6. The following are some of the notable exceptions:

Armenia, as usual, confuses the whole question. The Armenian Church celebrates Christmas on Old Style January 6. Thus their whole season starts about the time ours is ending.

In Iran, Christmas is prepared for with a partial fast that lasts the entire month of December to Christmas Day.

Holland starts Christmas on the last Saturday of November, when St. Nicholas arrives by boat, and finishes on the second day of Christmas, December 26.

Spain begins festivities on December 8 with the Feast of the Immaculate Conception and doesn't let up until Epiphany.

Sweden stretches the season for a whole month, from St. Lucia's Day on December 13 to January 13.

The United States is one of the biggest exceptions to the rule. Our Christmas starts with Santa's arrival at the big Thanksgiving parades and stretches through New Year's or, sometimes, January 6. That makes for a lot of shopping days.

Some Practical Advice for Department Store Santas

1. Santa must never kiss a child.
2. Santa's hands and nails must be immaculately clean at all times.
3. Santa must never bribe a child to be good by promising toys.
4. Santa must never threaten a child.
5. Santa must make no promises unless they can be fulfilled.
6. Santa must not frighten timid children with roaring laughter.
7. Santa should have tissue handkerchiefs available for children with sniffles.

Survey of Christmas Ideas, 1956
Sales Promotions, Inc.

"Christmas to an actor usually means an extra matinee."

Eddie Cantor

A Warning to Hunters

This article appeared in the Milwaukee *Journal* on December 26, 1950:

It seems that a successful deer hunter, with his quarry on the fender, stopped en route home to regale his cronies with the story of his triumph. The telling took longer than he planned, and certain low comedy characters utilized the pause to sow the seeds of his undoing. They sent for red paint and while the hunter recounted the glories of his hunt inside, they painted the nose of his slain buck a ruby red.

At this point, by no accident, the youngsters were homeward bound from school. And the enemies of our hero, not satisfied with leaving the red-nosed buck out there in naked view, stopped some of the moppets and horrified them with a whispered alarm. "Look! Rudolph!"

By the time our hero emerged, fifty youngsters were dug in for battle equipped with snowballs, rocks and righteous wrath. Well, he escaped with his life, and on Christmas Eve, it turned out that Rudolph was all right after all. So now the tale can be told.

Santa Claus Investigated

It might have been a movie like *Miracle on 34th Street* except it didn't have a happy ending.

In 1914 in New York City, John D. Gluck formed an organization called the Santa Claus Association, whose stated purpose was "to preserve children's faith in Santa Claus." It obtained from the Post Office letters addressed to Santa Claus and would investigate them to see if the cases were needy. If they were, it would try to help answer the requests for toys and presents and even sometimes meet rent payments. Obviously, this was financed by the contributions of Christmas-spirited citizens.

It sounds too good to last, and it was. In 1928 federal postal authorities refused to turn over any more mail and instituted an investigation into the organization. There were rumors of fraud and other irregularities, but nothing was ever proved. Still, the organization was criticized and disbanded. The organization's founder said, "All I ask is that these people don't sock it to us at this time of the year and spoil the faith of little children."

Things Named for Christmas

People have always named things after other things that they love. Christmas and the symbols of Christmas have appeared in many other names. Consider the following:

PLACE NAMES

Bethlehem is located in Pennsylvania, Kentucky, Indiana, New Hampshire, Maryland, Connecticut, and Georgia.

Holly is in Colorado, Michigan, and West Virginia.

Mount Holly is in New Jersey and Vermont.

Noel is in Missouri and Virginia.

Santa Claus is in Indiana and Idaho.

Christmas itself is in Michigan and Florida.

Christmas Cove is in Maine.

Mistletoe is in Kentucky.

There are two Christmas Islands: one in the Indian Ocean, administered by Australia; the other in the Gilbert Islands and claimed by the United States. Ironically, this second island with its peaceful name was the scene of nuclear test explosions in 1957, 1958, and 1962.

Christmas Ridge is an underwater mountain chain in the Pacific Ocean.

The Christmas bell is an Australian flower that is widely used in Christmas decorations down under. It blooms in the warm Decembers of the Southern Hemisphere. It has bright green leaves and a red flower, fringed in yellow, shaped like a bell.

The Christmasberry is also called California holly. It grows on the West Coast of North America. It is an evergreen tree or shrub with white flowers and, later, bright red berries.

The Christmas bush is another Australian decorative plant. It has many tiny flowers growing in soft clusters.

The Christmas cactus is also known, less pleasantly, as the crab cactus. It blooms in mid-December in its native Brazil and Central America. It has pink ornate flowers and light green, oval-shaped leaves.

The Christmas fern is a North American woodland fern, a dark evergreen.

The Christmas Rose, or black hellebore, is a Eurasian perennial. It has white or greenish blossoms that look much like wild roses. The leaves are evergreen.

ODD CHRISTMAS TREES

The pyramid-shaped assembly of pipes, valves, clamps, and so on, that stands over an oil well and controls the output of oil is called a Christmas tree.

The control panel of a submarine, with its flashing red and green lights, is also called a Christmas tree.

In CB radio jargon, a Christmas tree is a truck or any other vehicle with lots of bright lights (and a Christmas card is a traffic ticket).

To World War II aviators, a Christmas tree was the shower of bright metallic foil that they dropped over enemy targets to jam radar and communications systems. The name probably derived from the similarity to a well-tinseled tree.

At a drag strip, a Christmas tree is the set of flashing red, green, and yellow lights that signal the start of the race.

A DISEASE

Christmas Disease is a bleeding disease very much like hemophilia and similarly caused by a genetically determined deficiency of one of the several factors present in blood plasma that bring about normal clotting. Also like hemophilia, it is transmitted by carrier mothers (who themselves do not show symptoms) to their sons, half of whom are thus affected. The name is not taken directly from the season of Christmas but rather from the first known victim of the disease, a young lad named Stephen Christmas.

AN APPROPRIATE NAME

A book now out of print called A *Christmas Dictionary* was published in 1959, and was by the appropriately named author Holly Bell.

Robert E. Lee Writes to His Wife

December 25, 1861

I cannot let this day of grateful rejoicing pass without some communion with you. I am thankful for the many among the past that I have passed with you, and the remembrance of them fills me with pleasure. As to our old home, if not destroyed it will be difficult ever to be recognized. . . . It is better to make up our minds to a general loss. They cannot take away the remembrances of the spot, and the memories of those that to us rendered it sacred. That will remain to us as long as life will last and that we can preserve. . . .

Gift-givers of Christmas in Tradition

Austria	St. Nicholas or Christkind
Belgium	St. Nicholas
Brazil	Papa Noël
Chile	Viejo Pascuero
China	Lam Khoong-Khoong or Dun Che Lao Ren
Costa Rica	Christ Child or Santa Claus
England	Father Christmas
France	Père Noël or le Petit Jesus
Guatemala	Christ Child
Holland	St. Nicholas
Italy	Befana
Japan	Hoteiosho
Mexico	Three Kings
Norway	Julesvenn
Poland	Star Man
Puerto Rico	Both Santa Claus and the Wise Men
Russia	Babouschka
Spain	Wise Men
Sweden	Jultomten
Switzerland	Christkind, St. Nicholas, or Father Christmas and Lucy
Syria	Smallest Camel of the Wise Men's caravan
U.S.A.	Santa Claus

Gift-giving Days

Everyone in the United States gives gifts on Christmas (although family traditions may move the opening of presents back to Christmas Eve). Other countries, however, exchange their gifts on different days. The following are some prime examples:

Belgium	St. Nicholas' Day, December 6
England	Christmas or Boxing Day, December 26
France	Christmas for children's gifts, New Year's for adults
Holland	St. Nicholas' Day
Ireland	No real Christmas gifts, but pennies or trifles are given to Wren Boys on St. Stephen's Day, December 26
Italy	Epiphany, January 6
Mexico	Epiphany
Poland	Christmas Eve
Puerto Rico	Both Christmas and Epiphany
Spain	Epiphany
Sweden	St. Lucia's Day, December 13

A Modern Christmas Lament

In 1945 W. H. Auden, the great modern English poet, published *For the Time Being: A Christmas Oratorio*, a long poem that contrasted the events of the Nativity with modern attitudes. This excerpt from the final speech of the Narrator is very sad, especially when compared with the boisterous cheer and Christmas spirit of some of the older poetry we've looked at. This crisis of faith and brother love is one that modern human beings must learn to overcome.

Well, so that is that. Now we must dismantle the tree,
Putting the decorations back into their cardboard boxes—
Some have got broken—and carrying them up to the attic.
The holly and the mistletoe must be taken down and burnt,
And the children got ready for school. There are enough
Left-overs to do, warmed up, for the rest of the week—

Not that we have much appetite, having drunk such a lot,
Stayed up so late, attempted—quite unsuccessfully—
To love all of our relatives and, in general,
Grossly overestimated our powers.

The Knighting of the Sirloin of Beef by Charles the Second

This anonymous poem suggests how a Christmas joke might have given us the name of one of our favorite foods.

The Second Charles of England
Rode forth one Christmas tide,
To hunt a gallant stag of ten,
Of Chingford woods the pride.

The winds blew keen, the snow fell fast,
And made for earth a pall,
As tired steeds and wearied men
Returned to Friday Hall.

The blazing logs, piled on the dogs,
Were pleasant to behold!
And grateful was the steaming feast
To hungry men and cold.

With right good-will all took their fill,
And soon each found relief;
Whilst Charles his royal trencher piled
From one huge loin of beef.

Quoth Charles, "Odd's fish! a noble dish!
Ay, noble made by me!
By kingly right, I dub thee knight—
Sir Loin henceforward be!"

373

And never was a royal jest
Received with such acclaim;
And never knight than good Sir Loin
More worthy of the name.

How "Merry Christmas" Is Written Around the World

Argentina	Felices Pascuas
Armenia	Schenorhavor Dzenount
Belgium (Flemish)	Vrolijke Kerstmis
Brazil (Portuguese)	Boas Festas
Bulgaria	Chestita Koleda
China	Kung Hsi Hsin Nien or Bing Chu Shen Tan
Czechoslovakia	Vesele Vanoce
Denmark	Glaedelig Jul
Esperanto	Gajan Kristnaskon
Estonia	Roomsaid Joulu Puhi
Finland	Hauskaa Joulua
France	Joyeux Noël
Germany	Fröhliche Weinachten
Greece	Kala Christougena
Holland	Zalig Kerstfeest
Hungary	Boldog Karacsony
Iraq	Idah Saidan Wa Sanah Jadidah
Ireland (Gaelic)	Nodlaig Nait Cugat
Italy	Bono Natale
Japan	Meri Kurisumasu
Latvia	Priecigus Ziemas Svetkus
Mexico	Feliz Navidad
Norway	Gledelig Jul
Poland	Wesolych Swiat

Portugal	Boas Festas
Romania	Sarbatori Vesele
Russia	S Roshestvóm Khristóvym
South Africa (Afrikaans)	Een Plesierige Kerfees
Spain	Felices Pascuas
Sweden	Glad Jul
Turkey	Noeliniz Ve Yeni Yiliniz Kutlu Olsun
Ukraine	Chrystos Rozdzajetsia Slawyte Jeho
Wales	Nadolig Llawen
Yugoslavia (Croatian)	Srećan Božić
Yugoslavia (Serbian)	Hristos se rodi

A Christmas Tree

I have been looking on this evening, at a merry company of children assembled round that pretty German toy, a Christmas-Tree. The tree was planted in the middle of a great round table, and towered high above their heads. It was brilliantly lighted by a multitude of little tapers; and everywhere sparkled and glittered with bright objects. There were rosy-cheeked dolls, hiding behind the green leaves; there were real watches (with movable hands, at least, and an endless capacity of being wound up) dangling from innumerable twigs; there were French polished tables, chairs, bedsteads, wardrobes, eight-day clocks, and various other articles of domestic furniture (wonderfully made, in tin, at Wolverhampton), perched among the boughs, as if in preparation for some fairy house-keeping; there were jolly, broad-faced little men, much more agreeable in appearance than many real men—and no wonder, for their heads took off, and showed them to be full of sugar-plums; there were fiddles and drums; there were tambourines, books, work-boxes, paint-boxes, sweetmeat-boxes, peep-show-boxes, all kinds of boxes; there were trinkets for the elder girls, far brighter than any grown-up gold and jewels; there were baskets and pincushions in all devices; there were guns, swords, and banners; there were witches standing in enchanted rings of pasteboard, to tell fortunes; there were teetotums, humming-tops, needle-cases, pen-wipers, smelling-bot-

375

tles, conversation-cards, bouquet-holders; real fruit, made artificially dazzling with gold leaf; imitation apples, pears and walnuts, crammed with surprises; in short as a pretty child, before me, delightedly whispered to another pretty child, her bosom friend, "There was everything, and more."

Charles Dickens

Solution to a Christmas Dilemma

Robert Louis Stevenson, author of *Treasure Island* and *Dr. Jekyll and Mr. Hyde*, as well as many other stories, found a whimsical solution for the problem of having a birthday that falls on Christmas. He is writing to the young daughter of an American Land Commissioner in Samoa.

Vailima, June 19, 1891

I, Robert Louis Stevenson, Advocate of the Scots Bar, author of *The Master of Ballantrae* and *Moral Emblems*, stuck civil engineer, sole owner and patentee of the Palace and Plantation known as Vailima in the island of Upolu, Samoa, a British subject, being in sound mind, and pretty well, I thank you, in body:

In consideration that Miss Annie H. Ide, daughter of H. C. Ide, the town of Saint Johnsbury, in the county of Caledonia, in the state of Vermont, United States of America, was born, out of all reason, upon Christmas Day, and is therefore out of all justice denied the consolation and profit of a proper birthday;

And considering that I, the said Robert Louis Stevenson, have attained an age when O, we never mention it, and that I have now no further use for a birthday of any description;

And in consideration that I have met H. C. Ide, the father of the said Annie H. Ide, and found him about as white a land commissioner as I require:

Have transferred, and *do hereby transfer,* to the said Annie H. Ide, *all and whole* my rights and privileges in the thirteenth day of November, formerly my birthday, now, hereby, and henceforth, the birthday of the said Annie H. Ide, to have, hold, exercise, and enjoy the same in the customary manner, by the sporting of fine raiment, eating of rich meats, and receipt of gifts, compliments, and copies of verse, according to the manner of our ancestors:

And I direct the said Annie H. Ide to add to the said name of Annie H. Ide the name Louisa—at least in private; and I charge her to use my said birthday with moderation and humanity, *et tamquam bona filia familiae,* the said birthday not being so young as it once was, and having carried me in a very satisfactory manner since I can remember;

And in case the said Annie H. Ide shall neglect or contravene either of the above conditions, I hereby revoke the donation and transfer my rights in the said birthday to the President of the United States of America for the time being;

In witness whereof I have hereto set my hand and seal this nineteenth day of June in the year of grace eighteen hundred and ninety-one.

SEAL
Robert Louis Stevenson

Witness, Lloyd Osbourne
Witness, Harold Watts

Christmas Grades

The distinguished Professor of English William Lyon Phelps gave an unusually difficult examination to his students just before the Christmas holidays. One befuddled student turned in a blank page with his season's greeting:

God knows the answer to these questions.
Merry Christmas!

In the spirit of the season, Prof. Phelps responded:

God gets an "A." You get an "F."
Happy New Year!

377

A Christmas Wish

It is my heart-warm and world-embracing Christmas hope and aspiration that all of us, the high, the low, the rich, the poor, the admired, the despised, the loved, the hated, the civilized, the savage (every man and brother of us all through-out the whole earth), may eventually be gathered together in a heaven of everlasting rest and peace and bliss, except the inventor of the telephone.

Mark Twain

I'm Dreaming of a Green Christmas

J. P. McEvoy

That's right. *Green!* Who started all this breast-beating for a white Christmas? Irving Berlin. What was he doing at the time? Having a green Christmas out in Hollywood—writing movies for that green folding stuff. For many years I have met Berlin in the winter—in California, Florida, Honolulu—usually under a palm tree, never a snowbank. Irving Berlin is always as brown as a Waikiki beach boy. How does he get that year-round tan? Dreaming about white Christmases, but staying away from them.

Christmas in the Ghetto

Momma was so happy that Christmas, all the food folks brought us and Mister Ben giving us more credit, and Momma even talked the electric man into turning the lights on again. . . . How'd you know I wanted a wallet, God? I wonder if all the rich people who got mink coats and electric trains got that one little thing nobody knew they wanted.

Dick Gregory, from
Nigger: An Autobiography

Whom to Consult When You Find A Body Under the Tree

It is an old trick in literature to set the saddest events against the happiest backgrounds. Thus, Christmas appears in some of the most unlikely books and stories. This list of Christmas crime stories, compiled by Bill Vande Water, originally appeared in *Murder Ink, The Mystery Reader's Companion*, which was "perpetrated by Dilys Winn."

NOVELS

Agatha Christie:	*Murder for Christmas (Holiday for Murder)*
Charles Dickens:	*The Mystery of Edwin Drood*
Elizabeth X. Ferrars:	*The Small World of Murder*

Cyril Hare:	*An English Murder*
Georgette Heyer:	*Envious Casca*
John Howlett:	*The Christmas Spy*
Michael Innes:	*A Comedy of Terrors; Christmas at Candle-shoes*
Ed McBain:	*Pusher; Sadie When She Died*
James McClure:	*The Gooseberry Fool*
Ngaio Marsh:	*Tied Up in Tinsel*
Jack Pearl:	*Victims*
Ellery Queen:	*The Finishing Stroke*
Patrick Ruell:	*Red Christmas*
Dell Shannon:	*No Holiday for Crime*

SHORT STORIES

Margery Allingham:	"The Case of the Man with the Sack"; "The Snapdragon and the C.I.D."
G. K. Chesterton:	"The Flying Stars"
Agatha Christie:	"The Adventure of the Christmas Pudding" ("The Theft of the Royal Ruby"); "Christmas Tragedy"
John Collier:	"Back for Christmas"
August Derleth:	"The Adventure of the Unique Dickensians"
Arthur Conan Doyle:	"The Adventure of the Blue Carbuncle"
Stanley Ellin:	"Christmas Eve"
O. Henry:	"Whistling Dick's Christmas Stocking"
Edward D. Hoch:	"Christmas Is for Cops"
Ellery Queen:	"The Dauphin's Doll"
Damon Runyon:	"Dancing Dan's Christmas"; "Palm Springs Santa Claus"
Dorothy L. Sayers:	"The Necklace of Pearls"
Georges Simenon:	"Maigret's Christmas"
Rex Stout:	"Christmas Party"; "Santa Claus Beat"
Julian Symons:	"The Santa Claus Club"; "Twixt the Cup and the Lip"

A. C. Greene: *The Santa Claus Bank Robbery*

"Yes, Virginia..."

Dear Editor—

I am 8 years old. Some of my little friends say there is no Santa Claus. Papa says, "If you see it in *The Sun*, it's so." Please tell me the truth, is there a Santa Claus?

Virginia O'Hanlon

The year was 1897 but the question is a timeless one. The New York *Sun* assigned Francis P. Church, a veteran newspaperman who had been with the *Sun* for twenty years, to answer this seemingly unanswerable question. His reply is one of the most famous newspaper editorials of all time:

Virginia, your little friends are wrong. They have been affected by the skepticism of a skeptical age. They do not believe except they see. They think that nothing can be which is not comprehensible by their little minds. All minds, Virginia, whether they be men's or children's are little. In this great universe of ours, man is a mere insect, an ant, in his intellect as compared with the boundless world about him, as measured by the intelligence capable of grasping the whole of truth and knowledge.

"Yes, Virginia, there is a Santa Claus. He exists as certainly as love and generosity and devotion exist, and you know that they abound and give to your life its highest beauty and joy. Alas! how dreary would be the world if there were no Santa Claus! It would be as dreary as if there were no Virginias. There would be no childlike faith then, no poetry, no romance to make tolerable this existence. We should have no enjoyment, except in sense and sight. The external light with which childhood fills the world would be extinguished.

Not believe in Santa Claus! You might as well not believe in fairies. You might get your papa to hire men to watch in all the chimneys on Christmas eve to catch Santa Claus, but even if you did not see Santa Claus coming down, what would that prove? Nobody sees Santa Claus, but that is no sign that there is no Santa Claus. The most real things in the world are those that neither children nor men can see. Did you ever see fairies dancing on the lawn? Of course not, but that's no proof that they are not there. Nobody can conceive or imagine all the wonders there are unseen and unseeable in the world.

You tear apart the baby's rattle and see what makes the noise inside, but there is a veil covering the unseen world which not the strongest man, nor even the united strength of all the strongest men that ever lived could tear apart. Only faith, poetry, love, romance, can push aside that curtain and view and picture the supernal beauty and glory beyond. Is it all real? Ah, Virginia, in all this world there is nothing else real and abiding.

No Santa Claus! Thank God! he lives and lives forever. A thousand years from now, Virginia, nay 10 times 10,000 years from now, he will continue to make glad the heart of childhood.

Index

William the Conqueror assumes
English throne, 27
World War I, 33
yellow fever contracted, 32
Christmas, Stephen, 370
Christmas (Hunt), 272–73
Christmas at Candleshoes (Innes),
380
Christmas bells (flower), 42, 369
"Christmas Bells" (Longfellow), 194
Christmasberry (plant), 369
Christmas bush (shrub), 42, 369
Christmas cactus, 369
Christmas Carol, A (Dickens), vii,
260–68, 306, 315
Christmas Carol, A
(Dickens—poem), 277–78
Christmas Carol, A (film), 267
Christmas Carol, A (Rossetti), 274
Christmas Carroll, A (Wither),
275–76
*Christmas Carols, Ancient and
Modern* (Sandys), 181
Christmas Carols Association, 157
Christmas Carols New and Old
(Bramley and Stainer), 222
Christmas clubs, 61–62, 75
Christmas Concerto (Corelli), 235
Christmas Dictionary, A (Bell), 370
"Christmas Dinner, A" (Dickens),
257–58
Christmas disease, 370
"Christmas Dreaming" (Lee and
Gordon), 246
"Christmas Eve" (Ellin), 380
Christmas Eve (film), 290
Christmas Eve (Rimsky-Korsakov),
235
Christmas fern, 369
Christmas ginger snaps, 336–37
Christmas Holiday (film), 302
Christmas in Appalachia (TV
special), 311
Christmas in Connecticut (film), 291
Christmas in July (film), 291
"Christmas in Killarney" (Redmond,
Cavanaugh, and Weldon), 246
"Christmas in Nøddeba Rectory," 65
Christmas in the Holy Land (TV
special), 311
"Christmas Is for Cops" (Hoch),
380

Christmas Lighting and Decorating
(Saros), 357
Christmas log (*bûche de Noël*),
328–30
Christmas Martian, The (film), 303
Christmas Memory, A (TV special),
308–9
Christmas Night of '62 (McCabe),
278–79
Christmas Oratorio (Bach), 227–28
"Christmas Party" (Stout), 380
"Christmas Phantoms" (Gorki),
251–52
Christmas plates, 65
Christmas pudding, 68
Christmas rose, 369
"Christmas Song, The" (Torme and
Wells), 237
Christmas Spy, The (Howlett), 380
Christmas That Almost Wasn't, The
(film), 303
Christmas 'til Closing (TV special),
311
"Christmas Tragedy" (Christie), 380
Christmas Tree, The (film), 303
Christmas Tree, The (Lizst), 235
Christmas Tree Lane, 157
Christmas Tree Ship, 157
Christmas trees. *See* Tree
Christmas with a Country Flavor,
331, 349
"Christ the Lord Is Risen Today"
(Wesley), 189
Chocolate-dipped marzipan, 335
Church, Francis P., 381–82
Churchill, Winston, 34–35
Civil War, 194, 200
Classical music, 227–35
See also names of works
Clooney, Rosemary, 299
Clovis I (king of Franks), 26
Coca-Cola Company, 140
Coco, James, 313
Cocoa marzipan, 335
Cole, Nat "King," 237
Cole, Sir Henry, 58
Collier, John, 380
Colman, Ronald, 268
Columbia Broadcasting System
(CBS), 308, 311–15
Columbia Records, 242
Columbus, Christopher, 28
Comedy of Terrors, A (Innes), 380

Luther, Martin, 74, 151, 168, 174, 183–84

McBain, Ed, 380
McCabe, William G., 278–79
McClure, James, 380
Macdonald, George, 285
McDowall, Roddy, 312
McEvoy, J. P., 378
McIver, John, 313, 315
Mack, Helen, 295
MacMurray, Fred, 297
MacRae, Gordon, 254, 313
Magi. *See* Wise Men
Magister Ludi, 101
Magna Carta, 27
"Maigret's Christmas" (Simenon), 380
Malory, Sir Thomas, 26
Mame (Herman), 247
Marble Prophecy and Other Poems, The (Holland), 218
March, Fredric, 268
Marduk (god), 15, 163
Mari Llwyd, 102, 116, 159
Marks, Gerald, 246
Marks, Johnny, 242, 315
Marley, Dr. Miles, 261
Marlowe, Philip, 303
Marsh, Ngaio, 380
Marshall, E. G., 313
Martin, Hugh, 246
Martin Chuzzlewit (Dickens), 259
Mary, Mother of Jesus, 6, 12, 44, 56–57, 78, 85, 104, 119, 124, 125, 130
Marzipan, 334–35
Mason, James, 311
Masquing, 28–29
Mass of the Carols, 102–3, 126
Mass of the Rooster, 60, 103, 113, 144, 157
Mass of the Shepherds, 103, 123, 162
Matthau, Walter, 315
Matthew, St., 3–4, 7, 9, 12, 14, 227
Matthews, Timothy R., 219
Maxwell, Marilyn, 243, 295
May, Robert L., 242
Medici family, 137
Medieval castle (homemade), 350–51
Meet John Doe (film), 295–96
Meet Me in St. Louis (film), 246
Melchior, 10, 62

"Mele Kalikamaka" (Anderson), 246
Mendelssohn, Felix, 191
Menotti, Gian-Carlo, 307
Merlin (magician), 26
Merrill, Bob, 312, 313
Merry Christmas Herbal, A (Simmons), 353
"Merry Christmas" in other languages, 374–75
Merry Wives of Windsor, The (Shakespeare), 224
Mesopotamia, 15–16, 163
Messiah (Handel), 155, 201, 230–33, 312
Metropolitan Opera, 229
Mexico, 103–4, 371
   piñata, 120
   posada, 124–25
Middle Ages, 27, 39, 53, 68, 75, 130, 133, 135, 209, 221, 255–57
Midnight Mass, 47, 54, 56, 63, 73, 76, 79, 104–5, 119, 128
Mikalas, Svaty (St. Nicholas), 59
Millay, Edna St. Vincent, 285
Miller, Roger, 314
Milton, John, 272
Milwaukee *Journal*, 367
Mince pies, 68, 105–6
Minnelli, Liza, 312
Miracle on 34th Street (film), 99, 239, 296–98, 300, 367
Miracle on 34th Street (TV special), 313
Misrule, Lord of, 39, 54, 100–1, 110
Mistletoe, 68, 96, 107–9
Mitchell, Cameron, 289
Mitchell, Thomas, 294, 313
Mitchum, Robert, 292
Mithra (god), 17
Mithraism, 17
Mohr, Father Josef, 213–16
Monk, W. H., 172
Montgomery, James, 169, 171
Montgomery, Robert, 303
Moore, Dr. Clement Clarke, 139–40, 241, 280–83
Moore, Glen, 247
Moravian Christmas cookies, 335–36
Morgan, Dennis, 291
Morgan, Frank, 300
Mormon Tabernacle Choir, 157
Morris, Chester, 299
Morris, Ralph E., 100

394

399

and Germany and origins of
modern Christmas in, 74–75
Santa Claus as creation of, 138–40
stamps, 145
United States Post Office, 56
Unreason, Abbot of, 39
Utrillo, Maurice, 364

Vaccaro, Brenda, 314
Van Dyke, Henry, 254–55
Van Heusen, Jimmy, 246
Vaughan Williams, Ralph, 235
Venezuela, 157–58
Vera-Ellen, 299
Vernon, Jackie, 312
Very Merry Cricket, A (TV special),
315
Victims (Pearl), 380
Victoria, Queen, 153
Viejo Pascuero, 60, 371
Vienna Boys Choir, 241, 311, 313
Virgin Mary. *See* Mary
Visit from St. Nicholas, A (Moore),
139, 146, 241, 280–83
Vladimir of Russia, 130
"Von Himmel hoch" (Luther), 183

Wade, John Francis, 203–4
Wagner, Richard, 229
Waits (carolers), 158–59
Wakefield Cycle, 256
Wales, 67, 102, 159
"Waltons, The" (TV series), 309,
312
Washington, George, 31–32, 156
Wassail, 159–61
Water, Bill Vande, 379
Watts, Deacon, 200
Watts, Isaac, 200–1
Wayne, John, 299
Webster, Paul Francis, 246
"We Have Heard the Joyful Sound"
(Kirkpatrick), 174
Weihnachtsmann, 137
Weldon, Frank, 246
Welles, Orson, 313
Wells, Robert, 237
Wenceslas, Duke, 187
"We Need a Little Christmas"
(Herman), 247
Wesley, Charles, Rev., 189–91
Wesley, John, 189
West, Rebecca, 364

Westminster Abbey, 233
"We Three Kings of Orient Are"
(Hopkins), 222–23
"We Wish You a Merry Christmas"
(traditional carol), 223–24
"What Child Is This?" (Dix), 172,
224–25
"When I Survey the Wondrous
Cross" (Watts), 201
"While Shepherds Watched Their
Flocks by Night" (Tate),
225–26
"Whistling Dick's Christmas
Stocking" (Henry), 380
"White Christmas" (Berlin), 242,
244–45, 292
White Christmas (film), 244, 299
Whiting, Richard, 106
Wigilia, 161–62
Wiley, H. L., 29–30
Williams, Richard, 268
William the Conqueror, 26
Willis, Richard S., 199
Wills, Chill, 293
Willson, Meredith, 239, 297
Winchell, Paul, 315
Windows, stained "glass," 355
Winkworth, Catherine, 168
Winn, Dilys, 379
Winninger, Charles, 289
Winterhalter, Hugo, 245
Winters, Shelley, 312
Winter solstice celebrations, 15–16
"Winter Wonderland" (Bernard and
Smith), 245
Wise Men, 9–10, 43, 44–46, 62–63,
70, 75, 86, 88, 112, 118, 125,
126, 129, 145–46, 150, 196, 371
See also Balthasar; Caspar;
Melchior
Wither, George, 275–76
Wolsey, Cardinal, 110
Wood, Natalie, 297
Woolley, Monty, 290, 300
World War I, 33
World War II, 35, 68, 154
Wreaths
Advent, 40, 74
Della Robbia, 349
Wren, hunting the, 82–83, 85
Wright, Teresa, 313
Wyman, Jane, 303
Wynken de Worde, Jan van, 175